Legisprudence Library

Studies on the Theory and Practice of Legislation

Volume 6

The objective of the *Legisprudence Library* is to publish excellent research on legislation and related areas (such as regulation and policy-making) from the standpoint of legal theory. This series' title points to an emerging, comprehensive conception of lawmaking which focuses on the justification of laws and the overarching principles which should guide legislation and norm-giving altogether, with the rationality, the reasonableness and the quality of legislation being its major concerns. Taking on legal theory as its pivotal perspective, the series attempts to fill a significant gap in the field of legislative studies, where political science and sociological approaches remain dominant through date. Inasmuch as it fosters legal-theoretical research in lawmaking, it also contributes to widen the scope of standard jurisprudence, which has been up to recent times overwhelmingly centred on the judicial application and the interpretation of law, thereby underestimating the central role of lawmakers within the legal system.

Contributions preferably address topics connected to legislation theory, including (but not limited to) legislative rationality, legislative technique, legistics, legislative effectiveness and social compliance of laws, legislative efficiency and lawmaking economics, evaluation, legislative and regulative impact assessment, regulation management, legislative implementation, public access to legislation, democratic legitimacy of legislation, codification, legislative reasoning and argumentation, science and expertise within lawmaking, legislative language, symbolic legislation, legal policy analysis, lawmaking and adjudication, or judicial review of legislation and legislative process. Comparative and system transcending approaches are encouraged. Purely dogmatic descriptions of positive law or legislative proceedings are not taken into consideration though connections with legislative and legal practice are welcomed. The series welcomes monographs and edited volumes.

More information about this series at http://www.springer.com/series/11058

Virgilio Zapatero Gómez

The Art of Legislating

Springer

Virgilio Zapatero Gómez
Facultad de Derecho
Universidad de Alcalá de Henares
Alcalá de Henares, Spain

Translated by Jorge Yetano Roche

Translation from the Spanish language edition: "El arte de legislar" by Virgilio Zapatero,

ISSN 2213-2813 ISSN 2213-2856 (electronic)
Legisprudence Library
ISBN 978-3-030-23390-7 ISBN 978-3-030-23388-4 (eBook)
https://doi.org/10.1007/978-3-030-23388-4

Cover design: eStudio Calamar, Berlin/Figueres

This Springer imprint is published by the registered company Springer Nature Switzerland AG.
The registered company address is: Gewerbestrasse 11, 6330 Cham, Switzerland

Preface

Any contemporary state presents itself as committed to the "rule of law". The notion of rule of law is perhaps the most powerful and repeated political ideal within the current global discourse on legal and political institutions—this notion constitutes, in fact, the yardstick against which the legitimacy of a state is commonly evaluated and asserted (Tamanaha 2004, 2012). Of course, the meaning of the term "rule of law", like that of all open-textured terms, has a wide grey or twilight zone where old oligarchies and modern autocracies might eventually find a place. Yet, despite being a contested concept, the rule of law nevertheless retains a clear core of meaning that is generally recognised.

In the search of this minimal content of the notion of the rule of law, Friedrich Hayek's approach is a good starting point. In his view, the Rule of Law, once "stripped of all technicalities, (...) means that government is bound in all its actions by rules fixed and announced beforehand—rules which make it possible to foresee with fair certainty how the authority will use its coercive powers in given circumstances and to plan one's individual affairs on the basis of this knowledge" (Hayek 1976, pp. 103–104 [80]). Though not sharing all of Hayek's conclusions, Joseph Raz also endorses this formal starting point (Raz 1979) and stresses that the rule of law is a crucial virtue of the state which should not be confused, as often happens, with other important principles, such as democracy, justice, social equality, or human rights. Surely these other values and ideals refer also to virtues of the political system, but it is advisable to keep them conceptually separated from the ideal of the rule of law.

The rule of law means, in a manner, what it literally expresses: the government of laws. In legal and political theory, it implies that the state governs through laws and is subjected to them—or, put otherwise, that every state intervention must be backed by laws and live up to the principle of legality. Obviously, laws may be changed, but any change must always respect previously established legal procedures. As a result, all state authorities must make their decisions within the boundaries set by a given normative framework, not upon the basis of their subjective preferences, their ideology, or their sense of what is just or unjust. Apparently, the rule of law does nothing more than this: to delimit the playground, to set the rules of the game, and to make these rules respected.

Underpinning this formal conception of the rule of law lie such important ideas as legal certainty and security, and the predictability of government powers. The ultimate objective served by the rule of law may well vary depending on the ideological perspective of its advocates (see e.g. Waldron 2008, pp. 6 ff). For authors like Raz or, in this respect, also Hayek, the rule of law makes citizens' freedom and self-determination possible, enabling them to pursue their own life plans. For others, the objective of the rule of law is tightly associated with equality, in both its horizontal (between fellow citizens) and its vertical dimensions (between citizens and government) (Gowder 2014a, b). And yet other authors lay emphasis on the link between development and the rule of law, claiming that the rule of law is a reliable trigger of societal development and stability (Carugati 2014). For all of them, anyway, the rule of law is a key virtue of any legal system.

Even a seemingly formal and aseptic slogan like "the government of laws, not of men" gives rise to a number of principles which must be respected in the making of laws—regardless of their particular contents. These principles include requirements that, on the one hand, affect the very concept of law: no law exists unless it is based on rules (Hart 1968, pp. 99–125). And they also affect, on the other hand, the form of laws themselves: the rule of law vanishes, or is significantly weakened, whenever norms are drafted in such a way that they cannot be known in advance, for this lack of certainty hampers citizens' self-determination and makes it impossible for them to carry out their own life plans. Finally, the rule of law can be said to fail if legal norms are applied without due observance of legally established procedures and warranties. Thus, a basic conception of the rule of law must positively respond to these three questions: Is government limited by laws? Do state powers honour the tenets of formal legality when they act? Are laws impartially applied?

This book is mainly concerned with formal legality and with the question of how to achieve good laws—a topic which was famously addressed by the eighteenth century enlightened thinkers (Zapatero 2000), and on which a number of prominent legal scholars of our times have also elaborated: think, e.g. of authors like Fuller (1969), Raz (1979), or Waldron (1999). Historically, the baseline canon of "good legislation" demanded generality, publicity and accessibility, and comprehensibility of laws; prospectivity or non-retroactive norms; consistency or non-contradiction; the actual possibility of complying with legal obligations and prohibitions; stability; or congruency between enacted laws and their application. All these are valuable ideals that should not be abandoned in today's legal systems, particularly in view of the silent revolution which is transforming our legality-based "states of law" into jurisdictional states. Such ideals remain entirely alive and are still worth pursuing for those who believe—as I do—in representative democracy and thus in the dignity of legislation.

The idea of writing this book originally emerged during my parliamentary and governmental experience. From 1982 until 1993, I was the person in charge of legislative co-ordination for the Government of Spain. Those were years of very intensive legislative production. The 527 laws we elaborated during this period (along with thousands of decrees) profoundly modified all sectors of the legal order inherited from Franco's dictatorship and laid the foundations of a new social and democratic system. To an academic like me, this was really exciting and enriching—a unique experience—and I thought that, upon my return to the university, I should reflect on this experience and elaborate on it, in an attempt to contribute to improving not only scholarly awareness of how laws are made but also, and above all, their quality. I am deeply convinced that legal education and training of jurists should not only be limited to the teaching of how laws are interpreted or applied by courts, but also extend to how it is possible to make good laws. This was the ultimate goal I pursued some years ago when writing this book. The fact that the Spanish edition (Zapatero 2009) is sold out and the suggestion of my colleague Daniel Oliver-Lalana of translating it for the Springer's *Legisprudence Library* have given me the impulse to publish this English version, in the hope that it may be of interest to an international audience.

Madrid, Spain
April 2019

Virgilio Zapatero Gómez

References

Carugati MF (2014) What is the rule of law for? Democracy, development and the rule of law in classical Athens. Buffalo Law Rev 62:118–155
Fuller LL (1969) The morality of law, 2nd, revised edn. Yale University Press, New Haven
Gowder P (2014a) Democracy, solidarity, and the rule of law: lessons from Athens. Buffalo Law Rev 62(1):1–67
Gowder P (2014b) Equal law in an unequal world. Iowa Law Rev 99:1020–1081
Hart HLA (1968) El concepto de derecho. Abeledo Perrot, Buenos Aires [The concept of law. Clarendon Press, Oxford, 1961]
Hayek FA (1976) Camino de servidumbre. Alianza Editorial, Madrid [Road to Serfdom. Chicago University Press, Chicago, 1944]
Tamanaha BZ (2004) On the rule of law: history, politics, theory. Cambridge University Press, Cambridge
Tamanaha BZ (2012) The history and elements of the rule of law. Singapore J Leg Stud 2012:232–247
Raz J (1979) The authority of law: essays on law and morality. Clarendon Press, Oxford
Waldron J (1999) The dignity of legislation. Cambridge University Press, Cambridge
Waldron J (2008) The concept and the rule of law. Georgia Law Rev 43:1–61
Zapatero V (2000) El arte ilustrado de legislar. Introduction to: J. Bentham, Nomografía o el arte de redactar leyes. Centro de Estudios Constitucionales, Madrid, pp XV–LXXXII
Zapatero V (2009) El arte de legislar. Thomshon-Aranzadi, Cizur Menor

Contents

About the Author

Virgilio Zapatero Gómez (Dr. Iur., Dr. h.c. mult.) is emeritus professor at the University of Alcalá de Henares (Spain), where he has previously held the chair of legal philosophy. He has been representative at the Spanish Constitutional Convention (1977/1979); MP at the Spanish Congress of Deputies (1979/1993); Secretary of State (1982/1986); Ministry of Parliamentary Affairs of the Spanish Government (1986/1993); representative at the Parliamentary Assembly of the Council of Europe (1993); Rector of the University of Alcalá de Henares (2002/2010); and President of the Madrid Council of University Rectors (2006/2010).

He has extensively published on legisprudence, as well as on legal theory and philosophy, in leading Spanish-speaking academic journals. His books include, among others, the following: *El arte de legislar* (Pamplona: Thomson-Aranzadi, 2009); *El derecho como proceso normativo: lecciones de teoría del derecho* [Law as a normative process: lessons in legal theory] (Madrid: UAH, 2010, 2nd edition); *Nomografía o el arte de redactar leyes de Bentham* (Madrid: CEPC, 2004); *Fernando de los Ríos: biografía intelectual* (Valencia: Pre-Textos, 1999, 2nd edition); or *Socialismo y ética* [Socialism and Ethics] (Madrid: Debate, 1980).

Professor Zapatero has prepared reports on "Human Rights in Central America" (1997) and "Human Rights in Colombia" (1998) on behalf of the European Commission, and also drafted a Deontological Code for the International Federation of the Red Cross and Red Crescent Societies (IFRC) (2000).

He holds Doctor Honoris Causa degrees by several universities including the Universidad Ricardo Palma (Lima, Peru), the Universidad Nacional Autónoma de León (Nicaragua), or the Universidad Autónoma de Santo Domingo (Dominican Republic).

He has been awarded a number of prizes and distinctions, such as *La Gran Cruz de la Orden de Carlos III;* the *Medalla de Alfonso X El Sabio;* the *Medalla de la Orden del Mérito Constitucional* (Spain); the *Gran Cruz de la Orden del Libertador Simón Bolívar* (Venezuela); the *Gran Cruz de la Orden de San Raimundo Peñafort;*

the *Gran Cruz de la Orden de Bernardo O'Higgins* (Chile); the *Distinción de la Federación Iberoamericana de Ombudsman* (FIO); the *Master de Oro del Forum de Alta Dirección;* the *Gran Cruz del Mérito Naval;* and the *Medalla de la Orden de Sikatuna* (Philippines).

Chapter 1
Introduction: The Study of Legislation

The history of law is marked by alternate periods of overflow and channeling (Morand 1987, p. 502). If the answer to the spread of customs and to the unpredictability and inaccessibility of judicial decision-making was the discovery, with the French Revolution, of written laws as the only source of justice—and of codification as the ideal instrument of knowledge—, what could be the answer our modern society finds to the problem of managing a body of norms that will most likely continue to grow in volume and cause more ink to flow over its quality, efficacy, effectiveness and efficiency? Deregulation programs have attempted to redress an alleged overflow of legislation, pointing only to its over-cost and inefficiency. But we live nowadays in communities that are organised by laws, inside a regulatory State that articulates its policies through legal norms (Eskridge and Peller 1991, p. 707 ff; Farber and Frickey 1991, p. 875 ff), and to which we still attribute the task of steering society. And as long as this is the case, the pertinent question is not whether or not there are too many norms, but rather if they all satisfy the minimal demandable parameters of quality so they can fulfil the functions we have assigned to them, which are the functions of a social, democratic, and rule of law-based state.

The increase in the volume of regulation, the poor quality of legal texts, the doubts about the effectiveness of norms and the perceptions about their inefficiency and low efficacy have contributed to the germination of the most daring interpretations, or even to the sheer abandonment of law. Deregulation has been presented as the solution to the straying of regulation. But this is not an innocent response, because deregulation is nothing else than a re-regulation that has often served to mask a political agenda aimed at the restriction of democracy, the dismantling of the welfare state (see Tolchin and Tolchin 1983), and the substitution of the visible—and therefore politically accountable—hand of the government by the invisible hand of the market.

The regulations that were eliminated are precisely the ones that protected us from the greed of irresponsible corporations that force the very economic system to the edge of the cliff, or those that guarantee breathable air, drinkable water, edible food, safety and higiene in working places, protection against nuclear disaster, assurance

V. Zapatero Gómez, *The Art of Legislating*, Legisprudence Library 6,
https://doi.org/10.1007/978-3-030-23388-4_1

in old age, and a long etcetera of rights promised by the welfare state—after the severe, worldwide financial crisis exploded in 2008, few can now ignore what deregulation entails. But even if deregulation is not the answer, some of the problems that prompted it are real and demand deeper reflexion to find a possible solution within the framework of the social and democratic *Rechtsstaat*. The aim of this effort cannot be a deluge of new regulations but rather to equip ourselves with the ones that are necessary, and whose effectiveness, efficacy and efficiency can be guaranteed. In this sense, it could be very healthy to turn our eyes back to the process of legislating, so we can discover where and why rationality goes astray.

The preoccupation for the quality of laws has existed for many centuries, as demonstrated by the works of Plato *(The Laws)*, Aristotle *(Politics)*, Cicero *(On Laws)*, Pletho *(The Book of Laws)*, or Aquinas *(Summa Theologica)*, among many others. However, these works were written for another kind of cultural universe, for a context very different to our own. What is missing in them are certain elements essential to modernity, without which it was not probable that a technique or art of legislating would have ever developed. The legislating state had not yet made its appearance, the crisis of certainty had not yet fallen over our societies as it did towards the end of the seventeenth century (cf. Tomás y Valiente 1993), and rationalism had not yet extended into politics—all these conditions only did fully mature well into the eighteenth century. Rationalism applied to politics, the demand for more certainty and security in the face of the legal particularism of the *Ancien Régime*, and the state's ambition to monopolise normative power were the factors that fuelled the development of a will to rationalise and systematise the legal order. Such a will manifested itself in two complementary directions: codification, which would make it possible to know the existing law, and the art of legislating, which promised better laws. Both of them reached their peak during the age of Enlightenment (see Zapatero 2000). The names of Muratori (1753), Montesquieu (1964), Beccaria (1821), Condorcet (1980, 1821), Abbot Mably (1797), Schmid D'Avenstein (1776), Filangieri (1787), Rousseau (1973), Diderot (1989), Comte (1837) in France, or Bentham (1843, 1981, 2000) in the Anglo-Saxon context, are some examples of those enlightened minds that occupied themselves with the art of legislating, an art that was meant to liberate humanity from the despotism of monarchs (Rousseau) and the no less fearsome despotism of judges (Montesquieu). Certainty, legal security, liberty in short, did not only require an effort in codification and limitation of the executive and judicial powers; it also demanded taking good care of the writing of norms. This was ultimately the fundamental obsession of the enlightened. The legislator had to be taught to weigh words as if they were diamonds, for our liberties depend on them. Had it not been for this conviction, for the hope in this art of legislation, much of the legisprudential production of the Enlightenment would never have existed.

Of course, pointing out the deficiencies of some of these ideas today, two hundred years later, is not very difficult. But the really interesting question here is to know if the problem faced by the enlightened—to guarantee security and liberty by means of properly written laws—is relatively solved or not. Unfortunately, it would seem rather that the multiplication of sources in our modern legal orders resembles the particularism of the *Ancien Régime*, that normative motorisation has created oceans of norms, that the famous principles theorised by Dworkin (1978) revive in our systems the old and unreliable *interpretatio* and that the "rule of the constitution" is opposed to the rule of law.[1]

Drowned by the most dogmatic methodological and axiological positivism, the enlightened vocation for artful legislating was substituted by the vocation for interpretation. The jurist, from then on a scientist of the law (Díaz 1974, p. 65 ff), is interested predominantly in positive legal norms, in so far as they are valid, formally in force, and as long as they continue to be so. Hence, legal dogmatism has made the norm as it has been promulgated the inalienable and exclusive center of attention. Curiously enough, although positivism has put laws in a place of honor within the legal realm, modern positivists have been far less interested in legislation than in the functioning of courts and the performance of judges. They sustain the traditional thesis that defines law by its institutional sources, but the institutions they are more interested in are courts, rather than parliaments (Waldron 1999). Eventually, the legislator was overthrown and the judge was enthroned instead. The reasons for this short-sightedness can be found in various factors such as the voluntarist conception of law, the ideal of the purity of the science of law or the myth of the rational legislator, all-knowing, all-powerful, whose produce may not even be discussed or improved.[2] But, as Waldron (1999) points out, at the root of this disregard for legal reflection is also a mistrust of parliaments, those assemblies riddled with inexperienced people who, unlike judges, are politically active. And so, this incoherence, this reductionism has led to a certain disdain for the study of the normative process; that is, the study of the moment of the birth of the norm. That is how the traditional approach of legal thought has not only circumvented—as Peces-Barba (1988, p. 29 ff) explains—the problem of the relationship of power and law but, a fortiori and consequently, has dispensed with the study of the capital process of the conversion of politics into law.

It has been necessary to wait for the old problems that gave rise to the art of legislating in the eighteenth century to reappear in some way, so that even if timidly, the preoccupation for the study of the process of drafting norms can be rekindled. It was possibly in the United States where, during the New Deal, the concern for legislation recovered more strongly.[3] The revolt against common law formalism began to conceive law as a tool at the legislator's disposal to achieve certain social objectives, and to rely on social engineering as a conscious effort to change society and its institutions through the legal order. The work of figures such as Justice Holmes (1897), Pound (1911, 1942), or Gray (1909) already agreed on the need to adopt this new approach regarding common law. This new path was complemented by the writings of Louis Brandeis, Frankfurter (1927) or Landis (1938), who developed a positive vision of government based on the principle of institutional

[1]See Díaz's (1999, p. 101 ff) critique of this unwarranted and biased contradistinction.

[2]On this point, see García Amado (2000, p. 304 ff), as well as Marcilla (2005, p. 251 ff).

[3]For an overview of this new approach in the U.S., see Eskridge and Frickey (1994).

competence (the government was better equipped, better informed and better prepared than the judges to make general decisions), and leaned on this principle to justify the necessary deference of judges to government and parliament. But it was the work of Hart and Sacks (1958) that, from the 1950s to the present, has had a decisive influence on the teaching of law and the judicial interpretation of law in the United States. From then until the 1990s, most law students had *The Legal Process* as textbook. Its study has fostered the interaction between law and political science, has conditioned legal interpretation theories in the post-war period, and has significantly stimulated research on the lawmaking process. In spite of its more modern critics, the work of Hart and Sacks has established itself with an unusually robust vitality.

As to Europe, it has been in the second half of the twentieth century, and especially in the 1970s, when the studies on legislation have regained status, largely because of the application of the methodology of political science to law.[4] Peter Noll's influential book *Gesetzgebungsehre* (1973) is usually regarded as the beginning of a change of course to which a series of important works have contributed decisively.[5] It is to be expected that also in Spain (López-Calera 1988, p. 79), once the initial phase of transition and consolidation of democracy has been completed (a phase in which what was really at stake was the fundamental aspects of an advanced social and legal order), the preoccupation for the theory of legislation that is timidly emerging will vigorously develop.[6] Some studies specifically dedicated to the matter, as those of Galiana (2008, 2003, 2001, 2000) and Marcilla (2005), already point in that very desirable direction.

As I have explained elsewhere (Zapatero 1994), the scope of this kind of studies depends on whether their conception of the norm-making process is "minimalist" or "maximalist". This will determine if the studies concentrate on logical and linguistic problems only, if they include the political and institutional dimensions of the process of legislating, or if they go even further, encompassing the ethical dimension. In the work of Marcilla (2005, p. 275 ff) we can find a detailed discussion of the advantages and inconveniences of each of these possibilities—and of the reasons why she is inclined towards a maximalist conception. As far as the present book is concerned, its purpose is none other than to contribute to improving laws *("la ley")* as the most respectable source and the most worthy instrument of government. With this in mind we think of a theory of legislation that is far more humble than the Enlightenment's science of legislation, which wanted to tell the legislator what to do. Without giving up the discussion on the justice and morality of norms, the main

---

[4]On the rebirth of legislative jurisprudence in the U.S. and Europe, see Bar-Siman-Tov (2019); cf. also Oliver-Lalana and Wintgens (2019).

[5]To name but a few, see e.g. Giuliani and Picardi (1987), Amselek et al. (1988), Pagano (1988), La Spina (1989), or, more recently, Wintgens (2012), Albanesi (2013), Müller and Uhlmann (2013), and Karpen and Xanthaki (2017).

[6]See, among others, Atienza (1997), GRETEL (1986, 1989), Montoro (1989), Sainz and Ochoa (1989), Corona et al. (1994), Díez-Ripollés (2013[2003]), Menéndez and Pau Pedrón (2004), Zapatero (1994, 1998, 2000), Pérez Luño (1993), Laporta (1999, 2004), García Amado (2000), Fuertes (2008).

object of this work is to study how we can achieve legislation that lives up to what Lon Fuller (1969) called the internal morality of law; how we can make laws more efficacious, more effective and more efficient; how to articulate the process of norm production so that norms are the expression of the will of citizens; or how to better build the relationship between legislators and judges to make the rule of law a reality. And it is from this perspective that a theory of legislation can contribute to our legal systems by providing them with a little more linguistic, logical-formal, pragmatic, teleological and perhaps also ethical rationality (Atienza 1997).

It makes sense to ask ourselves how useful it might be to bring together, under the same label, fields of research and perspectives as different as those required for this type of study (Mader 1988; Posner 1983). Wróblewski (1979) points out that, in general terms, the effects of a science of legislation can be felt in three different directions: in the education of those who formally and informally influence legislative decisions, in the preparation and analysis of normative texts and through the participation of experts in the shaping of public opinion around legislative decisions. But I would also mention the contribution of the science of legislation to improving the training of lawyers. The manifesto *Pour une nouvelle génération de légistes*[7] that was published in 1979 in Belgium requesting the creation of a Belgian Institute of Legistics is based on this observation: the present legal training is essentially reduced to the application of law, that is to say, to the appreciation of past or future social behaviour in their relation with already existing rules; but there is something wrong when the reverse side of law, which refers to the invention of rules capable of guiding social behaviour in the direction desired by political power, remains hidden in legal training. Neglecting this perspective results in a mutilation of the capabilities of lawyers who, in many cases, not only interpret rules but also produce them. Producing rules is, curiously enough, what they have not been taught to do. That is why legal training should no longer be limited to the instruction of good judges and good lawyers but also teach the art of making good laws (Fleiner-Gerster 1982, p. 18).

Alchourrón and Bulygin (1993, p. 410) think that there are no specialists or technicians in legislative science for the simple reason that there are no academic centres to prepare them, and there are no such centres because there is no body of doctrine, i.e. there is no theory that systematically and methodically studies the problems posed by legislation and how to solve them. Maybe it is not impossible to change this, and maybe it's already changing. For a scientific approach to have a real influence, Wróblewski insists, two conditions must be met: first, science must have useful information contribute to the legislative process and, second, its influence at the decisive stages of the process must be guaranteed by appropriate bodies. The first condition depends on the results of scientific research in the areas of interest to normative production, while the second depends on the establishment of suitable institutional mechanisms and the functioning of the constitutional framework.

[7]See the Belgian *Journal des Tribunaux* of 17 November 1979.

The first condition can be considered largely fulfilled: that is, that science has something to say to the legislator, something to contribute to the regulatory process. Indeed, research on the language applied to law can provide criteria on the best use of normative language. The study of the structure of rules has already provided the legislator with models that standardise the presentation of legislative texts. The reflection on the development of public policies allows a better understanding of social demands and their subsequent conversion into political decisions. Comparative law studies enable a serious debate on what the best method for drafting regulations is. Sociology of law can contribute to the analysis of the efficacy of rules. Evaluation agencies offer increasingly refined analyses of the effectiveness of rules. The application of economic theory to the world of law provides a better understanding of the cost-benefit ratio of each legislative decision. Constitutional and parliamentary law, together with better knowledge of how collective decisions are made, can improve the normative process. And so we could list all the useful information that scientific disciplines make available to those in charge and that a theory of legislation could synthesise to help the legislator make better laws, endowed with the "internal morality" (Fuller 1969, p. 339 ff) that requires them to be necessary, clear in their formulation, efficacious, effective, efficient and therefore somewhat closer to the ideal of justice.

The problem, then, is not whether science has something important to offer, but whether the legislator is willing to accept it. Political rationality has its own laws, its own particular logic. To what extent is a legislator willing to "be advised" and are the necessary administrative and political structures in place to facilitate this cooperation? Something may be starting to change in our political systems, allowing us to keep hoping for a closer collaboration of the various specialists involved in the legislative process.

Indeed, governments are increasingly concerned about the process of producing regulation and its results. The increase in the quantity of norms in recent decades has led developed countries to believe that centralised management and monitoring of legislative activities are needed. As the OECD (1989) observes, the creation of these new organisms occurred in the 1970s although most of them were not operational until the 1980s. Three-quarters of OECD governments have set up high-level bodies to assist in the planning, direction, coordination and review of the normative system. Such bodies are dedicated to promoting better regulation in the future and to reforming regulatory procedures with a view to improving their efficiency and effectiveness. They all share the common goal of generating greater concern about the implications of normative decisions. National regulatory policies are being developed with the emergence of these organisms dedicated to the management of regulatory processes. But it is also true that in most countries these policies have been part of a broader plan, a set of structural adjustments aimed at contracting state and law. Now is the time to reconsider: the already serious consequences of the deregulation strategy mark an excellent opportunity to redirect the "willingness" of governments to improve their regulatory process. It is well worth the try if we consider that what is at stake here is our model of social order and coexistence that is the social and democratic state of law.

References

Albanesi E (2013) Teoria e tecnica legislativa nel sistema costituzionale. Editoriale Scientifica, Napoli

Alchourrón CE, Bulygin E (1993) Teoría y técnica de la legislación. In: Análisis lógico y derecho. Centro de Estudios Constitucionales, Madrid, pp 409–425

Amselek P et al (1988) La science de la législation. PUF, Paris

Atienza M (1997) Contribución a una teoría de la legislación. Civitas, Madrid

Bar-Siman-Tov I (2019) The global revival of legisprudence: a comparative view on legislation in legal education and research. In: Oliver-Lalana AD (ed) Conceptions and misconceptions of legislation. Springer, Cham, pp 275–294

Beccaria C (1821) Tratado de los delitos y de las penas (trans: de las Casas JA). Imprenta de Joachin Ibarra, Madrid

Bentham J (1843) Nomography, or the art of inditing laws. In: Bowring J (ed) The works of Jeremy Bentham. William Tait, Edinburgh, pp 231–298

Bentham J (1981) Tratados de Legislación Civil y Penal. Editora Nacional, Madrid

Bentham J (2000) Nomografía o el arte de redactar leyes. Centro de Estudios Políticos y Constitucionales, Madrid

Comte FCL (1837) Traité de Législation, ou Exposition des Lois Générales suivant lesquelles les peuples prospèrent, dépérissent ou restent stationnaires, 3rd edn. Hauman, Cattoir et Cie, Bruxelles

Condorcet MJ (1821) Observaciones sobre el libro XXIX de “El espíritu de las leyes”. In: de Tracy D (ed) Comentarios sobre “El espíritu de las leyes”. Imprenta de Fermín Villalpando, Madrid

Condorcet MJ (1980) Bosquejo de un cuadro histórico de los progresos del espíritu humano. Editora Nacional, Madrid

Corona MJ, Pau F, Tudela J (eds) (1994) La técnica legislativa a debate. Tecnos, Madrid

de Mably L'A (1797 [1776]) De la legislation ou Principes des Lois (Œuvres Completes), vol 9. Chez Bossange, Masson et Besson, Paris

Díaz E (1974) Sociología y Filosofía del Derecho. Taurus, Madrid

Díaz E (1999) Curso de Filosofía del Derecho. Marcial Pons, Madrid

Diderot D (1989) Observaciones sobre la instrucción de la Emperatriz de Rusia a los Diputados respecto a la elaboración de las leyes. In: Escritos Políticos de Diderot. Centro de Estudios Constitucionales, Madrid

Díez-Ripollés JL (2013) La racionalidad de las leyes penales. Práctica y teoría, 2nd edn. Tirant lo Blanch, Valencia

Dworkin R (1978) Los derechos en serio. Ariel, Barcelona. [Taking Rights Seriously, Harvard University Press, Cambridge (MA), 1977]

Eskridge WN, Frickey PP (1994) An historical and critical introduction to ‘the legal process’. In: Hart HM, Sacks AM (eds) (1958). The legal process. Basic problems in the making and application of law. Foundation Press, Westbury

Eskridge WN, Peller G (1991) The new public law movement: moderation as a postmodern cultural form. Mich Law Rev 89:707–791

Farber DA, Frickey PP (1991) In the shadow of the legislature: The common law in the age of the new public law. Mich Law Rev 89:875–906

Filangieri G (1787) Ciencia de la Legislación. Imprenta de Manuel González, Madrid

Fleiner-Gerster T (1982) Rapport introductoire. In: Principes et méthodes d'élaboration des normes juridiques. Actes du douzième Colloque de Droit Européen (Friburg, 13–15 octobre 1982). Conseil de l'Europe, Strasbourg

Frankfurter F (1927) The task of administrative law. Univ Pa Law Rev 75:614–621

Fuertes M (2008) Once tesis y una premática para restablecer la dignidad de la ley. Revista de Administración Pública 177:119–155

Fuller LL (1969) The morality of law, 2nd revised edn. Yale University Press, New Haven

Galiana A (2000) La relevancia de la técnica legislativa en la elaboración de las leyes. Anuario de Filosofía del Derecho XVII:247–272
Galiana A (2001) La metódica de la legislación: el proceso de formación de la voluntad legislativa. URV, Tarragona
Galiana A (2003) La legislación en el Estado de Derecho. Dykinson, Madrid
Galiana A (2008) La ley, entre la razón y la experimentación. Tirant lo Blanch, Valencia
García Amado JA (2000) Razón práctica y teoría de la legislación. Derechos y Libertades. Revista del Instituto Bartolomé de las Casas 9:304–318
Giuliani A, Picardi N (1987) L'educazione giuridica (V): Modelli di legislatore e scienza della legislazione. Edizione Scientifiche Italiane, Peruggia
Gray JC (1909) The nature and sources of the law. The Columbia University Press, New York
GRETEL (Grupo de Estudios de Técnica Legislativa) (1986) La forma de las leyes. Centro de Estudios Constitucionales, Madrid
GRETEL (Grupo de Estudios de Técnica Legislativa) (1989) Curso de técnica legislativa. Centro de Estudios Constitucionales, Madrid
Hart HM, Sacks AM (1958) The legal process. Basic problems in the making and application of law. Tentative ed, Cambridge, MA. [Foundation Press, Westbury, 1994]
Holmes OW (1897) The path of the law. Harv Law Rev 10:457–478
Karpen U, Xanthaki H (2017) Legislation in Europe. A comprehensive guide for scholars and practitioners. Hart-Bloomsbury, Oxford
La Spina A (1989) La decisione legislativa. Lineamenti di una teoria. Giuffrè, Milano
Landis J (1938) The administrative process. Yale University Press, New Haven
Laporta F (1999) Materiales para una reflexión sobre la racionalidad y crisis de la ley. Doxa 22:321–330
Laporta F (2004) Teoría y realidad de la legislación: una introducción general. In: Menéndez A, Pau Pedrón A (eds) La proliferación legislativa: un desafío para el estado de derecho. Thomson-Civitas, Madrid, pp 29–88
López Calera N (1988) La science de la législation en Espagne. In: Amselek P et al (eds) La science de la législation. PUF, Paris
Mader L (1988) La législation: objet d'une science en devenir. In: La science de la législation. PUF, Paris
Marcilla G (2005) Racionalidad legislativa. Crisis de la ley y nueva ciencia de la legislación. Centro de Estudios Políticos y Constitucionales, Madrid
Menéndez A, Pau Pedrón A (eds) (2004) La proliferación legislativa: un desafío para el estado de derecho. Thomson-Civitas, Madrid
Montesquieu CLSB (1964) L'Esprit des lois. Et la querelle de l'Esprit des lois, 1748–1750. In: Oeuvres Complètes, Liv. XXIX (De la manière de composer les lois). Aux Èditions du Seuil, Paris
Montoro MJ (1989) Adecuación al ordenamiento y factibilidad. Presupuestos de calidad de las normas. Centro de Estudios Constitucionales, Madrid
Morand A (1987) I problemi dell'inflazione normativa: il punto di vista di un osservatore svizzero. Il Foro Italiano 11:497–512
Müller G, Uhlmann F (2013) Elemente einer Rechtssetzungslehre, 3rd edn. Schulthess, Zürich
Muratori LA (1753) Dei Difetti della Giurisprudenza. G. Pasquali, Venezia
Noll P (1973) Gesetzgebungslehre. Rowohlt, Reinbeck bei Hamburg
OECD (1989) Directory of regulatory review and reform organizations in OECD member countries. OECD, Paris
Oliver-Lalana AD, Wintgens LJ (2019) Legisprudence. In: Sellers M, Kirste S (eds) Encyclopedia of the philosophy of law and social philosophy. Springer, Cham
Pagano R (ed) (1988) Normative europee sulla tecnica legislativa. Camera dei Deputati, Roma
Peces-Barba G (1988) Introducción a la Filosofía del Derecho. Debate, Madrid
Pérez Luño AE (1993) El desbordamiento de las fuentes del derecho. Real Academia Sevillana de Legislación y Jurisprudencia, Sevilla

Posner R (1983) Statutory interpretation in the clasroom and in the courtroom. Univ Chicago Law Rev 50:800–822
Pound R (1911) The scope and purpose of sociological jurisprudence. Harv Law Rev 24:140–168
Pound R (1942) Social control through law. Yale University Press, New Haven
Rousseau JJ (1973) El contrato social. Aguilar, Madrid
Sainz F, Ochoa J (1989) La calidad de las leyes. Parlamento Vasco, Vitoria
Schmid D'Avenstein GL (1821 [1776]) Principios de Legislación Universal. Imprenta Roldán, Valladolid
Tolchin SJ, Tolchin M (1983) Dismantling America. The rush to deregulate. Houston Miflin Company, Boston
Tomás y Valiente F (1993) Introduction to C. Beccaria, Tratado de los delitos y de las penas (1774) (trans: de las Casas JA). Joachin Ibarra, Madrid. Chamber Printer of H.M, IX-LXI (facsimile edition, Spanish Ministry of Justice, Madrid)
Waldron J (1999) The dignity of legislation. Cambridge University Press, Cambridge
Wintgens LJ (2012) Legisprudence. Practical reason in legislation. Ashgate, Aldershot
Wróblewski J (1979) A model of rational law-making. Archiv für Rechts- und Sozialphilosophie 65 (2):188–201
Zapatero V (1994) De la jurisprudencia a la legislación. Doxa 15/16:769–789
Zapatero V (1998) El club de los nomófilos. Cuadernos de Derecho Público 3:61–94
Zapatero V (2000) El arte ilustrado de legislar. Introduction to: Bentham J, Nomografía o el arte de redactar leyes. Centro de Estudios Constitucionales, Madrid, pp XV–LXXXII

Chapter 2
The Dignity of Laws

2.1 The Doubts of Our Time

The twentieth century, which some have defined as a firing squad in permanent operation, has also been the century of the revolution of legal and constitutional rights. Generations of rights—civil, political, economic, social and cultural—have followed one another inexorably (Peces-Barba 1999, p. 154 ff, 207 ff; 1998), relying on an economic model that has generated the surpluses needed to develop the idea of citizenship. This is what happened in Europe after the Second World War, in the United States of America with President Roosevelt's New Deal (Sunstein 1990), or in Spain as a result of the legislative development of the Constitution of 1978. The success of the model has been remarkable in terms of the percentage of public expenditure allocated to social programs, in the degree of income distribution, or in the policy of compensation for the new forms of poverty of our time; in short, a system of liberties has been built that also manages to generate increasing levels of equality. But for some time now, this formula of "social peace with democracy" has become the object of doubts, if not of radical criticism and political conflicts. The idea has spread that this model of social state—the most extensive and legitimate instrument for the political resolution of social problems—has turned out to be problematic, and the undisputed confidence in its promises has become blurred.

A certain kind of leftist political thought has not been alien to the radical criticism of the social state. But it was after the first economic recession in the 1970s that a whole set of ideas emerged with force which called for a "recycling" of the welfare state—a climate of opinion encouraged from the right-wing sectors of society. It has gone too far, they said, the state is oversized. And certainly, whoever compares our present states with those of past centuries will clearly perceive the extent to which the functions of the state have increased. From a state that was simply expected to administer justice, to maintain internal order and to guarantee the integrity of exterior borders, we have moved on to a welfare state that constantly multiplies its functions and commitments. And with this overload the model does not work, it is said,

V. Zapatero Gómez, *The Art of Legislating*, Legisprudence Library 6,
https://doi.org/10.1007/978-3-030-23388-4_2

because it disincentives both investment and work (Offe 1982, p. 68 ff). Trust in the state as an instrument of social direction and change has been replaced by mistrust of the state, and there is growing suspicion, in the best of cases, over the innocuousness of its laws and regulations: if you distrust the government as much as I do, they are telling us, you might not find it absurd to ask yourself this question: What are governments and their regulations for? And so we soon moved on from suspicion to stigmatisation. Are profits down? It's the regulation's fault. Are prices up? It's the regulation's fault. Is there a problem with the competitiveness of our industry? It's the regulation's fault. Are we lacking a research, development and innovation policy? It's the regulation's fault.

This has been and still is the intellectual atmosphere that we breathe at the beginning of the twenty-first century, in which a growing scepticism toward norms has developed (Mignone 1997). It is said that there are too many rules; that the rules are obscure and imprecise; that they rarely achieve the objectives they pursue or, in any case, achieve them at excessively high costs; and that they are increasingly burdened with a major democratic deficit that erodes their legitimacy. And this is how the close examination of the quantity, quality, effectiveness, efficiency,[1] and legitimacy of norms seems today to invite to a certain normative abstinence of the state, and to look outside the law—i.e. in the market—for the social control benefits it traditionally offered.

Besides disclosing the ideological background that underpins the political slogan of deregulation, those who defend the model of the social state should embark on a careful investigation of the profound changes that are taking place, and that affect the role and meaning of law—at least as it has been traditionally understood in our democratic systems. And in this task, a return to the studies of legislation can not only help to better understand such changes and their implications but also to facilitate the governance of our societies within the structures and principles of the rule of law. Let us point out some of these transformations that make it advisable to consider the process of normative production much more seriously.

2.2 Legitimacy Problems

Modernity saw in the state and in law the material and formal source of laws. Later, the State of Law or *Rechtsstaat*—with its classic principles: national sovereignty, division of powers, rule of law, and a catalogue of fundamental rights—allowed the

[1]In fact, the concern for the problems of effectiveness and efficiency of norms is shared by political figures adhering to different ideologies. And so, both conservative and progressive governments have instituted legislative and regulatory evaluation bodies—especially since the 1980s (see OECD 1989). As a proof of the growing interest for the improvement of regulation, important initiatives have been taken in numerous countries, most notably under the auspices of the OECD and with the involvement of the EU: see e.g. OECD (1999, 2010a, b, 2018a, b, 2019; cf. also Chap. 11 in this volume).

establishment of a coherent system to legitimise its norms (Díaz 1966). But this form of organisation we call the state, of unquestionable success and reputation until very recently, is subject to a process of erosion caused by the confluence of two current phenomena: globalisation and liberalisation (Putzel 2009).

Globalisation theorists—both those who focus on economic liberalisation (Wolf 2004) and the advocates of *global governance* (Giddens 1998)—share a remarkable scepticism towards the state. In the first case, because they choose to promote policies of pure and simple economic liberalisation. In the second case,[2] because they understand that the government of society and economy is no longer the prerogative of states; rather, states must now share this prerogative with other kinds of local, regional and even non-governmental organisations. It is not easy to endorse the policies they propose, especially if we analyse the relatively scarce results they promise when it comes to reducing inequality or improving peace and security in the world. Yet, these theories offer us a more accurate description of the progressive erosion of the state and, therefore, of the diminishing protagonism of law as the legitimate instrument of social direction.

These new capital transformations under way that affect the essence and function of the state itself are added to the historical process of increasing internationalisation of political, economic and social relations, which has been altering the classic theory of the sources of law: beyond the literal wording of the constitutional texts, reality tells us that states no longer sovereignly regulate the behaviour of their citizens.[3] Thus we see how there has been a growing internationalisation of the production of norms by virtue of which—and I am referring to countries such as Spain—more than half of our system or regulations is produced outside our borders: I am talking about all that multifaceted variety of international bodies to which states merely adhere, or where, at best, they represent one more voice at a negotiating table which they cannot even leave. Not to mention the thousands of regulations and directives issued by the European Union (Zapatero 1996). Finally, in this process of progressive de-nationalisation of the law, we must not forget the growing process—not always properly controlled—of delegating normative powers through the most varied techniques (among which the so-called "self-regulation" deserves special study), not only to public but also private bodies, which is giving rise to the appearance of a *soft law* that makes it almost impossible to reduce the notion of "law" to "state law".

These are some of the elements that make up the current situation, which has been described as a new legal pluralism (Arnaud 1981, p. 23 ff; Arnaud 1994). The result of the erosion of the state and its replacement by the market, of the "governance" through the coalition of governments and the more picturesque variety of entities within civil society (Braithwaite and Drahos 2000), of the growing internationalisation of the production of norms, and of its privatisation without further control cannot be—for the moment—other than the weakening of the vital

[2]Cf. e.g. Held (2004), Kaldor (2003); or Beck (2003).

[3]On the new "global regulators", see e.g. Zapatero (2003, 2006).

link between citizens and laws, which is the source of the latter's legitimacy (Hierro 2001b, p. 34).

2.3 The Dispute Over Quality

In addition to the growing marginalisation of citizens in the production of the laws that apply to them, we have to deal with the eternal complaint about the lack of quality of legislation: obscurity, ambiguity, gaps or loopholes, antinomies, lacking systematicity. . ., the long list of shortcomings that have always hampered normative language. The constant demand for greater clarity is not the fruit of a perfectionist or aesthetic craving. It reveals a well-founded concern: if laws are intended to shape the behaviour of citizens according to models established by the legislator, if they are to contribute to strengthening the value of legal certainty and security,[4] these models must be comprehensible, and therefore clearly established.

Experience shows to what extent the comprehensibility of norms is an ideal that is not easy to achieve: the inevitable open texture of normative language, the fallibility and sometimes the sheer incompetence of those who draft norms, the constraints imposed by the political system throughout the normative process, or the technification of the relations to be regulated hinder the path towards the formal, logical-linguistic rationality of norms, and may even sink them directly into irrationality. Thus, in addition to political problems, there are technical problems—of poor legislative technique—which affect the quality of norms (Alchourron y Bulygin 1993, p. 423). They are linguistic problems (ambiguity and vagueness) and logical problems, which can in turn be divided into systematic problems (gaps, contradictions and redundancies) and dynamic problems (promulgation and repeal); and it is these linguistic and logical issues that generate a considerable number of defects in legislation, which are ascribable not only to the politicians who pass the laws in government or parliament but also—to a significant extent—to the jurists who draft them.

But the dispute over the quality of rules is not only caused by the flood of intricate and incomprehensible laws. In some cases the doubts are even more radical: there is a suspicion that too often norms don't achieve the results they seek and there is a fear that, when they do, the cost may sometimes be unacceptable (Galiana 2008, p. 228 ff). These doubts became a premise of those legal-philosophical approaches (Savigny, Montesquieu, Ehrlich, Gurvitch. . .) that set out from the idea of a merely "receptive" legislator, i.e. a legislator whose only function and only possibility is to limit himself to translating into legal texts the *living law* already existing in society. But even those who welcome an interventionist legislator, committed to social change and confident in his ability to accommodate reality to the normative mirror, are often dubious about the effectiveness of legislation. The debate among experts on

[4]See e.g. Corsale (1979), de Palma Fernández (1997); or Arcos Ramírez (2000).

a law as well-intentioned as the one aimed to eradicate gender violence is one of the last examples in our country.[5]

As Dicey (1914) stated after studying the nineteenth century legislation of the British Parliament, laws often don't generate the benefits promised by their promoters nor produce the disasters foreshadowed by their adversaries. As a consequence of the financial difficulties now faced by states, this kind of scepticism has resurfaced with force. Indeed, the development of the ambitious social programs initiated after the Second World War has caused, since the 1980s, serious financing problems for governments whose resources are always lagging behind social demands. It is only logical that, in a context of scarcity, particular care should be taken to examine whether laws achieve the objectives they pursue and whether they achieve them at reasonable costs. There are therefore three different situations that should be distinguished more clearly: whether the norm is obeyed, whether it achieves the objectives it pursues and, if so, what are the costs involved in its application. To this purpose we could perhaps agree to the differentiated use of the terms efficacy, effectiveness and efficiency.

Efficacy has been understood by the general theory of law as the correspondence between the model of behaviour foreseen in the norm and the real behaviour of its addressees. And so it is said that a rule is efficacious when it is obeyed.[6] But if this is the criterion that has traditionally been relevant to the legal theorist, it is not the only one that is of interest to the citizen or to the legislator himself. The latter is increasingly concerned, first and foremost, with the effectiveness of rules. This is because the legislator does not dictate rules for the simple purpose of modifying or reaffirming the behaviour (or the feelings) of citizens: for the legislator, ordered behaviour is only the necessary means to achieve a certain state of affairs. Hence, the rule may be efficacious (obeyed) but ineffective (because it does not achieve the desired objective). The efficacy of the rule has to do with the positive or negative attitude that citizens adopt towards it. The effectiveness of the rule, on its part, depends on whether the decision-maker has correctly established the causal relationship between the desired result and the conduct demanded from citizens. And this operation, as we will see when discussing the implementation of norms (see Chap. 11), is a crucial (and controversial) aspect of any theory of legislation based on trust in law as a means of social control and direction.

A final but no less important parameter by which citizens increasingly judge the rationality of rules is that of efficiency. In a context of scarcity the legislator has to pursue the desired results at the lowest possible cost. The idea of better governance at lower costs is today a demand of the citizens of any country if it is true, as we believe, that efficiency is a necessary, but insufficient, condition for achieving the ideal of justice (Calsamiglia 1993). And in this field, the application of economic analysis to law can only be welcomed.

---

[5]In Spain, comprehensive or transversal "superstatutes" were enacted in the 2000s to fight gender violence (2004) and to effectively assure gender equality (2007).

[6]For a more precise notion of legal efficacy, see especially Navarro (1990) and Hierro (2001a, 2002).

Traditionally, legal scholars have dealt little with the efficacy of norms and rarely with their effectiveness and efficiency, and regular jurisprudence has not focused on the different scope and implications of these notions, despite the fact that they prove critical for lawmaking. The traditional jurist has not paid attention to the fact that the possible failure of the mechanism of social control we call "law" does not stem only or fundamentally from the degree of obedience or disobedience that follows the promulgation of each norm. Even norms which are generally obeyed or complied with may fail in accomplishing their objectives, i.e. may be ineffective; or may entail costs that are yet unknown, difficult to calculate or simply too high as compared to the benefits of legislation. And this may in turn fuel the suspicion, widespread in our societies, that law is a defective instrument of social control which sometimes does not supply what is needed and sometimes supplies it at unaffordable prices.

2.4 The Alleged Inflation

But curiously enough, as the state fades, citizens and experts themselves have the feeling that there are more rules than necessary and that the legislator is pouring on a daily basis more rules into society than it is capable of complying with or even knowing (Pérez Luño 1993). There is a growing feeling that, as a result of an increase in the presence of the state in our lives, the number of laws and other regulations has grown without reason; that we are experiencing a kind of "legislative orgy", a "legal pollution", a "normative tidal wave" or an explosion of regulation (Eskridge and Frickey 1987) with repercussions on the functioning of our rule of law system (Menéndez and Pau Pedrón 2005).[7] It is logical, then, to ask ourselves whether this feeling has solid foundations or whether the new climate has anything to do with the neoliberal onslaught.

In absence of precise studies that measure the normative density of our societies with reliable methodologies, the partial and provisional data available allow us to confirm that the number of norms that have been poured out daily on our societies has certainly grown. And so, limiting ourselves to parliamentary laws—a minimum part of the normative volume, according to Sabino Cassese (1992)—the number of laws in force in Italy in the 1990s ranged from 100,000 to 150,000, while a Budapest Legislative Institute estimated that 5587 laws were in force in Germany—except for the laws of the *Länder* (Schreckenberger 1986); and 5877 in France (Arbos 1991). The data are more eloquent if we take the rest of normative instruments into account.[8] From a privileged observatory for this purpose such as the OECD

---

[7]The "norm explosion" topic was recurrently discussed in the 1970s and 1980s: see, to name but a few examples, Barton (1975), Berner (1978), Hillermeier (1978), Sendler (1979); or Starck (1979).

[8]In this context, valid indicators might be the number of laws, the number of norms in general, or the number of provisions in normative texts. In addition, it is possible to distinguish, as Tomasic (1979) did, between important laws and minor legislative reforms. Yet another indicator—which

Table 2.1 Normative activity in Spain (Spanish Official Gazette) (1980–2018)

Year	Organic laws	Regular laws	Decree-laws	Decrees	Ministry orders	Total
1980	13	83	16	1447	931	2490
1990	1	31	6	783	465	1286
2000	9	14	10	2206	479	2718
2010	9	44	14	667	1390	2124
2018	5	11	28	151	648	843
Total	37	183	74	5254	3913	9461

(1993), it is stated that Member States are reaching a point at which regulatory activity may end up being the victim of its own success: the volume and complexity of norms is reaching unprecedented levels and thus creating management problems for both the public and private sectors. In any case, the data provided by the OECD invite to reflection. In the United Kingdom, for example, the basic legal reference for company law was increased from 500 pages in 1980 to 3500 pages in 1991. In France, the volume of the Official Gazette doubled between 1976 and 1990. In the U.S., the Federal Code was increased from 20,000 pages in 1960 to 120,000 pages in 1990. In Finland, the number of pages devoted to the publication of norms in the Legal Gazette was 2981 pages in 1990, 3459 pages in 1991, 4076 pages in 1992 and 4796 pages in 1993. The situation is very similar in all OECD and Latin American countries.[9]

As far as Spain is concerned, the activity of the Official State Gazette (*Boletín Oficial del Estado,* BOE) from 1980 to 2018 provides interesting information on this subject (Table 2.1).

We can see how the total volume of pages of the Official State Gazette has increased.[10] But to gauge the size of the phenomenon we are referring to, it is necessary to remember that the Official State Gazette does not reflect all the regulatory activity that affects citizens: most of the rules produced by our autonomous regions *(Comunidades Autónomas)* as well as the norms drawn up in

---

facilitates comparative assessments—might be the number of pages in the official journals or gazettes devoted to publishing norms.

[9]In Latin America, in general, and in Argentina in particular, "the phenomenon presents special virulence. Every politician feels compelled to dictate countless new laws, replace or reform the existing ones and project future laws in prodigious abundance. Such is the magnitude of the problem that, in order to promulgate the first 5000 laws, our legislators took 44 years (from 1862 to 1906), for the next 5000 laws they hardly consumed 9 years (1906–1915). In the last 20 years 7000 laws where dictated, not counting the numerous decrees and other general norms that may well be categorised under the general term of legislation" (Alchourron and Bulygin 1993, p. 410).

[10]As for the headers in Table 2.1, according to the 1978 Spanish Constitution (CE) "organic laws" are those relating to the development of fundamental rights and the regulation of the electoral system, as well as to the autonomous regions' constitutions *(Estatutos de Autonomía)* (Art. 81 CE); "decree-laws" are pieces of legislation issued by the Cabinet in cases of extraordinary and urgent need (Art. 86 CE).

Brussels[11] are not published in the Official State Gazette. On the other hand, the normative technique of creating and repealing norms—aggravated by the abuse of tacit derogations—is producing not only a redundant accumulation of norms but, as C.E. Alchourron and Bulygin (1993, p. 419 ff) point out, an indetermination (at least in the knowledge) of the normative system; that is, the impossibility of quantifying and knowing the number of norms that are actually in force.

Over the last decades, much has been discussed about the *regulatory state*, a vague and imprecise expression with different and even contradictory meanings (see Chevalier 2004; cf. also Majone 1991). For some, the state is only the centre of societal integration: without the regulatory and neutral functions performed by the state, society would be condemned to disorganisation and social disintegration. But a regulatory state is commonly understood as a state that intervenes powerfully and directly to realise the promises of the welfare state, in the form of social benefits and public services. And there are also those who understand the regulatory state to be a state that neither produces goods nor provides services but only regulates the free play of market forces (cf. Majone 2000). Leaving aside the inherently prescriptive component of the different understandings of the "regulatory state", they all have something in common: not only do they account for the marked need of norms—perhaps of other types of norms (cf. Porras Nadales 2002; Timsit 2004)—but also show to what extent the growing juridification has much to do with the structure of the political system (e.g. with its centralised or decentralised organisation), with the traditions and culture of the country in question, or with the political moment experienced by society (von Beyme 1985). And if this is the case, it is obvious that nowadays the regulatory state is intimately linked to the increasing involvement of the state in the fulfilment of the promises of the social *Rechtsstaat*. There is something inevitable in this growth of the volume of norms, especially until the 1970s. Ogus (1994) attributes the ever increasing number of laws and regulations that developed countries have witnessed in the twentieth century, in the first place, to the role that the state has played in relation to the economy as a consequence of the implementation of Keynesian theories. The second cause—always according to Ogus—is the expansion of political rights, which implies a strong social demand for quick answers to the problems of the moment. Thirdly, major technological advances pose a threat to health and safety of people and therefore require regulatory intervention. Finally, the rights revolution and the correlative explosion of citizens' expectations have triggered many state policy interventions.

It is therefore not possible to raise the issue of the so-called regulatory explosion outside its context. We are in a new situation in which the state is no longer merely the guardian of private business but intervenes in society; a situation in which the state, without giving up its function of social control, also assumes the direction of

[11]The situation of overflow in EU law is so significant that a program was implemented to eliminate all the norms that had become unnecessary. See the *Rapport de la Commission au Conseil européen sur l'adaptation de la législation existante au principe de subsidiarité* COM(93)545 final (29 Nov 1993).

society itself. The increase in the quantity of norms and the very diversity of norm types are not something that we can understand as a malformation of the legal system, but as a result of a certain configuration of the relations between the state and society. In this sense we can say that the increase in the number of norms is a specific phenomenon of our time; a phenomenon intimately linked to the rule of law.[12]

2.5 The Dignity of Regulation

In the face of conservative anarchisms and the opportunism of those who only believe in the virtues of the state in times of business turbulence, the realisation of the commitments of the social state and the rule of law (which is not reduced to the pure welfare state) implies regaining confidence in the state and defending the dignity of regulation.[13]

To regain confidence in the state is to understand that there are certain individual needs that can only be met through cooperation. The food we eat, the medicines we need, the water we drink, the clothes that cover us, the roads that communicate us, the vehicles that transport us and even the air we breathe require the coordination of thousands of actions by thousands of individuals. And this is not possible without a market that, in turn, in order to function, requires the determination of a regime of property, contracts and liability. We also know that there is little, if anything, that we can do individually to assert our interests against large corporations, and that we need someone to correct imbalances in power and eliminate monopoly positions. We are also aware that it is not within the reach of isolated individuals to face the consequences of natural disasters and to confront the financial, energy and humanitarian crises that periodically threaten us. It is also beyond our individual strengths to ensure the survival of our planet or the peaceful development of scientific and technological advances. All developed societies have to solve, as political bodies, at least this type of coordination problems—which, if not properly addressed, might lead societies to disintegration.

[12]It is in the framework of this kind of state that three different processes have taken place that are worth remarking. In the first place, the function of the state changes. It is no longer limited to creating an order that allows the free play of market forces, but rather intervenes actively in the market to correct its errors. Secondly, the legitimation system of the state changes as a result of the materialisation of law: the state is legitimised by the results achieved in society by means of regulation. And finally, the state structure changes: what is important in laws is no longer their generality but the definition of the social goals they aim at, an operation that requires abandoning the Kelsenian ideal of a "pure" law and embracing the participation of other social sciences, both for the production and the interpretation of norms. For this reason, as Teubner (1987, p. 3 ff) notes, juridification not only entails growing numbers of norms, it also means that the interventionist social state produces a new type of law, i.e. regulatory law.

[13]I borrow the titles of this section and this chapter from Waldron (1999).

But the fact that it is absolutely necessary to take decisions in these fields does not entail that the content of these decisions is obvious and undisputed. If anything characterises our societies it is the plurality of conceptions and projects around the solution of the problems identified. Alongside the inescapable moral pluralism, there is a no less resistant ideological pluralism that generates different definitions of social problems and different solutions. There are two main circumstances of politics, according to Waldron (1999, p. 151 ff): the need to act as a political body to guarantee our individual or collective existence, and the disagreement between citizens on the solutions to the problems of society. If we did not need to coordinate our actions or were always in agreement as to the solutions to be applied, we could dispense with politics. But this is not the case, so we depend on institutions to solve the dilemma. The norms dictated by governments and the laws passed by parliaments are instruments of social direction that help us make decent decisions in a context of moral, political and ideological plurality. They are therefore the most worthy instrument of social direction.

With regard to laws as a specific form of regulation, defending their dignity implies confronting the growing wave of delegitimisation of parliaments, over which the strongest disqualifications accumulate today, due to a pruritus of modernity or to plain snobbery. For some, legislative assemblies are the realm of what Bentham called *sinister interests,* others see them as the domain of arbitrariness and incompetence. Parliamentarians themselves are no strangers to the climate of discredit in which these institutions live, but beyond their responsibility for the deterioration of the institution, there is an ideological background in the rampant anti-parliamentarianism of our time, a repugnance to the idea that we all deserve the same respect and have the same right to a voice and a vote when it comes to deciding the direction of society. What is ultimately being rejected or questioned is the very system of government based on majority rule.

The law of numbers—counting the votes to make decisions and pass laws—suffers from poor image lately: for some people it has no more credit than deciding by the flip of a coin. But the curious thing is that what we accept in many areas of life as a reasonable method of decision making can be repugnant to us when it happens in a parliament. Very few would dispute the legitimacy of a court that condemns or acquits by majority, nor do we question that counting the supporters is a reasonable procedure when it comes to awarding a public contract, a position or a prize in an open competitive regime. But it does seem to some that there is slackness in deciding by majority vote the content of an income tax law, investments for a certain region, or the mandatory nature of a school subject like "citizenship education" (*Educación para la Ciudadanía y los Derechos Humanos).*[14] There is a certain nostalgia for philosopher kings, omnipotent and omniscient, for impartial experts, there is the conviction that rational deliberation always leads to fairer and more consensual decisions. Well, if we do not trust impartial third parties, or philosopher kings, or

[14]In Spain, this school subject was introduced into primary and secondary education in 2006—with conservative sectors and the Spanish Catholic Church levelling fierce criticism at this measure.

are not willing to flip a coin, or believe that deliberation will always and in any case lead us to a unanimous position, the adoption of a law by a majority is still the most respectable method of decision when it comes to the government of societies. Because it treats everyone as equal, because it allows everyone to give their opinion, because it does not impose an opinion on minorities and because there are no irreversible decisions but the assurance that whoever is a minority today can in the future be a majority—respect for the minority is an imperative of coherence with the same ethical and political principles that define and justify democracies (Díaz 2008, p. 419 ff).

Our societies need more and more government and parliament. In addition to the economic reasons for regulatory intervention—to protect the efficient functioning of the market and to deal with periodic crises such as the one unleashed in 2008—there also are non-economic reasons for appealing to legal norms (Sunstein 1990, p. 55 ff).[15] These are the problems of distribution (salaries, basic incomes, compensation for dependent people), of the need to satisfy certain collective desires (a quality television, for example, or certain cultural goods that don't enjoy a strong demand) or of attending to the rights of future generations (protection of the planet and its diversity). Moreover, insofar as technological and scientific progress take us to an unknown world full of great possibilities but also of now still unimaginable dangers, insofar as powerful groups have enormous influence over our food or medicines or over the safety of our jobs, can control our privacy, manipulate our interests or alter our own habitat. . ., we will need not less, but more and better norms to protect and improve our lives. Because legal norms are the connective tissue, the price we pay for living in a developed society (Tolchin and Tolchin 1983, p. 22). The achievement of these objectives and the respect for the rules of democracy are the very justification for the intervention of public institutions and, therefore, for the dignity of norms.

References

Alchourron CE, Bulygin E (1993) Análisis lógico y derecho. Centro de Estudios Constitucionales, Madrid
Arbos X (1991) La crisis de la regulación estatal. Revista de Estudios Políticos 71:259–280
Arcos Ramírez F (2000) La seguridad jurídica: una teoría formal. Dykinson, Madrid
Arnaud AJ (1981) Critique de la raison juridique. Oú va la sociologie du droit? LGDJ, Paris
Arnaud AJ (1994) Production de la Norme Juridique. Droit et Société 27:293–301
Barton J (1975) Behind the legal explosion. Stanford Law Rev 27:576–584
Beck U (2003) The analysis of global inequality: from national to cosmopolitan perspective. In: Kaldor M et al (eds) Global civil society. Oxford University Press, Oxford, pp 45–55
Berner G (1978) Inflation im Recht. Bayerisches Verwaltungsblatt 24:617–625
Braithwaite J, Drahos M (2000) Global business regulation. Cambridge University Press, Cambridge

[15]For a critical review of Sunstein's ideas, see Williams (1991).

Calsamiglia A (1993) ¿Debe ser la moral el único criterio para legislar? Doxa (Cuadernos de Filosofía del Derecho) 13:171–178
Cassese S (1992) Introduzione allo studio della normazione. Rivista trimestrale di diritto pubblico 2:307–330
Chevalier J (2004) L'État régulataire. Revue française d'administration publique 111:473–482
Corsale M (1979) Certezza del Diritto e crisis de la legittimità. Giuffrè, Milano
de Palma Fernández JL (1997) La seguridad jurídica ante la abundancia de normas. Centro de Estudios Políticos y Constitucionales, Madrid
Díaz E (1966) Estado de derecho y sociedad democrática. Cuadernos para el Diálogo, Madrid
Díaz E (2008) La filosofía política de Gregorio Peces Barba. In: Entre la ética, la política y el derecho. Homenaje al profesor Peces Barba, vol I. Dykinson, Madrid, pp 407–428
Dicey AV (1914) Law and Public Opinion in England during the Nineteenth Century, 2nd edn. Macmillan, London [Lecciones sobre la relación entre derecho y opinión pública en Inglaterra durante el siglo XIX, trans. M. Salguero and I. Molina. Granada: Comares, 2007]
Eskridge WN Jr, Frickey PP (1987) Legislation scholarship and pedagogy in the post-legal process era. Univ Pittsbg Law Rev 48:691–731
Galiana A (2008) La ley: entre la razón y la experimentación. Tirant, Valencia
Giddens A (1998) The third way. Polity Press, Cambridge, 1998
Held D (2004) Globalization: the dangers and answers. Open Democracy, 27 May 2004
Hierro L (2001a) Eficiencia y justicia. In: Justicia, igualdad y eficiencia. Centro de Estudios Constitucionales, Madrid, pp 63–90
Hierro L (2001b) El imperio de la ley y la crisis de la ley. In: Estado de Derecho. Problemas actuales, 2nd edn. Fontamara, México DF, pp 14–40
Hierro L (2002) La eficacia de las normas jurídicas. Ariel, Barcelona
Hillermeier K (1978) Eindämmung der Gesetzflut. Bayerisches Verwaltungsblatt 24:321–323
Kaldor M (2003) Global civil society in an era of regressive globalization. In: Kaldor M et al (eds) Global civil society. Oxford University Press, Oxford, pp 3–33
Majone G (1991) Lo Stato regulatore. Rivista Italiana di Scienza dell'Amministrazione 3:3–62
Majone G (2000) La Communauté européenne, un État régulateur. Montcrestien, Paris
Menéndez A, Pau Pedrón A (eds) (2005) La proliferación legislativa: un desafío para el Estado de Derecho. Colegio Libre de Eméritos/Thompson-Civitas, Madrid
Mignone C (ed) (1997) La crisi della legislazione. Studiosi y politici a confronto. Cedam, Padua
Navarro PE (1990) La eficacia del Derecho, Una investigación sobre la existencia y funcionamiento de los sistemas juríedicos. Centro de Estudios Constitucionales, Madrid
OECD (1989) Directory of regulatory review and reform organizations in OECD member countries. OECD, Paris
OECD (1993) Regulatory Management and Reform in OECD Countries: major conclusions. In: Note by the Secretariat of Public Management Committee. 7th Session of the Committee. OECD, Paris
OECD (1999) Regulatory reform in the United States. Government Capacity to Assure High Quality Regulation. http://www.oecd.org/gov/regulatory-policy/2478900.pdf
OECD (2010a) Better Regulation in Europe-The EU 15 Project. http://www.oecd.org/gov/regulatory-policy/better-regulation-in-europe-the-eu-15-project.htm
OECD (2010b) Reviews of regulatory reform: Australia 2010: towards a seamless national economy (OECD Reviews of Regulatory Reform). OECD, Paris. https://doi.org/10.1787/9789264067189-en
OECD (2018a) Reviews or regulatory reform. Regulatory reform in Canada. Government capacity to assure high quality regulation. OECD, Paris. Available at: http://www.oecd.org/gov/regulatory-policy/1960472.pdf
OECD (2018b) Regulatory policy outlook. OECD, Paris. https://doi.org/10.1787/9789264303072-en
OECD (2019) Better regulation practices across the European Union. OECD, Paris. https://doi.org/10.1787/9789264311732-en

Offe C (1982) Ingovernabilità e mutamento delle democrazie. Il Mulino, Bologna
Ogus AI (1994) Regulation. Legal form and economic theory. Clarendon Press, Oxford
Peces-Barba G (1998) Historia de los Derechos. Dykinson, Madrid
Peces-Barba G (1999) Curso de Derechos Fundamentales. Teoría General. Universidad Carlos III-BOE, Madrid
Pérez Luño AE (1993) El desbordamiento de las fuentes del derecho. Discurso en la Real Academia Sevillana de Legislación y Jurisprudencia. Sevilla
Porras Nadales AJ (2002) El derecho regulativo. Revisa de Estudios Políticos 117:49–72
Putzel J (2009) Globalization, liberalization, and prospects for the state. Int Polit Sci Rev 26 (1):5–16
Schreckenberger W (1986) Krise der Gesetzgebung. In: Gesetzgebung. Grundlagen, Zugänge, Anwendung. Kohlhammer, Stuttgart, pp 21–41
Sendler H (1979) Normenflut und Richter. Zeitschriftt für Rechtspolitik 12:227–232
Starck C (1979) Übermass und Rechtsstaat? Zeitschriftt für Rechtspolitik 12:209–214
Sunstein CR (1990) After the rights revolution. Reconceiving the regulatory state. Harvard University Press, Cambridge
Teubner G (1987) Juridification: concepts, aspects, limits, solutions. In: Teubner G (ed) Juridification of social spheres. A comparative analysis in the areas of labor, corporate, antitrust and social welfare law. Walter de Gruyter, Berlin, pp 3–48
Timsit G (2004) La régulation. La notion et le phénomène. Revue française d'administration publique 109:5–12
Tolchin SJ, Tolchin M (1983) Dismantling America. The rush to deregulate. Houston Miflin Company, Boston
Tomasic R (1979) The sociology of legislation. In: Legislation and society in Australia. The Law Fundation of New South Wales (Allen and Unwin Academic), Sydney
von Beyme K (1985) The role of the state and the growth of government. Int Polit Sci Rev 6 (1):11–34
Waldron J (1999) The dignity of legislation. Cambridge University Press, Cambridge
Williams SF (1991) Background norms in the regulatory state. Univ Chic Law Rev 58:419–434
Wolf M (2004) Why globalization works. Yale University Press, London
Zapatero P (2003) Derecho del comercio global. Thompson-Civitas, Madrid
Zapatero P (2006) Searching for coherence in global economic policy making. Penn State International Law Review 24(3):595–627
Zapatero V (1996) Producción de normas. In: Ruiz Miguel A, Díaz E (eds) Enciclopedia Iberoamericana de Filosofía. Vol. 2: Filosofía política. Trotta/CSIC, Madrid, pp 161–186

Chapter 3
Laws Under Suspicion

All action is motivated conduct. However, the term "motive" is misleading and encompasses different concepts, as Schütz (1962, p. 88 ff) has pointed out. We can say that the motive for which the murderer committed the crime was to obtain the victim's money, in which case motive comes to equal the state of affairs to be achieved by the action: it is a motive *for*. Or we can also ask ourselves what led the murderer—his life circumstances, his education, his social and family environment—to want to get the money by such methods: in this case we have a motive *why*. The former imply goals to be achieved, objectives that are pursued and therefore look to the future; the latter are categories that allow us to explain the actions already carried out based on their causes, antecedents, environment, or psychic predisposition of the actor and therefore look to the past.

All too often in legal theory, the distinction between motives *for* and motives *why* is lost, which allows some theories to express most of the motives *for* through *why* sentences. In other words, there is not always a sufficient distinction between the purpose of rules and the reason for them: between the objectives and the causality of legislative decisions (Twining and Miers 1991, p. 202 ff). Marxism incurred this confusion in the nineteenth century with its conspiracy theory of laws, and today Public Choice theory, by systematically putting laws under suspicion, stumbles with it again.

3.1 Legislation and Public Interest

The classical theory of legislation believed that it was in the public interest to explain and justify legislative activity; but few concepts are as elusive as *public interest*. The rationalistic, idealistic or realistic versions of it, as proposed by Sorauf (1961), Schubert (1960) or Downs (1962) hardly allow us to determine whether a normative decision responds, or not, to the idea of public interest. What we can do, however, is to specify how the idea of public interest was used in the twentieth century when it

V. Zapatero Gómez, *The Art of Legislating*, Legisprudence Library 6,
https://doi.org/10.1007/978-3-030-23388-4_3

came to justifying normative interventions. In order to move from the laissez-faire state to our contemporary state, it was necessary for the state to assume a new social meaning, and for the citizens to imagine and assign a clear mission to the state, namely: the correction of certain undesired results that the market, left to its own nature, inexorably produced.

The market had been presented as the ordinary and efficient mechanism for allocating resources, given that these, prima facie, always tend towards those uses where their economic value is greater. The prerequisites for such an efficient functioning of resource allocation by markets are *competition* (individuals and firms accept prices as given, without other restrictions than those derived from technology and scarcity), *rivalry* (all the variables that economic agents can chose from are under their direct control, which implies the existence of a complete system of individual property rights over goods that force all economic interactions to take place inside the market and to be reflected on prices), *perfect information* and *complete markets* (there is a complete system of markets that allows agents to assign subjective possibilities to all possible future states of nature and to negotiate contracts whose specifications are contingent on the state of nature finally prevailing) (see Albi et al. 1994). When all these conditions were met, it was said, there was no reason for state intervention, which would at best be redundant and at worst inefficient. In this sense, and as Spencer would say, the government that governs the least is the one that governs best.

But the real world was not so perfect, and soon situations arose in which efficiency (not to mention justice) required public intervention: such situations were caused by so-called market failures. When these occur, the public interest appears to justify the intervention of the state. The "public interest" theories of regulation assume that regulation appears as a response to specific goals as expressed through certain agents—government and parliaments—who act as interpreters and servants of that interest (see Mitnick 1989, p. 109 ff [91 ff]). Since Pigou (1932), the welfare economy has been one of the most prominent public interest theories, and has constituted the solid foundation of many of the normative interventions of the social state, called upon to correct the famous failures of the market (Breyer 1982).

In this sense, it was understood that regulatory intervention was necessary, in the first place, when there was a need to establish certain natural monopolies. From the perspective of the social interest, it was thought that, to ensure an adequate supply or to satisfy demand, it could be more efficient to produce certain goods (railways, telephony, etc.) through monopolies than through companies operating in free competition. Secondly, it was considered necessary to intervene when there were certain public goods that needed to be maintained (national defence, foreign relations, legislative and judicial function) that the private sector—Nozick had not yet appeared—could not guarantee efficiently. Thirdly, the existence of externalities (social costs that cannot be adequately reflected in prices) also forced the intervention of public institutions. Fourthly, there are information failures: in order for the market to function efficiently, there has to be a complete system of information on the relevant characteristics of products and processes that companies themselves are not always willing to provide. Fifthly, there are problems of coordination (Ogus

1994, p. 42 ff), on which Olson (1965) aptly elaborated when discussing the logic of collective action: a good, typical example is the regulation of traffic (Calabresi 1984). Sixth, it was argued that public authorities must deal with exceptional market circumstances such as wars, cyclical crises, profound technological transformations, etc. Seventh, some situations significantly alter the tenets of free competition (monopolies, oligopolies, etc.). And, finally, the existence of common property resources (fishing grounds, natural resources in general, etc.) and the need to preserve them required their regulation. Thus, from the perspective of social efficiency, the theory of public interest has traditionally asserted that governments should intervene whenever we are faced with a situation of natural monopoly, public goods, externalities, common property resources, or imperfect or too expensive information. In other words, governments' active intervention is needed, precisely, in order to achieve maximum social efficiency.

But to this list of failures—which justify the intervention of public authorities to restore the efficient functioning of the market—, political philosophy has added another series of non-economic reasons that justify intervention (Ogus 1994, p. 46 ff). In some cases it is the ideal of distributive justice, in its different versions: liberal, statist or social-democratic. In other cases, the private decision is replaced by the public decision for purely paternalistic reasons (the use of a helmet or seat belt, for example). And sometimes the need to intervene is based on the existence of certain community values. It is therefore clear that the justification for the intervention of public authorities has not only arisen for economic reasons, but that there are non-economic grounds too. Both reasons of efficiency and reasons of justice—or a combination of the two—, have traditionally constituted the basis of the so-called public interest theory. Such have been, and still are to a large extent (cf. Sunstein 1990), the *reasons for* of legislation.

3.2 Capturing the Legislator

In the perspective of the public interest arising from the Pigouvian approach, a benevolent and omniscient state is assumed to produce public goods, to internalise social costs and benefits, to effectively regulate industries, to redistribute income according to Paretian optimality and so on (McCormick and Tollison 1984, p. 180). The history of regulation shows that its growth has been the result of a series of empirical adjustments to perceived abuses. But from the 1970s onwards, serious doubts began to raise about the disparity between the model described in the theory of public interest and the real functioning of governments. In a curious coincidence, liberals and interventionists began to highlight the difference between the model of government that corrects market failures and its real achievements. It was argued that governments, through their interventions, are not achieving the market correction objectives they claim to pursue and that, when they do, the costs are too high. In other words, beyond the ideal model of governments correcting market failures, real governments are not only ineffective, but—more often than not—also inefficient.

Those who maintain the public interest as a reason for legislative intervention defend it by simply pointing out that, if regulation does not serve the public interest, it is because politicians are venal or incompetent; that these are contingent failures that can and should be corrected (Mitnick 1989, p. 111 ff [93 ff]). In other words, failures are regretted while more and better regulation is recommended. It is thought, therefore, that the failures in practice are not the result of shortcomings in the basic objectives or the nature of the process but of technical problems coming from inadequate staff and procedures that would gradually improve as society became more skilled in the mechanics of public administration. Regulation has been created for a good public purpose; what happens is that it's not always managed properly with the result that it doesn't always achieve its goals.

This response given from the shore of the public interest theory was considered clearly unsatisfactory (Posner 1974, p. 337). First, public interest theories do not take into account a good number of real-life situations in which the socially undesirable results produced by legislation were often intended by the groups that promoted the adoption of the norm in the first place. Norms sometimes show an unequivocal purpose not to achieve the efficient functioning of the market but precisely to alter its functioning in a direction that the theory of public interest could hardly explain. Second, there is little evidence to support the explanation that the problem lies in the incompetence of regulators: bureaucracy is not necessarily inefficient in achieving the objectives pursued by legislation. Nor is it a decisive argument to say that the public sector pays its agents worse than the private sector: lower salaries are sometimes compensated by the acquisition of contacts and relationships that will open subsequent opportunities in the private sector—as illustrated by the "revolving door" technique practiced by some public servants who end up advising the business groups they previously regulated. Thirdly, the poor results of policy interventions cannot be directly related to the lack of sufficient motivation in the public versus the private sector: to some extent, the motivations for working honestly and diligently are not very different in the public and private sectors. And finally, it cannot be simply argued that the problem lies in the lack of accountability mechanisms for regulators: all regulatory agencies are subject to the control of the executive or the legislative powers—and they also have to compete with each other to increase the funds assigned to them. Therefore, we are not dealing with a good idea that was poorly managed, i.e. with the failed attempts to materialise the public interest, but rather, as Posner (1974) concludes, with the fact that regulation has its origin and explanation in pure private interests.[1]

[1]For Posner (1974, pp. 339–340), two factors are usually neglected which would actually improve the explanation as to why the government fails. The first one refers to the intractable character of many of the tasks assigned to regulatory agencies: they are asked the impossible, like ascertaining the costs of regulated companies or connecting their prices with their costs, and there are good reasons to believe that the right tools to measure and control such things simply do not exist. This is the first explanation to their failure. The second factor is the cost of the legislative supervision of the results produced by the agencies. The process of legislative production implies a long negotiation

Some political scientists have advanced the fundamentals of what could be a theoretical tool to explain the origin of rules. According to this theory, regulatory bodies tend to fall under the control of the very sectors they regulate, which eventually end up, in one form or another, manipulating the rules in their favour. And when this happens, rules are not the result of an effort to serve the public good but simply of the capturing of legislators by certain industries. Even if the capture thesis is in fact closer to the reality of the policy making process, it cannot be a satisfactory answer for several reasons. First of all, because it is sometimes not very different from some versions of public interest theory. Secondly, because even though it is called "theory", it is rather a simple hypothesis that lacks an adequate theoretical foundation—what is more, there is a whole series of facts that refute this theory.[2] And thirdly, the theory of the capture overlooks a good deal of evidence pointing to the fact that governments often defend the interests of consumer groups, rather than those of the regulated industries.

In any case, the capture theory,[3] together with the Marxist approach to the issue, meant the first major break with the social democratic vision that made the public interest the motive and justification of laws. In the 1970s, the idea that governments created norms not so much to achieve a public interest, but to protect certain private interests, was advanced. And so began the development of a conspiracy theory of legislation that would eventually turn motives *why* into motives *for*.

3.3 Public Choice and Its Premises

Neither the theory of public interest nor the theory of group interest seemed to give an account of how regulation works in reality, so the vocation of our century for economics began to explore the development of a new explanatory model of regulatory decision-making processes.

The theory to be built had a twofold objective, explanatory and predictive. It had to be, first of all, a positive model that tried to explain the interactions taking place in the public decision-making process and also tended to predict its outcomes. As

---

period that entails a very high cost. The government is left with no other option but to delegate more and more normative powers to the agencies, gradually losing control over them.

[2]For instance, not every agency pursued initially a public interest that, as time went by, was "perverted": some agencies where created, from their onset, to defend private interests of the regulated groups. Moreover, the theory lacks predictive potential, for it doesn't explain what happens when the same agency regulates different industries.

[3]The first one to suggest the idea that regulatory agencies have a life cycle that takes them to gradually subordinate the public interest to the private industries was Bernstein (1955). According to Bernstein regulatory agencies have their own "life cycle". In the first stage of their existence they usually perform their regulatory duty zealously, but after some time they gradually lose power and degenerate to the point of being captured by the regulated groups. This idea was popularised later by Ralph Nader.

regards its explanatory capacity, the model suggests a single hypothesis—the maximisation of individual utility—to explain decision-making; and the results to which this hypothesis leads are claimed to be verifiable through empirical contrast. But above all, what is important about the envisaged theory is its predictive capacity: theoretical models, as Downs (1973, p. 23) said, should be verified more by the accuracy of their predictions than by the realism of their assumptions. The key significance accorded to the predictive capacity of the model comes from Friedman's (1953) suggestion that the only purpose of economic theory is to generate verifiable predictions. Such predictions however are not intended to describe exactly future reality but refer, rather, to a "model world": they describe what the predictable behaviour would be if men were to act rationally, not in terms of goals (the hypothesis is the maximisation of utility) but in terms of the means to achieve those goals. But although rarely confessed, this new theory of legislation was also about building a normative model that attempts to prescribe what political institutions should do (Bottomley et al. 1991, p. 209), suggesting a whole range of constitutional and deregulatory mechanisms aimed at minimising the supposedly inefficient public intervention.

The first premise of the theory is methodological individualism: the theory of Public Choice—as pointed out by Buchanan (1984, p. 113)—is methodologically individualistic in the same sense as economic theory is. The basic subjects of actions and decisions are individual persons, not organic units such as parties, provinces or nations. Collective action is nothing more than the action of individuals when they choose to meet certain objectives collectively rather than individually (Buchanan and Tullock 1980, p. 38). Hence the focus should be on individual purposes and interests. The pursuit of a public interest independent of the interests of the individuals involved in the social choice would be like seeking the Holy Grail.[4]

The second premise is the rationality of individuals. The macroeconomic model of the theory of Public Choice—this is what we are fundamentally referring to—shares some assumptions with other theories about rationality. The first is the concept of instrumental rationality developed by Weber (1979, p. 20 ff), according to which individuals always adopt the optimal strategy to achieve their objectives—which are assumed to be transitive and stable. Of course, people sometimes make mistakes: they lack sufficient information, or time, or intelligence. It also happens that sometimes the objectives are not very clear or change over time. These criticisms serve as a warning against the more simplistic approaches to the matter, but in no way invalidate the idea of rational behaviour: after all, although there are many

[4]A somewhat more nuanced position is that of Downs (1973, p. 18), for whom "the organismic view of government is untrue because it is based upon a mythical entity: a state which is a thing apart" from individuals. On the other hand, the "individualistic" approach is incomplete "because it does not take coalitions into consideration": when a small group of people ally themselves to manage the state apparatus, "we can reasonably speak of the government as a decision-maker separate from individual citizens at large"; this way "we avoid both false personification of a mental construct and an over individualistic view of society".

cases of irrational behaviour, there are also plenty of instances in which people behave pretty much in agreement with the model of instrumental rationality.

The third premise of the model—and the weakest element in this theoretical proposal—is the concept of the individual as a maximiser of utility. Every economic theory, like every political theory, is based on a certain psychological conception of the human being: before elaborating on the state, Hobbes (1999) dedicates the first part of the Leviathan to man. Before presenting his theory of the general will, Rousseau (1973) speaks to us of the natural human. The Public Choice is based on the axiom that the individual is fundamentally selfish. Models of economic theories assume that people seek to maximise their own utility or interest, and that their economic well-being, strictly defined, is an important component of this interest (Buchanan 1984). It is not that the maximisation of one's own benefit is the only reason that influences human behaviour, but it is the one that best explains such behaviour and allows a better prediction of future behaviour.

The novelty of the economic theory of law at this point is the application of the logic of the market to the logic of politics. There are not two different logics in individuals, one public and one private. There is only one model of human being that applies the same logic of maximising utility in both the private and the public sphere: the burden of proof to the contrary—Buchanan (1984) concludes—should fall on those who suggest that different human models can be applied in the fields of economic and political behaviour. Or as McCormick and Tollison (1984) would say: politicians are no different from other people; they are economic agents who respond to their institutional environment in a predictable way, and their actions can be analysed in much the same way as economists analyse the actions of market participants. Consequently, the important differences between the market and the world of politics are not in the motivations of individual actors. There is no splitting of personality between our private and political selves, we do not seek to satisfy the public interest when we vote and the private interest when we shop in the supermarket. We seek private interest in both cases. Yet, although the story of Dr. Jekyll and Mr. Hyde is the subject of an excellent novel, it is nevertheless a poor basis for analysing political behaviour.

With such premises—individualism, rationalism and maximisation of utility—a new theory of legislation was constructed that seeks to replace the conventional social-democratic conception of law as an expression of the public interest with what they call *politics without romance*.

3.4 Politics Without Romanticism

One of the first applications of the model was to study the relationship between interest groups and legislation in terms of supply of, and demand for, norms.

The work that paved the way was George Stigler's *The Theory of Economic Regulation* (1971). For Stigler, the problem of regulation is not to discover what public interest the state must pursue with its laws: the problem is discovering when and why an industry or a company (or any other group of people of similar characteristics) is able to use the state for its own private benefit or is used by the state for the benefit of third party interests. What groups and industries seek in the state is the way to control its coercive power and use it to increase their profits. The contribution that the state can make to industries can materialise as direct subsidies in the form of money, controls that prevent or limit access to the sector for new companies, regulations on substitutes and complements in the production process, or pricing policies. This is what companies demand from public authorities. Now, the industry that seeks political power has to turn to the potential seller: a political party (Stigler 1971, p. 12). The political party has operating costs, the costs of maintaining an organisation and competing in elections. In turn, the industry seeking regulation must be prepared to give back what the party needs: votes and resources. It is very likely that the cost of any given piece of regulation will increase with the size of the industry being regulated.[5] And if a party raises prices too much, it is possible to opt for other parties for lower prices.

If Stigler wanted to explain why private groups seek state regulation, it was also necessary to explain why governments end up offering it. In the same line, although with different overtones, we find Sam Peltzman's (1976) explanation, which is complementary to Stigler's.[6] For Peltzman, politicians are also profit maximisers, they seek to maximise electoral majorities, which they achieve by "offering" rules to those who are willing to pay more for them in the form of votes and resources (Farber and Frickey 1991). Another particularly interesting contribution in terms of predicting regulatory behaviour, although from a different perspective, is that of Wilson (1980, pp. 367–370), who, among other things, tries to anticipate the behaviour of legislators by evaluating the costs and benefits of their policies. For Wilson, the benefits produced by policies can be concentrated (on a group) or diffuse: and the same happens with the costs. In view of this distinction, Wilson proposes the following prediction for normative policies: (a) if the benefits of a new regulation are diffuse among the population while the costs are concentrated among a group, the regulation will be blocked; (b) if the benefits are concentrated on a small group and the costs are diffuse, the regulator will tend to support the interests of the small group; and (c) if the costs and benefits are concentrated among competing groups, the regulator will act as an arbiter between them.

Posner (1993, p. 353 ff) perfectly sums up the behaviour of both interest groups and legislators: "the basic assumption of economics that guides the version of economic analysis of law that I shall be presenting is that people are rational maximizers of their satisfactions—all people (with the exception of small children and the profoundly retarded) in all of their activities (except when under the

[5]Regarding the problems that free-riders pose to group dynamics, see the seminal work of Olson (1965). For Olson, rational individuals, naturally selfish, will only act in the interest of the collective if the group is very small or if they are coerced into doing so. The most rational attitude, from this perspective, is to be a social cadger.

[6]Peltzman (1976) asks himself why do politicians offer laws, and his answer is because politicians want to maximise electoral majorities.

influence of psychosis or similarly deranged through drug or alcohol abuse) that involve choice". Obviously this goes also for legislators and therefore nothing they do is motivated by public interest as such. What they really want is to be elected and re-elected, so what they need is money. This money is easier to obtain from well-organised groups than from isolated individuals, because the rational individual has very little incentive to invest time and effort in deciding who to vote for. Only organised groups of individuals (companies or any other type of organisations also led by individuals) will be able to overcome the problems that collective action poses: information and the actions of free-riders. But such a group will not organise or act effectively unless its members have much to gain or lose from a specific piece of regulation. The basic tactic of an interest group is to trade the votes of its members and the financial support for the candidates in exchange for an implicit promise of favourable regulation (Muller and Murrell 1986, pp. 126–127).

Group interest theories, on the other hand, seemed to forget, initially, the important role played by public servants in the legislative process. Although those holding these posts are not elected and therefore the hypothesis of maximising votes does not apply to them, the principle of utility maximisation can indeed explain their behaviour. Regulation can also be understood as the result of rational choices that public officials make in order to maximise services, i.e. to satisfy their preferences, under variable constraints and with variable opportunities for reward (cf. Mitnick 1989, p. 137 [120]). Civil servants are seen not as public servants, but as utility maximisers as well. Inevitably, parliaments have to delegate the implementation of legislative policies to public officials (Buchanan 1984). But how do officials use their power? Possibly it has been Niskanen (1971) who has offered a more developed application of economic analysis to the functioning of bureaucracy. For Niskanen, the motives behind the behaviour of bureaucrats are the maximisation of their pay, job stability, working conditions and power or public recognition. The prototypic regulatory bureaucrat pursues either the goals of the agency he is assigned to (conservation, empowerment of the agency), or the goals of the clients or users of the agency's services, or personal goals. For all of these goals, what he needs is to maximise budgetary appropriations, expand the own administrative unit and increase legislation.

But, while focused on examining the behaviour of groups, legislators and officials, the role of governments, which are undoubtedly the protagonists of the process in parliamentary systems, still had to be explained. It was soon thought that the same methodology could be applied to them.

If the classical theory of legislation focused on analysing the motives *for* of governments and found that they were merely maximising the welfare of society, it was now the private motives—the motives *why*—of rulers that were of interest. And these were determined, like those of any other human being, by the impulse of selfishness: this duality—Downs (1973, p. 305 ff) says—is born from an axiom of selfishness according to which, in general, people carry out economic activities primarily with the aim of promoting their own private ends and secondarily to procure benefits for society. Therefore, when we investigate their behaviour, we should not limit ourselves to the examination of the social function they perform but should indicate what their motivations are. The neglect of this perspective has led, in

Downs' (1973, p. 309) opinion, to a false generality of the theory of public decisions: the premise according to which the government acts with the aim of maximising social welfare would mean that those who run it are completely altruistic in terms of their productive activity. They would be the only humans among all the members of society who lack private motivations unrelated to the fulfilment of their social function.

The perspective proposed by Downs (1973, p. 30) is very different. The aim is to find a rule that predicts the rational behaviour of governments. To find answers, the role of political parties needs to be investigated. If the traditional theory stated that political parties were trying to realise the general interest by satisfying the demands for social welfare, in the new perspective the parties were no longer more than a coalition of people trying to control the governmental apparatus. Politicians, according to this model, never look for positions to put in practice a specific policy: their sole objective is to obtain the advantages that the position grants. Politics is for them a simple way of reaching their private ends, and this can only happen if they are elected. This reasoning is based on the fundamental thesis that parties formulate specific policies that allow them to win elections, rather than winning elections in order to implement a specific program. Since without success in elections, none of the gages of public office is obtained, the main objective of any party is to win them. Hence, all their actions are aimed at maximising the number of votes in their favor and the policy is only of interest as a simple means to this end. And if governments are looking to maximise their votes it is because they believe that there is a relationship between the decisions they take and the way citizens vote: the voter defines his preferences among the contending parties "by comparing the stream of utility income from government activity he has received under the present government" with "those streams he believes he would have received if the various opposition parties had been in office" (Downs 1973, p. 53). Such is the harsh description given by Downs of the actions of politicians and governments: they are maximisers not of a public interest but simply of the votes that can allow them to conquer power or remain in it.

Thus, in this conception of public life, the behaviour of the actors in the normative process—interest groups, legislators, civil servants and governments—is best explained when the altruistic halo of politics is lifted to verify that political institutions do not function in the way presented by the theories of public interest. As Buchanan concludes (1984, pp. 131–132), "the romance is gone, perhaps never to be regained. The socialist paradise is lost. Politicians and bureaucrats are seen as ordinary persons much like the rest of us, and politics is viewed as a set of arrangements, a game if you will, in which many players, with quite disparate adjectives, interact so as to generate a set of outcomes that may not be either internally consistent or efficient by any standards".

3.5 A Few Exceptions

But, fortunately, the theory of Public Choice is not the end of this story: it has been questioned in many different ways.[7] First and foremost, it has been criticised for not explaining where preferences in the market come from, why they are so diverse or why they change. Parties may not have any preferences in certain cases, and there is no lack of altruistic attitudes among legislators, public officials or members of governments. That is why, very soon, the first adjustments to the thicker conclusions of the Public Choice began to emerge, although, in truth, without completely abandoning the backbone of the doctrine.

And so we see how, together with the omnipresent private interest, the existence of a public interest that could play a role in public decisions—though only a very limited one—began to be admitted. Such was the case of Anthony Downs himself who eventually admitted that the public interest is a component of public life and fulfils at least three important functions in it (Downs 1962). First of all, it is a concept that we citizens usually use in public dialogue and upon which we evaluate the actions of governments: and so we sometimes say that the government has fallen prey of powerful interests, and other times we say that the government has imposed the general interest on group interests. Public authorities, for their part, often use public interest as an argument to ask citizens to accept a total or partial waiver of their interests on the basis of a higher collective interest. And finally, public interest is used as a guide for the actions of officials and politicians.[8] But just because we use it doesn't mean it's clear what public interest really is (Mitnick 1989, p. 257 ff [242 ff]).

Breaking with Buchanan and Tullock (1980), for whom there are not two logics (private and public) but only one logic—that of rational selfishness that prevails in both the private and the public spheres—, Downs (1962) notes that each individual plays different roles and that each role has its own dynamics. As an individual, a person can detect when a public policy benefits his or her "private interests" and thus choose the alternative that is most beneficial to him or her personally. But at the same time this person is also a citizen and can, as such, differentiate between private and social interests. Not only are there private interests and public interests, but both may be in contradiction.

Having accepted the existence of public interests alongside private interests and that both kinds of interests may be in contradiction, the relevant question is which one will prevail in the event of a discrepancy between the two. Although it is not

[7]See e.g. Dunleavy (1991), as well as Baldwin et al. (1998).

[8]For Downs (1962, p. 10), the struggle for power forces each politician or public servant to develop a conception of public interest which justifies his particular decisions. From the perspective of the citizen, the task of politicians or public servants is to make decisions in favor of the public interest, and therefore it is rational to demand from them public interest arguments for their decisions, even if these were taken for other reasons. From the perspective of politicians, the development of a conception of public interest and its connection with the decisions they make is a way of fighting for power by obtaining the support of the majority.

easy to make predictions about this, we can perhaps say—Downs (1962, p. 28) presumes—that the idea of the public interest will prevail within governments when it comes to decisions in which the survival of the system is at stake, or when particular interests only remotely or indirectly are affected, or when their decision implies breaking certain minimum social consensus. On the contrary, private interests are likely to determine those actions of the legislator that relate to policies that have a direct effect on the citizens' income, on their working conditions, or on any other activity in which they are actively involved. The same could be said of the behaviour of civil servants and of the citizens themselves—not only governments are prone to utility maximisation (in terms of votes), but also we, the citizens, tend to maximise our utility by voting for the parties which benefit us most.

But for Downs, these modifications introduced in the theory of Public Choice by accepting the possibility of altruistic behaviour in public decisions (i.e. that sometimes politicians act in the public interest and not only seeking votes) do not imply a change of the model: the revised model simply recognises those few examples in which politicians' moral commitment to democracy as a social system is superior to short-term, selfish interests (Downs 1962, p. 32). But then, is this an exception that does not invalidate the model, or is it simply that the model of a theory of legislation based exclusively on selfishness does not have the necessary consistency? Or is it that the premises are wrong and what needs to be done is to change the model altogether?

3.6 In Search of Another Theory of Legislation

The economic analysis applied to legislation has a threefold objective: to explain the behaviour of the legislator, to be able to predict his decisions and, even if it is not openly stated, to prescribe a very specific legislative policy. Yet, there are very serious doubts about the explanatory and predictive capacity of this theory; and, as for its legislative recommendations, their acceptance or rejection depends on whether or not we share neoliberal ideology and policies. Following Edward L. Rubin, there are a few brief considerations to make in this regard.

Of the three premises on which the theory of Public Choice is based—methodological individualism, rationalism and selfishness of individuals—the first two may be said to be robust and well-established. The refusal to ascribe an entirely autonomous nature to collective agents, i.e. the affirmation that any good social theory has to start from the preferences of individuals, is not an idea whose paternity can be attributed to the economic analysis of law; it was already a consolidated idea long before. Also the premise of the rationality of the agents—what Max Weber called instrumental rationality—is a good starting point for any social theory, even if the possibility of irrational behaviour—due to lack of time, lack of information, prejudices that bias decisions, etc.—should not be excluded in human beings. In any case, methodological individualism and rationality of the agents are premises shared by the most consistent theories of public decision making.

The highly debatable point of the Public Choice theory as applied to legislation is its premise of the selfishness of the agent; a premise that affirms that all agents involved in the legislative process—officials, legislators, social groups—only seek to maximise their personal utility. Personal interest can certainly include very different goals such as earning money, achieving notoriety, being promoted, being respected, or even reinforcing the ego. But of all the meanings that we can give the term utility, Public Choice theory is obliged to choose the most material of them. In doing so, it has understood that voters cast their vote only with their economic interests in mind; that individual selfishness prevents people from joining together to achieve collective goals, or that legislators only make their decisions with their re-election in mind. A closer look at reality shows the weight that ideology and pure political affiliation have in the votes of many citizens. A more accurate and realistic description would also show the strength and mobilisation power that, despite free-riders, certain collective objectives possess, such as the protection of the environment, the fight against racial segregation, against death penalty, in favour of peace, etc. A more open-minded examination shows how legislators seek re-election, but also how they are loyal to their ideology, their values, their commitments and their moral code, which they can sometimes place above the search for re-election. In short, politicians are *a priori* neither better nor worse than any other citizen. Legislators and government officials are interested in many other things that the Public Choice theory does not talk about. And a theory that does not take into account all these realities will be a bad explanation of reality; it will be an incomplete theory.

The aim was to address these objections by admitting exceptions or nuances, proposing—as Anthony Downs did—a much broader concept of individual interest, which already includes economic interest, but also the search for power, prestige or pleasure. But then the Public Choice has to abandon its pretension of being able to predict legislative behaviour and its intellectual coherence: the whole theory becomes pure tautology and there is no way to exclude any other conceivable human motivation for decision making (see Rubin 2002, p. 323 ff). That is why, among all the meanings and contents of the notion of *utility*, the Public Choice opts for that of maximising re-election. This is not an empirical fact (since reality shows us that legislators have other motivations as well), but a hypothesis forced by the obsession with prediction: the need—Rubin (1991, p. 16) points out—to invoke a strict version of selfishness arises from an epistemological commitment to positivism, according to which the virtue of a theory consists in its ability to predict observable behaviour. A definition of a legislator's utility function that acknowledges public interest, ideology, wealth, fame, or promotion alongside re-election fails as a predictive theory because it includes everything.

But what would be the scientific value of a theory based on the hypothesis of maximising votes? Popper (1973, p. 40) has proposed the refutability or falsifiability criterion rather than the verification criterion as a demarcation line between empirical and metaphysical science: only those theories that can be refuted by experience are admissible. Well, as Posner (1993, p. 363) himself acknowledges, the economic analysis of law places greater emphasis on the confirmation than on the falsifiability criterion. This is partly because, he says, economic theory has become so rich and spongy that almost any hypothesis, even one that seems to refute a fundamental implication of the theory, as e.g. the very law of supply and demand does, could be adapted to it. That is why a theory that is not indeed falsable or refutable but only confirmable has a weak foundation. One can never be sure whether observations that confirm (i.e. that are consistent with) theory A are not, on the other hand, confirming a theory B that is comprised by or that overlaps with A.

Criticism of Public Choice, as a theory of legislation, does not make it logically worthless: its insistence on the economic component of decisions is a very important contribution to an issue that traditionally did not receive the necessary attention. What is in doubt is its imperial aspiration of wanting to explain everything on the basis of the selfishness of the agents. And as for its prescriptive component, we should not overlook the fact that the defence of the market that this approach entails has sometimes been accompanied by strong criticism of democratic institutions. Kelman (1988, pp. 202–203) has summed it up emphatically: "the public choice literature is decidedly not about the potentially mutable failure of democratic institutions to live up to their promise: rather, it is an effort to demonstrate that given certain suppositions about the way political actors (both voters and 'governors') behave, and given certain suppositions about the actual power government possesses, the democratic sphere is, at its core, an arena of theft, an unmitigated disaster that should be limited carefully, tolerated only if fundamentally powerless. Not only does the democratic sphere lose the falsely idealized, elevated status that it enjoyed in the mainstream centrist picture, but it becomes the embodiment of, if not evil, then abject failure. The 'market', in this view, transforms private greed into social progress and harmony, mutual benefit, and positive sum games; democracy transforms (indistinguishable) private greed into stagnation, wasteful rentseeking, and negative sum games". This way of explaining the problem is possibly extreme, but however, not without reason.

Other premises are available on which to base a theory of legislation that is more in tune with the reality of the legislative process and from which, on the other hand, recommendations may be derived to improve the current imperfections of the process. A theory such as the one suggested here assumes methodological individualism and the rationality of the agent as its starting point, but it differs radically in the idea that everything is explained through the egoism of human beings. Turning to phenomenology, Rubin (1998) starts the construction of such a theory from the idea of *meaning*. As reasoning creatures that we are, our first motivation is to attribute meaning to the things around us, to ourselves, and to the world in which we live. As Weber (1979) said, meaning is the most basic concept of sociology.

Our life world *(Lebenswelt)* is organised into fields of different importance—sub-universes of meaning—according to our current state of interests, each of which has its own specific center of density and fullness and its open horizons: I decide on a course of action in one sense and not in another, in light of what I consider significant for my deepest convictions and interests. Or as Schütz (1962, p. 213 ff) would say, "from the world that is within my present or potential reach, I choose as primarily important those objects that are or will in the future be possible ends or means for the realisation of my projects, or that are or will be dangerous, or enjoyable, or meaningful to me in any way". That is why individuals—and the agents involved in the legislative process are individuals—make their decisions by opting, within the horizon of their world, for that course of action that gives more meaning, here and now, to their own life. Sometimes what will make the most sense will be to maximise personal well-being (in the form of money or votes); on other occasions it will be, for instance, the protection of the environment, the rights of certain marginalised groups, the eradication of hunger, development aid, or animal rights. People certainly turn to earning money or winning elections when this gives meaning to their lives. But they also renounce money or votes when an altruistic decision fills their life with meaning.

Legislators are no different from the rest of human beings in this regard: they seek votes, certainly, but they also seek to be respected, to be loyal to their party and to their constituencies; they seek prestige and fame, they take care of their good name; they want to feel comfortable with themselves by adjusting their decisions to their moral code, by doing what they feel they have to do. And they often make such a decision even if it implies a cost in votes. Like any human being, they are sometimes selfish and sometimes altruistic. The decision will depend, in each here and now, on the way that the resulting behaviour gives meaning to life.

A theory of legislation based on this conception of agency, apart from being more in tune with reality, offers an alternative to Public Choice approaches and challenges the deregulation spirit undelying them, for it conceives norms as the most worthy instrument of social direction. And it is precisely this theory that allows us to improve the legislative process. In contrast to the recommendations of Public Choice scholars—in brief: priority to the market and maximum abstinence of the legislator—,[9] the starting point of this theory is to consider the legislative process as a process of public decision making that can be studied with the instruments of political science and public policy analysis (Rubin 2005). This approach makes it possible to reflect on issues that are particularly relevant to the lawmaking process, such as how to improve legislative decision-making procedures; how to use legislative language to make the wording of norms a little clearer; how to articulate the connection between the making of laws and their enforcement and application; how to structure and organise norms best; how to ensure an adequate implementation of laws…, in short: this theory would allow us to deal with everything the economic analysis of law has undervalued or neglected (see Rubin 1991, p. 25).

To sum up, what is needed is a theory that, instead of being exclusively concerned with the *motives why*, also focuses on the *motives for* of the activation of legislative processes, with a view to providing a better explanation of these processes and, ultimately, to improving them.

---

[9] As we will see later (Chap. 5), not all Public Choice scholars share the same views on the importance of laws—see e.g. Lessig (1998) on the distinction between an "old" and a "new" Chicago School.

References

Albi E et al (1994) Teoría de la Hacienda Pública, 2nd edn. Ariel, Barcelona
Baldwin R, Scout C, Hood C (1998) Introduction. In: A reader on regulation. Oxford University Press, Oxford
Bernstein MH (1955) Regulating business by independent commission. Princeton University Press, Princeton
Bottomley S et al (1991) Law in context. The Federation Press, Canberra
Breyer S (1982) Regulation and its reform. Harvard University Press, London
Buchanan J (1984) Política sin romanticismo. Esbozo de una teoría positiva de la elección pública y de sus implicaciones normativas. In: El análisis económico de lo político. Lecturas sobre la Teoría de la Elección Pública. Instituto de Estudios Económicos, Madrid
Buchanan J, Tullock GG (1980) El cálculo del consenso. Fundamentos lógicos de una democracia constitucional. Espasa-Calpe, Madrid
Calabresi G (1984) El coste de los accidentes. Ariel, Barcelona
Downs A (1962) The public interest: its meaning in a democracy. Soc Res 29:1–36
Downs A (1973) La teoría económica de la democracia. Aguilar, Madrid
Dunleavy P (1991) Democracy, bucreaucracy and public choice. Harverster, London
Farber D, Frickey P (1991) Law and public choice: a critical introduction. University of Chicago Press, Chicago
Friedman M (1953) The methodology of positive economics. In: Essays in positive economics. University of Chicago Press, Chicago [Ensayos sobre economía positiva. Gredos, Madrid, 1967]
Hobbes T (1999) Leviatán, o la materia, forma y poder de un Estado eclesiástico y civil. Alianza, Madrid
Kelman M (1988) On democracy-bashing: a skeptical look at the theoretical and empirical practice of the public choice movement. Va Law Rev 74:199–273
Lessig L (1998) The new Chicago School. J Leg Stud 27:661–691
McCormick RE, Tollison RD (1984) Análisis del Estado. In: El análisis económico de lo político. Lecturas sobre la Teoría de la Elección Pública. Instituto de Estudios Económicos, Madrid
Mitnick BM (1989) La economía política de la regulación. FCE, México [The political economy of regulation. Creating, designing, and removing regulatory forms. Columbia University Press, New York, 1989]
Muller D, Murrell P (1986) Interest groups and the size of government. Public Choice 48:125–145
Niskanen W (1971) Bureaucracy and representative government. Routledge, New York
Ogus AI (1994) Regulation. Legal form and economic theory. Clarendon Press, Oxford
Olson M (1965) The logic of collective action. Harvard University Press, Cambridge
Peltzman S (1976) Towards a more general theory of regulation. J Law Econ 19(2):211–240
Pigou AC (1932) The economics of welfare, 4th edn. Macmillan, London [La economía del bienestar. Aguiar, Madrid, 1946]
Popper KR (1973) La lógica de la investigación científica. Tecnos, Madrid
Posner R (1974) Theories of economic regulation. Bell J Econ Manag Sci 51(6):335–358
Posner R (1993) The problems of jurisprudence. Harvard University Press, Cambridge
Rousseau JJ (1973) El contrato social. Aguilar, Madrid
Rubin EL (1991) Beyond public choice: comprehensive rationality in the writing and reading of statutes. N Y Univ Law Rev 66:1–66
Rubin EL (1998) Putting rational actors in their place: economics and phenomenology. Vanderbilt Law Rev 51(6):1705–1728
Rubin EL (2002) Public choice, phenomenology and the meaning of modern state: keep the bathwater, but throw out that baby. Cornell Law Rev 87:309–361
Rubin EL (2005) The conceptual explanation for legislative failure. Law Soc Inq 30(3):583–606
Schubert GA (1960) The public interest. The Free Press, Glencoe
Schütz A (1962) El problema de la realidad social. Amorrortu, Buenos Aires

Sorauf FJ (1961) The public interest. Adm Sci Quat 6(2):246–248
Stigler G (1971) The theory of economic regulation. Bell J Econ Manag Sci 2:3–21
Sunstein CR (1990) After the rights revolution. Reconceiving the regulatory state. Harvard University Press, Cambridge
Twining W, Miers D (1991) How to do things with rules, 3rd edn. Weidenfeld & Nicholson, London
Weber M (1979) Economía y Sociedad. FCE, México
Wilson JQ (1980) The politics of regulation. Basic Books, New York

Chapter 4
The Design of Laws

For ancient legal positivism the law was command, and command was the expression of the will of the sovereign. Even Ovid's *Metamorphosis* would become law, it was said, if it was just brushed by the sovereign's sceptre. From this point on, there was little room for reflection on how to improve laws. The jurist, permanently complexed by a positivist version of science, was confined to be a mere exegete of the sovereign's will, and the enlightened ideal of the law as *voluntas ratione animata*—which had been settled during the eighteenth century—lost strength: so to speak, reason abdicated its function of "animating" legislation.

But the possibility and even the need to appeal to reason to guide the will of the sovereign never completely disappeared. It is true that rationalism in the eighteenth century had thought it possible to find the perfect law and that, after that first dreamy stage, reason was assigned a more limited role. But humanity has never lacked a current of thought that considered—and still considers—that law can become the expression of a rationality informed by experience, even if such a rationality is limited or "bounded". It may well be impossible to find *the* perfect law, but science can certainly help us make laws that are a little better than the ones we have. To reach this goal, we can apply the tools of public policy analysis to the legislative process (Rubin 1991/1992). These are good tools for updating the ancient ideal of law as *voluntas ratione animata*.

4.1 Laws and Reasons

The conversion of political science into action-oriented research from the 1950s onwards facilitated the attempt to translate mathematic, statistic and economic studies into the field of political decisions. Economic theory and statistics consider that, when a person's preferences are known, they can be ordered and ranked with the help of logical concepts such as asymmetry, connection or transitivity. Ordered in this way, an individual who intends to be rational has to examine all the

V. Zapatero Gómez, *The Art of Legislating*, Legisprudence Library 6,
https://doi.org/10.1007/978-3-030-23388-4_4

alternatives, compare them with some unit of measure—for example, utility—and choose the best option. A rational decision would therefore involve the implementation of a whole set of operations consisting of ordering and clarifying preferences, informing oneself of all the options, examining the possible consequences of each option and choosing the best one.

According to this ideal model of rationality, the rational subject takes optimal decisions in a context defined by the following characteristics (Simon 1958, p. 137 ff): she or he (a) is a human being, endowed with an intelligence that allows him or her to find the "real" solution to a given problem; (b) has clear and stable preferences; (c) knows all possible solutions; (d) can predict all the consequences of each option; and, finally, (e) has an objective criterion (utility, justice, security, etc.) according to which she or he is able to order all his preferences.

As Hayek (1945) emphasised, however, reality hardly fits this model (see Meny and Thoenig 1992, p. 139 ff). First of all, because information is scarce and expensive: perfect information does not exist in practice. It is difficult, if not impossible, to know all the causal relationships that are at the heart of a problem, nor is it possible to know all the possible options or to imagine all the consequences of each of them. Moreover, when it is possible to obtain this type of information, the cost of obtaining it is very high in terms of time and money. And even if we do gather all the required information, it is sometimes not easy to assimilate it, either because of our own limitations or because our prejudices make us neglect information that is contrary to our values or beliefs. Secondly, the criteria guiding our choices are few, and not always applicable to the kind of decisions to be made. For example, if we limit ourselves to purely economic criteria, we see how cost-benefit, cost-effectiveness, risk and opportunity cost analyses may be applicable to legislation in certain areas, especially to economic legislation, but such criteria may be inadequate in other areas—think e.g. of social rights legislation. Thirdly, the ability of each human being to generate a comprehensive inventory of possible solutions varies greatly. And finally, deciding is part of a process in which the subject is under strong psychological pressure, which affects the outcome of his or her decisional process.

This is not how decisions are taken when rules are drafted and, therefore, a model was proposed that is closer to reality and that would make it possible to save a core of rationality in the legislative process. For Simon (1958), many of the problems faced by the drafter are solved through routine decisions that almost automatically follow previously established protocols, as is often the case with decrees declaring disaster or catastrophic areas, for example. But of course, not all problems benefit from this type of pre-coded response: often, the political decision-maker has to look for solutions *ex novo*. The options considered—and therefore the solution that is eventually imposed—are not necessarily optimal, as there is not always sufficient information or a clear and stable measure available to allow comparisons between them. Therefore, a political leader only exceptionally tries to reach optimal solutions; usually he tries to find a satisfactory or *satisficing* solution.[1]

[1]In this connection, see further Wintgens (2013) and Sartor (2009).

And this is possible provided that those who have to decide are able to simplify the complex problems to be dealt with. The fundamental technique that allows organisations to tackle difficult problems—unemployment, immigration, housing, etc.—consists of dividing the problem into its corresponding sub-problems and attributing their management to different organisational units (within the same or different ministerial departments). In this way, the level of information required, the number of options to be considered and the criteria for comparison between them can be reduced. Thus, the *possible* rational decision comes from the person who operates with a small number of options, adopts a *reasonable* criterion and opts for a *satisfactory* solution. Maximising is unfeasible in practice, the best can sometimes be the enemy of the good and therefore maximisation is replaced by satisfaction.

But, although this is an important limitation of the initial aim to rationalise decision-making in public life..., does the model correspond to what is actually done by real politicians? Well, the model does not fully fit in with what actually happens in the decision-making process either. Public policies are not always decided through analysis and intellectual performance but also through the different mechanisms by which people exert control, influence or power over others; that is, through interaction. Politics is a power game, not an intellectual exercise, and the problem is whether this power game can be "rationalised". In his famous "The Science of Muddling Through", Lindblom (1959) tried to demonstrate how decision making in the administration can be rational, but of a kind of rationality different to what is often imagined. The rational decision can be reached through "successive limited comparisons".

The politician or the official, according to Lindblom, has to find a way to drastically reduce the need for information. To this end, two different methods are available. First, it is possible to concentrate only on those policies that differ in a relatively small degree to existing policies, which significantly reduces the number of alternatives to be examined and simplifies research. And the second method operates, as Simon (1958) suggested, by parcelling out the problems into sub-problems and attributing them to different administrative units that will deal only with more operative or manageable goals. This does not mean that definitive rational solutions can be found—politics rarely solves problems definitively: the formulation of a specific policy is nothing more than a process of successive approximations to a desired objective. The policy moves forward in small steps, little by little, incrementally, avoiding therefore serious mistakes. The experience of the past and the present provides a fairly good understanding of the consequences of each small step to be taken.[2] There is no need to make long-term predictions;

[2]In integrated societies, according to Lindblom (1959), radical changes are impossible or unlikely. Any extreme proposal is doomed to political irrelevance. This proximity of the options allows for a greater possibility of predicting the consequences as the options are compared with the current situation that is already known. The virtue, Lindblom says, of such a hypothetical division of labour is that every important interest or value has its guardian. And these guardians can protect the interests they care about by repairing the damage caused by other agents and better anticipating the damage before it occurs. Thus, he pointed out, even partisanship and narrow-mindedness, to use

moreover, this procedure makes it possible to put predictions to the test and, above all, to correct the small errors that may occur. It is thus through small adjustments, through a trial and error approach, that we can avoid major mistakes in decision-making and move forward, albeit slowly. This is the highest level of rationality to which we can aspire in our societies.[3]

But the approaches which we have referred to—those of absolute rationality and of limited rationality—are rather prescriptive of the behaviour of the legislator or official rule-maker. As for their descriptive capacity, it depends on very specific circumstances that would need careful study. In any case, it seems that at least four policy decision procedures could be differentiated, depending on their degree of eventual rationalisation: computation, judgement, compromise, or intuition (Thompson 1967; see also López González 1988, p. 23 ff).

First of all, there are some policy decisions that are taken mechanically, through routine procedures, because all the data on the problem to be solved is available and there is a high degree of consensus on the appropriate solution. For example, when natural disaster occur, very similar decrees are usually issued in which only the amount of the subsidy or the range of benefits granted vary, according to the magnitude of the disaster. Secondly, there are decisions that require a long process of research because, even though all involved decision makers have agreed on the policy objectives, the causes that would generate the desired effects are unknown: full employment, reducing traffic accidents or increasing the amount of dammed water..., are normally shared objectives which require a research task on the best employment, traffic or hydraulic policy. Thirdly, there are occasions in which, in the face of a problem whose causes are known, there is no agreement on the objectives: we know that the increase in the number of immigrants puts pressure on the employment policy, but there may not be agreement on the objectives to be pursued by immigration policy. In this case, it is very likely that the decision will be reached through political compromises,[4] which does not mean that the analysis of the problem cannot facilitate the clarification of positions and serve as a legitimate instrument of argument in the debate. And finally, the legislator may face a real problem for which he doesn't know the cause (because at the moment he lacks the

pejorative terms, can sometimes be positive for the decision-making process since they can ensure that what one agency forgets will be taken into account by another; each agency's members specialise in a different point of view.

[3]Lindblom's position can only be endorsed in the context of a highly integrated society, in which there is a broad social and political consensus that allows radical changes to be avoided and incremental changes to be advocated. And although this approach is certainly conservative, its insistence on the need to strengthen the "competition of ideas" would require important organisational changes in our systems so that as many ideas as possible can be expressed and contrasted, and hence can influence decision-making. It is necessary, he insists, to change the process of public policy-making so that the potential of democracy can be tested (Lindblom 1991, p. 157).

[4]Or, to borrow from Sunstein (1996), on could also speak of "incompletely theorized agreements".

relevant information, or the time and means to obtain it) and there is no consensus on the objectives to be pursued, so the decision has to be made intuitively.

There is, therefore, no single method of decision-making. It depends, to a large extent, on the characteristics of the problem upon focus and the context in which it occurs. But regardless of the conception one may have of the rationality of policies, whether the decision is made intuitively or by compromise, or whether it is decided by computation or by judgment, there is a strong coincidence in the need for the use of science in policy-making (and a law is the expression of a policy). Some—e.g. deliberative democracy theorists—consider it possible to deduce political considerations discursively, through an intellectual process, rationally. Others, like Lindblom (1991, p. 41 ff), consider scientific knowledge an absolutely essential instrument both for clarifying their own ideas and persuading others throughout the process. Some use the idea of the philosopher-king as a parameter of political rationality, others understand that interaction requires information, analysis and research in order to make efficiency and effectiveness in decision-making compatible with democratic control of decisions. But, in any case, it seems beyond doubt that recourse to experts, to a theory of legislation adapted to modern times (Twining and Miers 1991, pp. 198–199), to policy analysis, would contribute to recovering the ideal of law as *voluntas ratione animata*.

It is true that there is not yet a theory to direct the legislator. While the activity of judges or courts is guided by an impressive body of doctrine and studies on the performance of this function and its rationalisation, the legislative process lacks such orientations. What is more, the impression has been created in our societies that legislation is pure power play and that it cannot be rationalised. The starting point here is the opposite: it is not only necessary but also possible to articulate techniques, procedures and an organisation of the normative process that, correctly used by the drafters of norms, would allow progress to be made towards the goal of enlightening the political will with the help of reason.

A project of this type involves a legislative methodology based on problem-solving (Seidman 1992, p. 32),[5] which goes far beyond *legal drafting* because it requires, prior to drafting legislation, to carry out a whole series of tasks. The three most significant ones are: defining the problem to be solved, setting the objectives to be pursued, and evaluating the options available to the drafters of the norm. Each and every one of these tasks requires the use of empirical research by experts. These are tasks that normally precede in time the work of parliaments and cabinets or councils of ministers, and are usually entrusted to technical bodies. Just as judges and courts are required to properly ground their decisions, the documentation that accompanies a bill must serve to explain and justify the legislative decision (Seidman 1992, p. 7). This is possible if the theory of legislation can specify what constitutes a good foundation and justification of a law.

[5]For Seidman (1992) there are four distinct phases: definition, possible explanations, possible legislative solutions and finally implementation and monitoring of the proposed solutions.

4.2 Laws to Solve Problems

Fuller (1969) imagined a hypothetical ruler, *Rex*, who, trying to establish a just social order, fails in his project by resorting to singular, retroactive, impossible or contradictory rules. But Rex would also fail—it should be added—if, willing to comply with Fuller's "internal morality of law", he hadn't defined the problems he was trying to solve through regulation, had lacked precise objectives, had not examined the available options or adopted a decision that was not co-extensive with the objective and the problem in question. In such hypothetical circumstances his officials, even if they had the deepest knowledge of the mysteries of law and legal technique, would not have been able to provide him with the law he wanted.

If *Rex* does not succeed in knowing the relevant data that make up the problem that concerns him, if he misdiagnoses the problem, if he fails to clarify the objectives pursued by the norm, if he does not attack the root of the problem or if he conflicts with other stated objectives…., the official in charge of drawing up the draft norm will not be able to provide him with a suitable instrument, nor will the citizen find in the text the desired pattern of behaviour, nor will the interpreter have clear criteria for its application to each specific case. Herbert Hart (1968, p. 160) said that it's a characteristic of our human behaviour—and therefore also of legislators—that if we try to regulate some area of behaviour, our efforts will always be hindered by two interrelated obstacles or handicaps. The first is our relative ignorance of fact; the second is our relative indetermination of aim. Indeed, experience shows that when a law fails as a problem-solving mechanism, its failure usually originates long before the drafting begins, it occurs when the exact problem to be solved is not precisely defined (Gouvin 1994). Therefore, it is necessary to diagnose first and only then prescribe (Twining and Miers 1991, p. 116 ff).

By *definition* of a problem, we mean the process by which a problem, once recognised as such and included in the public agenda, is perceived by the different parties, is subsequently explored, articulated, quantified whenever possible and, in some cases—not all—given an authorised or provisionally acceptable definition in terms of its probable causes, components and consequences (Hogwood and Gunn 1984, p. 108). In democratic systems, the definition of a problem to be solved is not in the hands of a single person or a single centre of power. In our pluralistic societies, many individuals, groups and institutions are involved in defining problems. For this reason, given the plurality of participants and the open nature of our societies, each player in the political process brings to the social debate a particular perspective on the seriousness of the problem, its urgency, the causes that motivate it, or the consequences that can be deduced from it. Immigration, for example, can be defined from the perspective of the pressure on the host country's education or health systems, or it can be defined from the perspective of the situation of misery that causes it in the country of origin. In some cases the problem of immigration will be defined from the perspective of the capacity of public services; in others, the focus will be on solidarity, or security issues. Hence, the definition of a problem of this nature is never an academic issue but a political one.

It is this strong political content of every definition that generates the difficulties. A public policy program is not simply a solution to a problem for which all the data is known and an agreement on its existence and significance already exists: part of the problem is the way it's constructed and defined in advance (Lecca 1993, p. 186). The very definition of the terms of a problem is, in politics, a power game in which one does not only seek, as could happen in the scientific community, a disinterested knowledge of reality, but rather to achieve action-oriented knowledge, to make decisions that affect individuals and society. The definition of a problem in politics is pure rhetoric if it's not action-oriented. For the same reason there is no objective, indisputable definition. In other words, problem definition is an endless process: problems—terrorism, energy crisis, unemployment, immigration, etc.—are continually being redefined in our societies. Our way of defining them evolves, as new actors continually enter the public arena with their own perspectives. Changing power relations and new social needs generate successive "authorised" definitions. A good example is the debate on nuclear energy: a few years ago, following the accidents at Three Mile Island or Chernovil, it appeared to be a stigmatised option to solve the energy crisis; today, however, the debate on the advantages and disadvantages of nuclear energy remains open.

To our "relative ignorance" of the facts we must add the difficulty of knowing all future combinations of events, and therefore of making predictions. Every legal norm implementing a public policy is born with a vocation of permanence over time; but it is not always easy to elaborate a norm capable of dealing with situations or problems that are continuously evolving. The legislator or the official who prepares the draft law must try to overcome this difficulty by "imagining" how the situation will evolve. Drafters, that is, must resort to prediction, but prediction is extremely difficult (Hogwood and Gunn 1984, p. 145), and they do not always have enough time or information, nor does they necessarily understand the dynamics of a given process. On the other hand, it is clear that predictions in public policy analysis can be used not only to help make a decision but as a justification for decisions already taken for other reasons and on other grounds. The power of political predictions lies in the ability to present a picture with the most vivid colours—as is typical for both the catastrophism of the opposition parties and the exaggerated optimism of governments. It's this objective difficulty of predicting the evolution of a problem that sometimes explains why the legislator resorts to ambiguous or vague terms or to delegation as a way to deal with the uncertainty of the future.

It is true that defining a problem involves no small difficulties. But these difficulties cannot, however, be exaggerated to the extent of rendering futile any attempt to provide as much information, objectivity and rationality as is possible for the development of a norm. The contrary would be to condemn ourselves to arbitrary exercise of power. The use of relevant analytical techniques can and should equip systems with the kind of organisation that will ensure maximum diligence in normative decisions. It is also true that our interest here is the "authorised", official definition of problems by public authorities. In this sense, the definition we are looking for is the one that usually begins in government headquarters, is refined in the administrative phase, and, in case of government bills, is submitted to public debate among the different groups that participate in the parliamentary process. Sometimes a consensus is reached during this long process; sometimes a particular group imposes its definition. But it is clear that this process, that takes place in public ("under bright lights and with stenographers"), requires giving reasons and submitting each particular perspective on each problem to the "market of ideas" that any democracy implies. So, even if it is a subjective process, with a great political load, with conclusions that are always provisional and subject to "better reasons" that may eventually appear, this process is far from being useless work. Any definition serves to organise the debate, to give it coherence and to feed the circuit of information available to public opinion (Rouban 1993, p. 199).

So, either because it is a technical question that can easily be solved by a computer, or because it is a question of political importance that will be resolved interactively through reasoned debate or by the final imposition of the majority opinion, the drafter of a rule must proceed as carefully as possible, taking certain precautions in order to provide a definition of the problem to be solved.[6]

First of all, the definition of a problem should be carried out by, or shared with, experts and technicians who contribute their knowledge.[7] In any case, it is convenient to separate the person or persons who analyse a problem from the ones who make the final decision. Any normative decision can be broken down into three elements: an element of denunciation or enunciation of the problem; a programmatic element (what to do), and an instrumental element (the means to do it). These three aspects should be differentiated as far as possible. Formally, the person or persons who decide should not have complete control over all three stages (Lecca 1993, p. 194).

Secondly, we must look for the right opportunity, the ideal moment to define a certain problem. It is not the same to argue about the full enforcement of the death penalty following one of the horrific murders that regularly hit public opinion as it is to argue about it a few months after the shock. It's simply not possible to attempt a calm debate on the safety of air traffic the day after the accident suffered by the Spanair plane in August 2008, in which 154 people lost their lives; or to propose a decision on the nuclear moratorium in Spain at the same time as a radioactive leak in Ascó is made public (26 November 2007) or following the incidents in Vandellós (25 August 2008).[8] When a certain concern, dissatisfaction or unease has not yet been expressed in public opinion on any issue, the political leader has a tendency not

[6]Brian W. Hogwood suggests this checklist: (a) who says there is a problem here?; (b) is it a real problem, is it manageable by the government?; (c) what probability of agreement exists around the problem?; (d) is it the right time to give a definition?; (e) who defines the problem?; do they have a particular interest?; (f) are there alternative perspectives?; (g) what is the appropriate degree of aggregation?; (h) has the causal structure of the problem been understood?; (i) can the implications of the problem be specified and quantified?; and (j) when and how does the definition need to be revised? See Hogwood and Gunn (1984).

[7]This appeal to the experts is the insistent recommendation—which I fully share—of the works of Cass Sunstein (2004, 2005).

[8]Ascó and Vandellós are nuclear plants located in the Spanish province of Tarragona.

to deal with it and to devote himself to the most urgent problems: hence the fate—being filed away—of thousands of notes and reports that are made daily in the administration, detecting problems, pointing out their causes and proposing measures. If they are unrelated to the problems on the public agenda, such analyses and suggestions are irrelevant. When, on the other hand, a problem has caught the public eye's attention and has a strong impact, the public official immediately demands concrete solutions, but in that moment in time, urgency prevents a calm examination of the problem. Therefore, when circumstances allow for a calm assessment, the politician may well lack the incentive to take action (Lecca 1993, p. 188). Conversely, when public opinion demands immediate action, calm assessment might be impossible. In short, "where evaluation is possible it may not be relevant for politic action and when the latter demands it, evaluation may prove impossible". Such is the paradox and the challenge: to find the right moment for a correct definition of the problem.

Thirdly, defining a problem involves, among other things, finding its causal structure. Without the identification of the causes of the problem, it will be impossible to study the options and set the objectives of the norm. Without determining the causes of the problem to be solved—whether it is the increase in accidents at work or deaths from gender-based violence—the enactment of a rule will not be much different from shooting in the dark. When a particular problem has entered the public agenda and shocked the public, there is a risk that the problem is over simplified and the ensuing decisions are also simplistic.

There are at least three latent risks in this phase of the operation. Firstly, there is a tendency, when it comes to avoiding political responsibility or justifying the decision not to intervene, to explain problems on the basis of external causes. This is the recurring argumentation of those in power in this type of situation: to affirm that there is no jurisdiction or competence on the matter. In a globalised world such as the one we live in, and especially in polyarchic political systems, it is becoming increasingly easy for policymakers and legislators to elude their responsibility to act in the face of a problem: sometimes the European Union is responsible, sometimes the central government is responsible, or the autonomous regions (*Comunidades Autónomas*). An important part of the political debate is an attempt to put the causes of problems beyond the reach of the persons responsible. Only the attentiveness of an adult citizenship, an open political debate and transparency can make it difficult for power to hide behind fatalism or powerlessness to justify inaction. We must always be aware of this natural tendency of all power to arrogate to itself the paternity of prosperity and to argue its lack of competence when the time comes for difficulties.

A second risk lies in the belief that intervention is needed at any rate: to confuse the causes with the conditions (Gouvin 1994, p. 1338 ff). Whoever wants to define a problem with a view to its solution must carefully examine whether the problem in question can be corrected by means of legislation or whether it is an issue that is beyond human possibilities, such as physical and natural conditionings, which must be precisely assumed as data that sets limits to human action.

And the third risk is mono-causality. Traffic accidents can be caused by defects in road design, car design, car power, the education—or lack of it—of drivers, alcohol or tobacco consumption, etc. Similarly, work accidents can be due to the lack of safety measures at work, to certain working conditions or, let's say, to the consumption of alcohol at work. Well, when the intervention of power is called for, if the problem becomes particularly acute, the urgency of time and the pressure to intervene can alter the categories of a correct evaluation with the obvious risk of simplifying the problem and its causes. When immediate solutions are required, there is a high probability that the description of the problem will be simplified in order to simplify, in turn, the solution offered. The more pressure a problem of unemployment or healthcare puts on society, the greater the risk that the immigrant, for example, is signalled as the sole responsible. Mono-causality—the simplification of reality—leads, when one is not aware of it, to ineffective legislation that does not achieve the objectives it claims to pursue. And when simplification is a deliberate attitude of legislative actors, we are faced with a no less dangerous product: the pure manipulation of citizens.

It is true, as we have pointed out, that every definition is charged with subjectivity. One way of integrating it as a positive element in the decision-making process, is to have an organisational structure in which the evaluator does not decide, and the decision maker has to rely on the contribution of experts. Perhaps a good step in this direction is, we believe, the creation of Public Policy Evaluation Agencies working in support of both governments and parliaments.

4.3 Identifying Objectives

A different matter, although so closely linked with the definition of the problem that they sometimes fuse together, is the task of identifying the objectives to be pursued in the development of a rule (Rubin 1991/1992, p. 283 ff). Without defining its goals, neither the drafter of a rule can give it the appropriate form, nor can the governing body implement it, nor can the interpreter apply it, nor can the degree of efficacy and effectiveness of the rule be measured. On the other hand, if the objectives of a law are not made explicit, it is unlikely that a serious parliamentary procedure will be possible, it will stray in tedious debates on technical issues and will overlook the substance of the problem to be solved. Such is the importance of this task.

The first problem that arises, however, is terminological, since the term "objective" is sometimes used to refer to the interests that are hidden in the norm (what Alfred Schütz called the *reasons why*),[9] other times to the fundamental principles behind a political decision, and yet on other occasions to the consequences that the norm is intended to produce (the *reasons for*). It is therefore important to begin by clarifying the meaning we give here to the so-called objectives of a norm.

When we talk about the objectives of a rule, we are not referring to the interests that sometimes move legislators. In any regulatory policy, those responsible for its

[9] See above the introduction to Chap. 3.

development can, and in fact do, carry certain interests. In our pluralistic democracies, groups and individuals seek policies that benefit them. Similarly, any public decision-maker is likely to take into account his personal or group interests when making a decision, whether these are maximising votes, in the case of politicians, or maximising power, in the case of public officials. Public policies cannot be understood if the interests behind them are unknown: this is the positive part of the Public Choice analysis. But it is one thing to acknowledge the weight of private interests in the genesis of norms, and another to reduce the study of public policies to detecting these interests that *capture* norms. It is capital not to confuse interests and objectives of public policy, no matter how intertwined they might be.

It's also necessary to differentiate between objectives and reasons. Behind regulatory policies and the rules that implement them are certain reasons, moral and/or political principles that guide them. Public authorities are entrusted with the mission of promoting the realisation of certain ultimate principles or values (freedom, equality, solidarity, as well as their manifestations) which thus constitute the basis or reason for their actions. In the legislative process, in public debate, the legislator tries to offer arguments and reasons, but rarely displays his interests. Such is the core of the neo-republican conviction, its belief that rational debate and discussion make it possible to determine with precision the superiority of some values over others: by rejecting that decisions on values are merely a matter of taste, the republican perspective assumes that practical reason must be used to solve social problems (Sunstein 1985, pp. 31–32). However, even though reasons or principles can and must play a key role in the legislative process, objectives cannot be reduced to them.

By the term "objectives of the norm" we mean all the effects that we want to cause in the social environment,[10] the state of affairs that we want to reach with the adoption of a rule, what we have called the *reasons for*. At the drafting stage of a law, what needs to be identified are not, for the time being, the principles and interests that bubble in any public policy, but rather the objectives that are pursued with it. So understood, from the point of view of the legislator (Twining and Miers 1991, p. 202), the identification of the objective is indispensable. A public policy—and therefore a norm—without an objective would be like a regulatory spasm, and such spasms are truly exceptional. Every law implies an attempt to modify (or maintain) a certain aspect of social reality. It must be assumed—unless there is incontestable proof to the contrary—that parliaments are composed of reasonable people who reasonably pursue reasonable objectives. This continues to be the contribution of Hart and Sacks' (1958, p. 1378) work to the matter.

Identifying objectives is required firstly by the drafters of the rule in order to understand exactly what outcome the legislator wants to achieve with it. In the Anglo-Saxon system—with their peculiar method for normative drafting to which we will refer later (Chap. 8)—this phase of normative production is articulated

---

[10]It would also be necessary to distinguish between the consequences that are intended for reality and consequences that are intended to be produced on the legal system. See, in this regard, Twining and Miers (1991, p. 202).

through the instructions prepared and approved by the Cabinet. In the continental system, the procedure is more informal, without the requirement for a specific instance or a particular document to determine such objectives. Secondly, parliamentarians need objectives that have been clearly specified in advance in order to be able to adequately fulfil their task when debating, approving or rejecting a bill. And thirdly, citizens, who have the right both to know where their representatives want to take them and to judge the efficacy and efficiency of their decisions, also need to know the objectives of a law. Without setting the objective of draft laws in an authorised manner, it will not be possible to demand accountability, as is characteristic of a democratic system, for the inefficacy and the inefficiency of public administrators.

Some authors (see e.g. Rose-Ackerman 1988) attach great importance to the expression or statement of public policy objectives, and have even suggested that constitutional courts should review for the consistency of laws. Since laws must be internally consistent, i.e. their content must be aligned with the stated objectives, those legislative provisions that are manifestly inconsistent should be judicially invalidated. On the other hand, these authors stress that laws must also have an external consistency, understood as coherence between the objectives declared by the legislator and the personal and material resources made available for their implementation. Whether or not courts should review for legislative consistency is debatable. But anyway, a democratic system that aspires to increase the efficacy, effectiveness and efficiency of public policies and, at the same time, to ensure greater accountability of public managers or administrators, must take the public statement of legislative objectives (as well as legislative goal-setting in general) very seriously. The real difficulties this task entails—which lead us to the "relative indetermination" of purpose to which H. Hart referred—should not prevent people in positions of public responsibility from having to show their cards at some point in the process.

In order to fulfil its function, legislative goal-setting must avoid generalities, grandiloquent sentences or declarations, and be truly operational. As in the development of any public policy, the legislator in this case needs to be able to answer questions such as: where are we and where do we want to be?; what is preventing us from getting there?; what needs to be done to achieve the objective?; what must all other implicated parties do to make the operation a success?; how do we coordinate multiple objectives?; what would be considered a success?; how could we quantify it?; what conditions are required for a good result?; and finally, what would need to be done if the policy fails?[11] Very possibly, if the drafters of any regulation could have this kind of information prior to the drafting, the quality of laws would be significantly improved.

Once we have clarified what is meant by objectives and their usefulness, the second problem that arises is that of who should set them and how they should be set;

[11]Hogwood and Gunn (1984, p. 159 ff) offer a checklist with the following questions: (a) Where are you?; (b) Where do you want to go?; (c) What is stopping you?; (d) What do you need other Departments to do?; (e) What do you have to do yourself?; (f) How should you manage multiple objectives?; (g) What do you consider a success?; (h) Should the objective be quantified?; (i) What conditions does success depend on?; and (j) What will you do if the objectives are not achieved?

this brings us back to the problem of the participation of experts in the legislative process. The study of the relationship between the "political" and the "administrative" elements in the decision-making process is an age-old topic in administration science (cf. Weber 1979, p. 1070 ff), and the conception of politicians who establish objectives and technicians who determine the means to attain them is as popular as it is unrealistic (de los Ríos 1917). It cannot be expected that the politicians with responsibilities in the Executive—scarcely a thousand people in Spain including ministers, state secretaries and under-secretaries, general directors and members of their respective teams—have the real capacity to lead and supervise each and every one of the public policies for which they are responsible. Ministers have to allocate time to a wide range of tasks such as representation, travel, visits, attention to parliamentary responsibilities, attendance at meetings, etc. Very little time remains to study files and give instructions. In Spain, for instance, ministers do not even have the time to study in depth the approximately 50 dossiers that have to be approved by the Council of Ministers every week. Nor do they have or need to have specialised training in each field: they are "generalists" and not necessarily experts, which obliges them to have confidence in the administration. The rotation in the function imposed by the democratic play, on the other hand, causes policy makers to inherit many of the policies developed by their predecessors.

The conclusions Mayntz (1985) draws from the organisation in the Federal Republic of Germany are—leaving the inevitable peculiarities aside—largely generalisable. Not only do program initiatives come from the technical ranks, it is also the bureaucracy that does much of the work of preparing and formulating such proposals. Sometimes, the political leadership of a given department learns about the projects under development (not the most important ones, of course) only after they have already been drafted. Certainly, the political leader may reject them or change them radically: but this happens infrequently because the bureaucrats will usually not propose anything that cannot ultimately be accepted. The political leadership, in turn, will pay special attention, R. Mayntz says, to issues that are of critical nature, are politically controversial and virtually conflictive, have a special public impact, help to elude criticism of past gross errors, or are suggested by members of the parliamentary faction, the Cabinet or other influential political figures.

Therefore, in reality, the objectives are usually established through a permanent dialogue between politicians and technicians, and it's not easy to determine the weight of each part in this task. Bureaucracy usually only develops and proposes policies that are consistent with the presumed intention of the policymaker; politicians, in most cases, endorse policies generated within the bureaucracy. Nevertheless, how objectives are determined in the real legislative process is one thing and how this should be properly done, quite another. And while it would be a mistake to dispense with the participation of expert technicians at this stage, allowing politicians to forsake their responsibility to lead the normative process would be to renounce essential principles of democracy. That is why the Anglo-Saxon experience of an Office Parliamentary Council, operating on the basis of previous Cabinet policy instructions, is an interesting practice—we will return to this point in Chap. 8.

4.4 Various Solutions

Identifying the different ways to achieve a given objective is not an easy task: far from the fatalistic positions that politicians usually adopt, there is never a single solution to each of the problems on the agenda. The alternatives are numerous, sometimes innumerable. However, this purported exuberance of options, which may be correct in speculative terms, does not match in practice the small number of options that are in fact considered in our societies, so that the problem here is more one of scarcity than of abundance. It is said, for example, that of all the alternative paths available to achieve a given objective, the only options taken into account are the ones coming from those figures who have support within the organisation. Indeed, certain personalities have the capacity to raise options and others don't, depending on their prestige or power within the organisation. This fact already entails an initial simplification and impoverishment of the variety of possible solutions to each problem. And it also reveals the importance of properly organising the decision-making process: the greater or lesser variety of options examined by lawmakers can depend on how this process is organised.

A second reduction in the number of available options derives from the incremental strategies that are often followed by administrations. The bureaucracy in charge of elaborating public policies is well aware of the fact that it can only propose what is politically acceptable: and in societies that are integrated economically and politically, any proposal deemed radical or excessively deviated from the status quo will trigger fear and rejection in the social majority. This implies a further significant simplification of the options taken into account in the development of rules.

A third limitation comes more and more, in our societies, from the international context. In a globalised market with increasingly structured international blocks, the room for manoeuvre of national politicians is seriously constrained.[12] As we have pointed out elsewhere (Zapatero 1996), a good number of the rules in our national systems have already been drawn up outside our borders (European Union and other international organisations) and a large number of the remaining rules are transpositions of Community or international obligations. Particularly important in this respect is the harmonising role that the Council of Europe has been playing in a multitude of areas: no state can afford to overlook the political and moral obligation to align its national legislation with the framework of wider Europe. Finally, the very requirements of national economies to remain competitive force states to legislate while glancing sidelong at their commercial counterparts. The globalisation of markets, the affiliation of states to international organisations such as the Council of Europe or the European Union and the need to ensure the competitiveness of national economies are another major constraint on the options that are ultimately considered in the normative process.

All of this, among other factors, implies a simplification of the options in political, economic, social and cultural policies: so the solutions to problems, though

---

[12]See further Chap. 14 in this volume.

theoretically almost infinite, are in reality rather limited. The challenge at this point is not so much to simplify the countless options to be considered as to achieve an organisation and articulation of the political system in which plurality, open debate and transparency give rise to a sufficient number of options to avoid the fatalism of the single option.[13] Hence, it is important for the drafters to look for guidance in other sources, the most important of which are history and comparative law (Seidman 1992, pp. 66–67). History, because in politics not only are problems sometimes repeated, but different solutions have already been attempted. Comparative law because, in a globalised world with regional or supranational organisations, states usually have to solve the same kind of problems and, although solutions are rarely directly transplantable, there is a wider range of solutions to be considered when different legal systems are compared (Watson 1974; Seidman and Seidman 1996). Analogously, in countries with a federal structure, such as Spain, the regulatory initiatives of the autonomous regions may work as pilot experiences in problem solving.

4.5 Evaluation of Options

But it is not enough to identify a sufficient number of possible solutions, it is necessary to evaluate them and finally choose one. There are several criteria that can be used to make this kind of evaluation (Viscusi 1992), and, depending on which one is used, the option that is ultimately chosen will be different. Efficiency, perhaps one of the most criticised criteria among philosophers and academics, is also the most widely used by economists and public officials, especially in the U.S. since the Reagan and Clinton administrations.[14] This idea has been so successful that for some authors, like Posner, efficiency is an adequate criterion for justice, whereas for others, like Calabresi, it is, if not the only component, at least one of the most relevant components of the notion of justice (cf. Calsamiglia 1989, p. 150). The core aspect of the concept of efficiency is that there should be no waste; that, when it comes to public policies, the maximum benefit should be obtained with the allocated resources or, alternatively, that the cost of obtaining a benefit should be the minimum possible (Albi et al. 1994, p. 149 ff). It was Pareto who offered the first justification for this criterion: a policy is eligible if it improves the situation of one person without, at the same time, worsening the situation of another. And since very few policies can meet such stringent requirements, Kaldor, Hicks and others justified this approach on the basis of the compensation criterion: a specific policy is eligible before other options if its beneficiaries obtain enough benefit to compensate, even

[13]See e.g. Hogwood and Gunn (1984, p. 170 ff), discussing various tecniques to identify options.

[14]A history of the introduction of these techniques in the U.S. as well as their political repercussions can be seen in Sunstein (2004, p. 45), as well as in Tolchin and Tolchin (1983).

hypothetically, for the loss of those who suffer the consequences. Such is the purported basis of the cost-benefit analysis.[15]

According to this logic, all public administrators, when evaluating possible solutions, must carry out a cost-benefit analysis, understood as a detailed explanation of the consequences of the different options available to them (Sunstein 2004; cf. also 2018). Such an analysis would enable citizens to see whether the problem in question is large or small, what the cost of reducing or eliminating the problem is and what the benefits are. All this means giving experts a particularly important—albeit not decisive—place in the normative process. This is in the interests not only of efficacy but also of promoting a genuinely deliberative democracy: citizens should decide, have the final and sovereign word, but while doing so, they should always have in view, 'on the screen' so to speak, both the costs and the benefits of public decisions, so that no significant fact escapes private and public scrutiny.

The cost-benefit analysis attempts to evaluate monetarily the flows of benefits and costs associated with each of the policy options studied (Albi et al. 1994, p. 181 ff). This requires a clear definition of the objectives of the policy, a study of the alternative ways of achieving them, a list of the benefits and costs, the choice of a social discount rate (tasa social de descuento), the estimation of the potential uncertain or risky effects, the consideration of the distributive effects and the systematic presentation of the results of the study. The aim of all these actions is to have a thorough quantitative evaluation of all the facets of a problem and to make the expected results homogeneous so they are comparable by the common standard that is money, in order to help political representatives in the selection process.

Such an analysis does not provide the solution but it must help the politician answer the question of whether a particular option provides a net benefit to society and whether, prima facie, the policy in question should be approved or continued. The usefulness of cost-benefit analysis derives at least from the following circumstances.[16] First, it facilitates meaningful comparisons between different courses of action: the conclusion of such an analysis is a number, an amount of money that reflects the estimated net benefit of a proposal. Secondly, cost-benefit analysis favours the correct management of a program because it requires that the preferences of individuals is taken into account: the basic idea of cost-benefit analysis is that it reflects the economic benefit it provides to society and, therefore, it has to consider the value that users attribute to it. Thirdly, the cost-benefit analysis encourages a

---

[15]In the list of criteria for improving the quality of government regulation approved by the OECD Council in 1995, it was recommended that, before adopting a norm or decision, the following questions should be answered: (1) Is the problem correctly defined?; (2) Is Government action justified?; (3) Is regulation the best form of Government action?; (4) Is there a legal basis for regulation?; (5) What is the appropriate level (or levels) of Government for this action?; (6) Do the benefits of regulation justify the costs?; (7) Is the distribution of effects across society transparent?; (8) Is the regulation clear, consistent, comprehensible and accesible to users?; (9) Have all interested parties had the opportunity to present their views? See the OECD Reference Checklist for Regulatory Decision-Making (Appendix to OECD 1995).

[16]See Australian Government (1992).

careful examination of the real added value of each proposal. Fourthly, and especially, cost-benefit analysis can only enrich and improve the democratic function. In short, given that needs are unlimited and means are scarce, a cost-benefit analysis makes it possible to optimise the use of social resources.[17]

It is obvious, however, that cost-benefit analysis has limitations (Heinzerling 1998, p. 1981), and its conclusions need to be played down when it comes to making normative decisions. Viscusi (1993), among others, referred to the two main questions this technique leaves unanswered: the distribution of costs and the monetisation of benefits. Because indeed, the cost-benefit analysis helps the legislator choose the solution that brings a net benefit to the community. But it tells us nothing about which groups or groups bear the costs and which groups benefit, who loses and who wins, and this is a critical issue in any policy decision. The cost-benefit analysis is not concerned therefore with the redistributive potential of a given regulatory policy. On the other hand, it is clear that not all the objectives of a specific norm can be expressed in monetary terms. If this type of analysis is applicable in economic regulation, it presents serious difficulties when it comes to social regulation where goods and services are at stake that are often not commercialised in the market: how to evaluate monetarily the benefit for society of reducing the risk of AIDS or cancer?, the benefit of prolonging the life of a sick person?, keeping the atmosphere clean or national security?

This is why other complementary evaluation procedures are used, such as the cost-efficacy analysis that simplifies the cost-benefit one (Albi et al. 1994, p. 165 ff): when it is not possible to obtain good monetary estimates of the benefits of a given program—that is, when the objectives pursued cannot be evaluated monetarily—but we can calculate the social costs, the analysis compares the costs with non-monetary indicators of the effectiveness in expenditure. The monetisation of benefits is replaced by some index (such as a percentage in the reduction of crime, mortality or pollution, for example) that allows the efficacy of the alternative solution to be measured. Viscusi (1993) has also studied the advantages and limitations of this type of analysis. Cost-efficacy analyses are particularly useful to eliminate policy options that are clearly inferior. If one health policy saves six human lives at a cost of EUR one million and another saves five lives at a cost of EUR 1.5 million, the option seems, prima facie, clear: the cost per life is lower in the first case so the first option

[17]The concern for the improvement of the planning of policy interventions is encouraging governments to set criteria that allow for a more precise clarification of the objectives pursued with the development of a norm, as well as the options available to the legislator. An example is the UK Government (2003), which in its *Better Policy Making: A Guide to Regulatory Impact assessment* advises norm drafters to consider, among other questions, the purpose and intended effect of the measure; the options available; the cost-benefit assessment; the equity and fairness of the measure, and its impact on small enterprises and on competition; enforcement issues and sanctions; consultations (within government and public consultation); and monitoring and review.

would be preferable.[18] But the snag about this methodology is that it considers the achievement of a particular objective as an established fact: this method serves, once the objective is defined (maximisation of the number of lives), to find the most cost-efficient means to apply to the problem but it doesn't help to define the objective because it does not resolve whether or not such an objective is morally relevant.

There are other evaluation techniques among which risk assessment of each option is increasingly prominent.[19] Under the heading of risk assessment, the OECD (1994) highlights how health and safety regulation has grown in recent years to the point where it now accounts for no less than half of the total costs associated with regulation. This type of regulation seeks to reduce the collective risks to health and safety posed by all human activities, particularly work, transport, air, water, foodstuffs and housing.[20] Regulatory decisions in these areas are based on often poorly understood but rather essential assessments of the spread of a specific risk and the ability of public authorities to reduce it. Legislators have to make decisions in this area under pressure from an increasingly sensitive public opinion that has opted for the precautionary principle in its maximum expression: zero risk.[21] There are notable differences between how experts perceive risk and how citizens do it. As citizens, we are more easily carried away by heuristic availability (we see a risk more likely if we have a known example at hand), we overestimate the probability of a given risk (we tend to put ourselves in the worst case scenario even though, as in the case of the mad cow crisis, the probability is minimal), we have a real aversion to things getting worse, we rely more on the benevolence of nature than on the decisions humans make and we are unable to assume that risk is an inevitable part of our way of life (Sunstein 2005, p. 35 ff). This means that people often perceive risks more clearly than benefits and tend therefore to overvalue risk elimination policies (zero risk) without caring about the costs (that are hidden). In other cases, we will overestimate the benefits of a given policy (measures to combat avian influenza, for example) without knowing the real probability of the risk or even the magnitude of the risk involved.[22] Risk analysis, in the hands of specialists, would help to avoid political decisions driven by hysteria and irrational alarm.[23]

[18]It is not always clear, though: What happens when options involve discrimination on the basis of, for example, sex? Would the six-life option (prostate cancer) be correct instead of the five-life option (breast cancer)?

[19]There is a vast literarute on this issue, with one of the most notable contributions in this regard being the works of Sunstein (2004, 2005). Cf. also Black (2002), as well as, more recently, Dunlop and Radaelli (2017).

[20]Evidently the norms that regulate security are increasingly becoming comercial weapons that are used between regional or national markets. In the face of the absence or the difficulties of risk assessments, states deliberately create security obligations that are not aimed so much at protecting health and sanitation of their nationals, but at establishing obstacles to comercial exchange.

[21]For an emphatic critic of the precautionary principle as it is, in his opinion, applied in the member states of the EU, see Sunstein (2005).

[22]When examining the costly policies established for the prevention of shark attacks, Swanson (2001)—cited by Cass Sunstein (2004, p. 87)—points out that "it is thirty times more probable that a person is struck by lightning than bit by a shark".

[23]In Spain, a good example was the sanitary alert (25 April 2008) not to consume Ukranian sunflower oil—which caused an unwarranted social alarm.

But risk analysis is not easy from a practical, political and ethical point of view (see Michaelson 1996), nor is it easy to make comparisons between risks. The problem is to determine the value of risk reduction so that a decision can be made based on the marginal cost in terms of the level of risk reduction considered reasonable: how much more are we willing to spend on reducing cancer risk by x %? How many lives would we save if the same amount were spent on preventing road accidents? A risk assessment could, in certain cases, make it possible to improve the allocation of resources. If—and this is purely an example—the aim is to save as many lives as possible, perhaps by redirecting certain health policies towards the prevention of transport risks, it would be possible to save more lives at the same cost. The fact is risk assessments have begun to be considered and required in policy decisions, whether as guide for public decision-makers that lack the most fundamental risk-management criteria or as international harmonisation of risk assessment methods to prevent the creation of false barriers to trade.[24] One example is the British Government's *Guide to Risk Assessment* (UK Government 1993; see also Australian Government 1995).[25] Another example are the recommendations made by an ad hoc expert group appointed by the Commission of the European Communities in 1995: (a) all food hygiene directives must provide that the measures to be taken are based on a risk assessment; (b) the data required for risk assessment and their understanding must be widely improved and disseminated; and (c) the common principles of the risk analysis system and its critical control points must be used to underpin all food hygiene legislation on the basis of the risks considered.[26]

With all their limitations and deficiencies, these are some of the instruments available to public officials to evaluate the different solutions for a problem and

[24]Sunstein (2004, p. 160) suggests a list of eight points: (1) agencies should not only identify the advantages and disadvantages of reducing risks, but also try, as far as possible, to quantify the relevant (non-monetary) effects; (2) the quantitative description should complement and not displace a qualitative description of the relevant effects; (3) to improve the overall assessment, agencies should try to convert non-monetary values (involving, for example, lives saved, improvements in health and aesthetic values) into dollar equivalents; (4) agencies entrusted with life and health assessment should be controlled by laws or decrees establishing minimum and maximum limits; (5) agencies should be allowed to make adjustments in their analysis based on the various qualitative factors; (6) agencies should be required to demonstrate that the benefits justify the costs. If they fail to do so, they should be asked to demonstrate that the action is nonetheless reasonable, on the basis of a publicly given explanation; (7) in ordinary circumstances, the appropriate response to any social fear that is not based on evidence and the wave effects associated with it, is education and appeasement of the social mood, rather than an increase in regulation; and (8) unless otherwise provided by law, a judicial review of risk regulation should require a general demonstration that the regulation has produced more benefit than harm, based on a reasonable assessment of benefits and costs.

[25]Cf. also *The Analysis and Regulation of Safety Risk. A survey of the practices of National and Commonwealth regulatory Agencies* (Australian Office of Regulation Review 1995).

[26]See the EC Commission's *Rapport du groupe d'experts independants pour la simplification legislative et administrative*, COM (95) 288 final (21 June 1995). In this connection, see also the OECD's (2010) report *Improving the Governance of Risk.*

select the most satisfactory one. And in this task, the active participation of experts and specialists with useful knowledge is inexcusable.[27]

But does all this mean that the cost-benefit analysis is the most relevant criterion when evaluating the options and making policy decisions? Not at all. It would be if we were to adopt a radical utilitarian perspective for which the ethical criterion par excellence is the maximisation of the general welfare. It is true that the general welfare is morally relevant and a government must choose, *prima facie*, the project that increases the general welfare: this is what our most common and deepest intuitions tell us about the role of governments. Yet cost-benefit analysis is not a moral criterion but a decision-making procedure (Adler and Posner 1999). The moral criterion guides us towards the objective we should strive for; the decision-making procedure shows us the way to achieve it. And above and beyond the maximisation of the general welfare there can be, and in fact are, other criteria of superior moral value. There are policies that simply cannot be evaluated on the basis of costs and benefits. And when these are susceptible to such assessments, efficiency does not and cannot have the last word. It is ultimately the moral criteria—for some the maximisation of welfare, for others, like Rawls, the attention to the less favoured, or the equality in certain levels of welfare (Dworkin 2003), or simply the respect for certain rights—that will often make it necessary to push the results of the cost-benefit evaluation in to the background. In the evaluation of normative options, efficiency is a morally relevant criterion, but not necessarily the *decisive* criterion.

4.6 In Favor of a Legislative Policy Office

Considering a given law as the manifestation of a specific public policy allows us to conceive its elaboration from the perspective of a problem that needs to be solved: laws, like parliaments, exist to solve problems. We start from the definition of the problem, we study its causes, investigate the possible solutions, evaluate them and choose the most satisfactory among them. But it is clear that the legislator does not have the knowledge or the time to carry out such a calm analysis as proposed here. On the other hand, the legitimate political confrontation makes it difficult to separate facts and values; and, without this separation, it is difficult to correctly define and evaluate the different solutions. These circumstances have historically reduced the theory of legislation, as the enlightened thinkers used to say, to "the cry that reason addresses to the throne". Legisprudential proposals remain mere good intentions unless they are actually reflected in a well-organised legislative process. It is therefore necessary to ask whether there is any kind of organisation of this process that would allow this methodology to be applied.

[27]See Wildavsky (1979), as well as Lindblom and Cohen (1979), among many others.

As far as Spain is concerned, experience shows us how in our parliamentary system the discussion does not begin with the existence of a problem, an analysis of its causes or an assessment of possible solutions. The parliamentary process begins with a draft bill on which the debate focuses. Sometimes, the legislator has only this text and a meagre background documentation; the minimum necessary to comply with the requirements of Art. 88 of the Constitution.[28] Anyone who tries to find here an analysis of the kind we are suggesting will waste his time. And if he does find it, he should know that this kind of documentation is usually prepared after the text has been drafted, i.e. only to provide some justification for the proposed decision. In this way, the parliamentary debate is lost in technicalities and trivialities without the MPs being able to understand what exactly the law is about and what they are deciding upon—of course, this may not hold true for exceptional legislative scenarios.

The structure of the legislative process in parliamentary democracies would theoretically allow for a better connection between legislative theory proposals and legislators. As is well known, and paradoxically enough, one of the characteristics of parliamentary democracies is that in 90% of cases, the legislative initiative corresponds to the Executive. Conversely, it is characteristic of presidentialist systems that legislative initiative depends almost exclusively on parliament itself. For this reason, in our systems, the quality of laws depends to a large extent on the quality of the projects drafted by the Executive. Parliament can make a good project technically worse, but it can hardly improve a bad one. Therefore, if we want to improve the quality of our laws, the greatest effort must be concentrated on the drafting of bills before they are submitted to the Houses, and even before they are drafted. This is where the methodology suggested here is fully applicable.

The most recurrent organisational proposals—inserting public policy analysis into the parliamentary process (Rubin 1991/1992); requiring written justification for bill proposals (Seidman 1992); strengthening judicial oversight of laws (Sunstein 1990); experimental, test or sunset laws (Lowi 1969); or institutionalising a systematic review of existing laws—might make more sense in presidentialist systems such as the United States. In parliamentary systems, however, the best solution is to be found in proposals such as Gouvin's (1994, 1995) to create an Office of Legislative Policy. For the reasons stated above, such an office should reside in government headquarters.[29] This could be the formula for ensuring that laws—at least important laws—have been subject to a careful analysis such as the one we have proposed here. Of course, the last word comes always from the Houses; but if the organisation of the normative process is improved, it will be more likely that their decision will be the fruit of reason informed by experience; or, as the classics would have said, *voluntas ratione animata*.

---

[28]Art. 88 of the Spanish Constitution states: "Government bills shall be passed by the Council of Ministers, which shall refer them to Congress, accompanied by a statement setting forth the necessary grounds and facts in order for them to reach a decision thereon".

[29]This is not incompatible with the creation of a parliamentary office of legislative policy, even in both chambers (if a double control is desired), which analyses MPs' legislative initiatives.

References

Adler MD, Posner EA (1999) Rethinking Cost-Benefit Analysis. Chicago Working Papers in Law and Economics 72. https://papers.ssrn.com/sol3/papers.cfm?abstract_id=164902
Albi E et al (1994) Teoría de la Hacienda Pública, 2nd edn. Ariel, Barcelona
Australian Government (1992) Introduction to cost-benefit analysis for managers. Australian Government Publishing Service, Canberra
Australian Government (1995) The analysis and regulation of safety risks. A survey on practices of national and commonwealth agencies. Australian Office of Regulation Review, Canberra
Black J (2002) Critical reflections on regulation. Aust J Leg Phil 27:1–35
Calsamiglia A (1989) Justicia, eficiencia y optimización de la legislación. Documentación Administrativa 218/219:111–151
de los Ríos F (1917) La crisis del Parlamento. Discurso de apertura de curso de la Universidad de Granada. Universidad de Granada, Granada
Dunlop CA, Radaelli CM (eds) (2017) Handbook on regulatory impact assessment. E. Elgar, Cheltenham
Dworkin R (2003) Virtud soberana. La teoría y la práctica de la igualdad. Paidós, Barcelona. [Sovereign virtue. The theory and practice of equality. Harvard University Press, Cambridge (MA), 2002]
Fuller LL (1969) The morality of law, 2nd revised edn. Yale University Press, New Haven
Gouvin EJ (1994) Truth in savings and the failure of legislative methodology. Univ Cincinnati Law Rev 62:1281–1376
Gouvin EJ (1995) A square peg in a vicious circle. Harv J Legis 32:472–492
Hart HLA (1968) El concepto de derecho. Abeledo Perrot, Buenos Aires[The Concept of Law, Clarendon Press, Oxford, 1961]
Hart HM, Sacks AM (1958) The legal process. Basic problems in the making and application of law. Tentative ed, Cambridge, MA. [Foundation Press, Westbury, 1994]
Hayek FA (1945) The use of knowledge in society. Am Econ Rev 35(4):519–530
Heinzerling L (1998) Regulatory costs of mythic proportions. Yale Law J 107:1981–2070
Hogwood BW, Gunn L (1984) Policy analysis for the real world. Oxford University Press, Oxford
Lecca J (1993) Sur le rôle de la connaissance dans la modernisation de l'Etat et le Status de l'Evaluation. L'Evaluation en question. Revue Française d'Administration Publique 66:185–196
Lindblom CE (1959) The science of muddling through. Public Adm Rev 19:79–88
Lindblom CE (1991) El proceso de elaboración de políticas públicas. MAP, Madrid
Lindblom CE, Cohen D (1979) Usable knowledge: social science and social problem solving. Yale University Press, New Haven
López González E (1988) Técnicas de control de ejecución en la dirección estratégica de la Administración Pública. MAP, Madrid
Lowi TJ (1969) The end of liberalism. The Second Republic of the United States. W.N. Norton, New York
Mayntz R (1985) Sociología de la Administración Pública. Alianza, Madrid
Meny I, Thoenig J-C (1992) Las políticas públicas. Ariel, Barcelona
Michaelson J (1996) Rethinking regulatory reform: toxics, politics and ethics. Yale Law J 105:1891–1925
OECD (1994) Gestion et reforme de la reglementation: sujets de reflexion dans les pays membres de l'OCDE. OECD, Paris
OECD (1995) Recommendation of the council of the OECD on improving the quality of government regulation (adopted on 9 march 1995), including the reference checklist for regulatory decision-making and background note. OCDE/GD (95) 95. OECD, Paris
OECD (2010) Improving the governance of risk. Reviews of regulatory risk and regulatory policy. OECD, Paris

Rose-Ackerman S (1988) Progressive law and economics and the new administrative law. Yale Law J 98(2):431–368
Rouban L (1993) L'Evaluation, nouvel avatar de la rationalisation administrative? L'Evaluation en question. Revue Française d'Administration Publique 66:199–208
Rubin EL (1991/1992) Legislative methodology: some lessons from the truth-in-lending act. Georgetown Law Rev 80:233–307
Sartor G (2009) A sufficientist approach to reasonableness in legal decision-making and judicial review. In: Bongiovanni G et al (eds) Reasonableness and law. Springer, Dordrecht, pp 17–68
Seidman A, Seidman RB (1996) Drafting legislation for development: lessons from a Chinese project. Am J Comp Law 44:1–44
Seidman RB (1992) Justifying legislation: a pragmatic, institutionalist approach to the memorandum of law, legislative theory and practical reason. Harv J Legis 29:1–77
Simon H (1958) Organizations. John Wiley & Sons, New York
Sunstein CR (1985) Interest groups in American public law. Stanford Law Rev 38:29–87
Sunstein CR (1990) After the rights revolution. Reconceiving the regulatory state. Harvard University Press, Cambridge
Sunstein CR (1996) Legal reasoning and political conflict. Oxford University Press, New York
Sunstein CR (2004) Risk and reason. Safety, law and the environment. Cambridge University Press, Cambridge [Riesgo y Razón. Seguridad, ley y medio ambiente. Katz, Buenos Aires, 2006]
Sunstein CR (2005) Laws of fear. Beyond the precautionary principle. Cambridge University Press, Cambridge
Sunstein CR (2018) The cost-benefit revolution. Harvard University Press, Cambridge
Swanson S (2001) High-profile attaks feed fears, experts say. The Chicago Tribune (5 September 2001)
Thompson J (1967) Organizations in action. McGrave, New York
Tolchin SJ, Tolchin M (1983) Dismantling America. The rush to deregulate. Houston Miflin Company, Boston
Twining W, Miers D (1991) How to do things with rules, 3rd edn. Weidenfeld & Nicholson, London
UK Government (1993) A guide to risk assessment (the deregulation iniciative. Regulation in balance. A guide to risk assessment). Cabinet of Trade and Industry, London
UK Government (2003) Better policy making: a guide to regulatory impact assessment. Regulatory impact unit. Cabinet Office, London
Viscusi W(K) (1992) L'Amelioration du respect de la reglementation: strategies et applications pratiques dans les pays membres de l'OCDE. OECD, Paris
Viscusi W(K) (1993) Comment améliorer la base analytique des decisions en matière de réglementation. OECD, Paris
Watson A (1974) Legal transplants. An approach to comparative law. University Press of Virginia, Charlottesville
Weber M (1979) Economía y Sociedad. FCE, México
Wildavsky A (1979) Speaking the truth to power: the art and craft of policy analysis. Little Brown, Toronto
Wintgens LJ (2013) The rational legislator revisited. In: Wintgens LJ, Oliver-Lalana AD (eds) The rationality and justification of legislation. Springer, Cham, pp 1–31
Zapatero V (1996) Producción de normas. In: Ruiz Miguel A, Díaz E (eds) Enciclopedia Iberoamericana de Filosofía. Vol. 2: Filosofía política. Trotta/CSIC, Madrid, pp 161–186

Chapter 5
Legislative Policy

5.1 To Intervene or Not to Intervene

In her *Guide to Good Regulation*,[1] Prime Minister Margaret Tatcher demanded that answers to these questions be given before the drafting of a law: what would happen if no action were taken?, what risks would it imply and what would be their importance? It was at that time that such questions became fashionable within the regulatory institutions. It came to be known as the *necessity test*.[2] If until then it was expected from public authorities to face the problems that arose within their societies, from then on, one of the first options to take into account was simply to do nothing.

The causes for this change of attitude are very diverse. Sometimes the underlying reason may be a reluctance to take responsibility for an intervention: it is easier to avoid responsibility for an omission than it is for an action. But it is also true that sometimes public authorities are faced with problems that are difficult or impossible to deal with (Stone 1966, p. 50 ff), normatively speaking, because they refer to events that take place in privacy, or because of the intangible and delicate nature of certain relationships, or because of the limitations of power in the face of the magnitude of the interests at stake, or because of the impact of intervention when prejudices are deeply entrenched, or because of the strength of a well-established status quo. There are social problems that are simply unmanageable by law and others that are difficult to solve. Therefore, before embarking on the normative adventure, it is necessary to examine whether or not the problem in question can be addressed by regulation with certain guarantees of success (Sabatier and Mazmanian 1979, p. 541). Regulatory intervention will be risky if there is a lack

[1] UK Government (1993).

[2] Some checklists including questions related to the necessity of norms can be consulted in the GRETEL Group's *Course on Legislative Technique* (1989). Such tests are commonly used in many countries. See Chap. 11 (especially Sect. 11.3) in this volume.

V. Zapatero Gómez, *The Art of Legislating*, Legisprudence Library 6,
https://doi.org/10.1007/978-3-030-23388-4_5

of causal theory that adequately connects the behaviour to be regulated and the objective to be achieved, if there is a great diversity in the behaviours to be regulated, if the target population is very large, or if the modifications to be made in a specific pattern of behaviour are profound. These are regulatory constraints which have always existed and which justify the necessity test.

Also today, new and important limitations to the action of states have arisen as a result of the growing internationalisation of economic, social and political relations and the liberalisation of the movement of people, goods and services. The consequences of this process are the elimination or weakening of borders; the emergence of new actors that escape the normative power of states, such as large corporations and transnational corporations; the insertion of states into supra-state political units such as the European Union, or the existence of problems, such as security and environment, that can only be dealt with by inter-state or supra-state alliances. These are also new facts that give significance to the question of whether or not public authority should intervene.

But behind the appeal to the so-called *necessity test* are not only these logical doubts about the real limits of law but also often a conception and a political ideology that tries to justify in the twenty-first century the return to renewed forms of the old nineteenth century laissez-faire. It is argued, today as then, that a whole series of problems are either insoluble or can better find a solution when left to their own. In any case, these problems are better solved with minimal interference from public authority. This is what Mrs. Tatcher's administration recommended when it ordered its officials to think twice before intervening because "intervention may not improve things; the situation may resolve itself, or perhaps people have misunderstood the problem; society can correct the situation without changing the rules. Changing the rules might just displace the problem. Market forces such as branding and consumer loyalty, competition and innovation can be a faster and safer way to solve the problems that have been identified" (UK Government 1993). It is a well known fact that those who have the ability to establish the terms of the problem are more likely to impose its solution. The discussion on the need for intervention was raised here in the name of efficiency, and it was hoped that abstention or intervention in homeopathic doses by public authorities could be justified. However, it should be stressed that efficiency is not the only principle that can guide the decisions of regulatory authorities.

The drafter of a norm has to look for the answer to the necessity test by other means. There are those who consider that the functions of public authority are the resolution of conflicts, the regulation of behaviour, the organisation and legitimisation of power, the structuring of living conditions in society and the administration of justice (Llewellyn 1940, p. 1355 ff). Others would offer a list of functions that would include protection of family, promotion of public health, social peace, compensation for damages, facilities for commercial exchange, recognition and management of private property, defence of basic freedoms, protection of privacy and control of private and public legal activities (Summers 1971). And there yet are those who prefer to talk about functions such as social integration, conflict management and resolution, social orientation, legitimisation of power, distribution of wealth and education (de Lucas 1994, p. 97 ff). The list of functions is greater or shorter according to different countries or historical moments. But the answer to the necessity test is not to be found only in the list of functions that the law actually performs in a given society but in the purposes that the institutional framework (especially the Constitution) assigns to public authorities. That is why the solution is not always to answer the question of what would happen if no action were taken but whether we are legally obliged to take it or not. The answer must be found by the public policy maker in the values, in the guiding principles and in the mission that the Constitution imposes upon public authorities.

A different—and debatable—question altogether is which tools should be used to intervene with. Political science has carefully studied the different resources available to any government for carrying out its policies. Hood (1983, p. 4 ff), for example, imagines governments as holders of four core resources that, in turn, can lead to many combinations. These are money, nodality, organisation and authority: he calls them NATO system (nodality, authority, treasure and organisation). By nodality we understand the location of government at the most important crossroads of existing information in society. Strictly speaking, a *node* is the intersection of different channels of information; and governments are obviously a hub through which a remarkable amount of information flows. This wealth of information is one of the most powerful instruments available to them for social control and management. The term money or treasure refers to the government's possession of a stock of economic resources that can also be used as an instrument of social control: extracting it from the pockets of some citizens and returning it to other members of society either in the form of currency or services. The term organisation means that the public authority has the legal attribution of providing itself with material and human resources (civil servants, soldiers, workers, etc.) in order to achieve directly the goals it pursues.[3] Recourse to authority implies the possession of legal powers, the powers to command, prohibit, guarantee, adjudicate, etc. It is on this authority that a theoretically inexhaustible tool such as regulation is based. And it is here, at this point, that the test of necessity is fully pertinent: must we or must we not intervene normatively, with that tool we call regulation?

[3]Lowi (1968, 1970, 1972), on his part, classifies all the possible government actions in constitutive, distributive, redistributive and regulative policies. Constitutive policies are those by which public authority creates institutions and bodies and then establishes the necessary procedures for the production of all other public functions. Distributive policies are those that allocate land, subsidies or fees among citizens. Redistributive policies are used to manipulate the environment by giving or taking resources that strengthen or weaken the position of citizens. Regulatory policies have a targeted and direct impact in the behaviour of citizens by increasing or reducing the range of alternatives at their disposal. See also Gustavsson (1980).

5.2 The Market as a Regulatory Policy

The behaviour of citizens is conditioned by at least four types of limits (Lessig 1998, p. 662 ff). Legal norms or rules are one of them: they aim to direct the behaviour of citizens by establishing directives through officially authorised bodies. Social norms are a second source of regulation: they contain patterns of behaviour that, without having been promulgated by an official source, tell us, for example, that we cannot tell or laugh racist jokes, or whether or not to tip the waiter. Markets also regulate the behaviour of citizens through prices, widening or narrowing, depending on the case and the individual, the possibilities for action. And finally, nature or the world in which we live limits or expands our possibilities for action. These four modes of regulation work together and constitute the sum of the forces that guide the behaviour of human beings. The four forces are interconnected and, although they operate in different ways and with different intensity, the greater or lesser protagonism of each of them conditions the others: more legal norms, fewer social norms and less market, for example. The greater or lesser confidence in the strength of each of these four types of regulation determines the type of legislative policy to follow.

For the so-called Chicago School, the least effective out of these four types regulation, are rules: their provisions are crude, their response to problems is slow and their results are frustrating. The other three kinds of regulation do better, that is why the Chicago School focuses on them and dispenses with legal rules as much as possible. Regulatory policy—at least for the *old* Chicago School—rests on recognising and maximising the market's regulatory potential in the conviction that it will find the right answer to any social problem on its own, just in time and in an efficient manner.

But to say that the market alone can find a precise, quick and efficient answer to every problem does not mean that we can possibly imagine a market without state and without law. Even within the deepest and most intense neo-liberal dream, as Nozick's (1988), the market needs laws to be constituted as such. Markets are neither self-constituting nor self-regulating: they have always been regulated markets since their inception (Shearing 1992, p. 68 ff). Or, as Croizier (1991, pp. 116–117) puts it, the market does not exist in a pristine state of nature that abusive interventions by governments have come to pervert and distort. On the contrary, markets are human constructions that, in order to emerge and develop, require very precise, concrete and delicate normative interventions. For the invisible hand to appear, to which Adam Smith referred, it is necessary for the very visible hand of the state to do its work by defining an operating framework. The market is not something given, pre-social or pre-political. There is no un-constituted market to return to; nor is there an already constituted market whose maintenance and proper functioning exempts us from applying certain rules. The market is such a delicate human invention that, without the intervention of public powers, it wouldn't be born and, once it was born and without such care, it would volatilise and disintegrate in a matter of seconds.

The emergence of a market requires certain functional prerequisites to be offered and maintained by the state (Lowi 2001, p. 134 ff). Firstly, law and order to ensure legal certainty. Secondly, rules governing the right to property, which is based on a legal fiction: first, there is a need for rules establishing what is mine and what is yours, then the market appears. Thirdly, the institution of contracts is required and without rules that regulate them, that establish the consequences of not complying with what has been agreed, there are no contracts, and without contracts there is no market. Fourthly, we need rules to regulate public goods: we can and will discuss and discuss intensively which goods should be public and which should not, but, in any case, all the markets that ever existed and will ever exist need certain public goods. Fifth, there is a need for rules on liability for damage: no sane person would participate in a market without knowing what and how much liability he assumes. All these functional prerequisites of market economies do not arise by spontaneous generation but are due to intense and constant state intervention.

But these are not the only interventions that are needed for markets to emerge. The collapse of the former communist system has highlighted the profound interventions that were necessary—and remain necessary—to dismantle a planned economy and build a market economy instead. China's experience has also led its leaders to conclude that their reform, in addition to the regulation of contracts and property, required a whole series of laws to create the institutions without which it would be difficult if not impossible for the market economy to appear (Seidman and Seidman 1996). And so they have reached the conclusion that in order to have control over currency and credit, they need banks; to ensure the fiscal responsibility of the government, they need to articulate the right regulation for budgetary discipline; to ensure the preparation of their workers, they need an education system; to ensure the mobility of the workforce, they need a system of retirement and disability pensions; to achieve a developed agricultural sector, it is necessary to institutionalise some agricultural services; to protect the environment from the voraciousness of private enterprise, they also need to equip themselves with control agencies; and a long list of other requirements. The conclusion is clear: no market works in a vacuum, each market operates in the context not only of a myriad of rules but also under the guidance of institutions that make it possible.

The point is not, therefore, to choose between market or state, but rather how much market is appropriate, how to constitute it and how to preserve it. It is therefore in this context of regulated markets that the question of whether or not public authorities should intervene in a regulatory capacity and what would happen if they didn't should be raised and answered.

Advocates of a norm-making policy based on minimal intervention often argue that it's up to the greater efficiency of the market to solve much, if not all, of society's problems (Self 1993). Most individual needs are met through the exchange of goods, services and skills that each of us possesses to varying degrees. The market is thus presented as the ordinary mechanism for allocating resources provided that some ideal conditions are met: complete information on prices, clear and precise establishment of property rights, rational selfishness of individuals, absence of transaction costs, absence of externalities in the functioning of the market itself, homogeneity of products and the impossibility for an individual—whether buyer or seller—to determine the price of the product (Buchanan 1985, p. 14). And when these strict conditions are met, we are facing a perfectly competitive market which, following the course indicated by the invisible hand, produces an efficient allocation of resources, in the sense that these will always tend towards uses where their economic value is greater (Polinsky 1989, p. 11 ff).

But rarely does such a perfect market actually occur. Consumers or users often lack the correct information about the products they consume, the medicines they take or the goods and services they purchase on the market. Property rights over certain goods such as the air we breathe, the water we drink or other natural resources are not always perfectly defined. More often than the economic theory of law would care to admit, citizens are altruistic and prefer to sacrifice their immediate economic interest for causes such as eradicating hunger, helping those who have to migrate from their homes or supporting the development of certain countries. Likewise, and even if they are congenitally selfish, people are not always rational in their decisions. On other occasions, the transaction costs of making certain collective decisions are high, not to mention the externalities that are generated daily in the form of attacks on nature or the power of certain corporations to impose the price of the energy we consume, the telephones we use, etc. In such cases, when the market is not efficient, the regulatory policy of minimum intervention considers that public authorities can and should intervene, but they must do so only as the market would have, that is, maximising efficiency.[4] What lies behind this idea, however, is a very particular normative theory that, when asked whether it is necessary to intervene, answers more or less in this way: *abstain from intervening, but if you must, if there is no choice but to do so, legislate as an efficient market would, that is to say, using only the techniques of private law, mimicking the market itself through the new regulation.* Everything else is superfluous.

The regulatory policy of minimum intervention aims at achieving maximum efficiency through three emblematic instruments of private law. The first secure instrument is well-defined property rights. An efficient system of ownership needs to have these three characteristics: (a) universality, according to which all resources should be owned by someone (public ownership would thus be inefficient); (b) exclusivity, which implies the possibility of preventing others from consuming a specific good or service from another source; and (c) transferability, so that resources can flow towards the most efficient uses (Paz-Ares 1981, p. 640). The function of law is to establish a system of ownership which, by internalisation of external benefits and costs, achieves an efficient functioning of the market. Thus, where there is an externality, the first solution must be to internalise costs through a clear and precise delimitation of property rights: "the concentration of costs and benefits on the holder creates the right incentives for a more efficient use of resources" (Paz-Ares 1981, p. 649). Obviously, if each resource must be allocated

[4]See Paz-Ares (1981, p. 636 ff). Cándido Paz-Ares' important article—on which I largely draw in the next pages—offers an excellent discussion of the role that private law institutions (such as property rights, liability, and contracts) play within the economic analysis of law.

to the provider that obtains the maximum value from it, the problem of wealth redistribution has no importance and no sense for the economic analysis of law.

The second major institution of private law is liability. If the function of law is the internalisation of external effects, what should be done to deal with damage caused by an accident and affecting property rights? Given the impossibility of resolving this problem through the market (it is not possible to contact a priori with all the potential victims of an accident and "buy" their right not to be injured), the legal system has to regulate the situation as the market would have done if this transaction had been possible, i.e. by assigning the right (right to compensation) to the party in whose hands it is most valuable and by charging the costs to the party who is able to avoid them with the lowest possible expenditure. The defendant is guilty of negligence—as Paz-Ares (1981, p. 660) summarises—if the amount of damage caused by the accident, multiplied by the probability that the accident might occur, exceeds the cost of the precautions that the defendant could have taken to prevent the occurrence of the accident. In this way, by pursuing the most efficient solution, *market deterrence* is also achieved, that is, the reduction of the number of accidents.

The third great institution that can enable efficient solutions is contract law. The market assumes that all resources will tend towards the hands in which they reach maximum value. But such a shift will not occur when there are transaction costs that equal or exceed the profit that would be generated by the exchange. Instruments must therefore be put in place to minimise transaction costs. Here is where the significance of contract law resides. Contract law performs three main functions: to specify which agreements between the parties are binding and which are not; to define the rights and duties created by contracts which, while enforceable, are ambiguous in their terms; and to indicate the consequences of unjustified breach of the contract. Without such prior specifications by way of law, transaction costs would be high—sometimes prohibitive—and resources would not be directed towards their more valuable use.

The question, therefore, of whether and how to intervene, is answered by stating that the only efficient response is to resort to private law techniques with which the market can be imitated and to offer those solutions that the market would have found by itself if it had functioned correctly.[5] In short, the question of what would happen if

[5]Posner (2003, p. 230) sums it up like this: "In settings in which the cost of voluntary transactions is low, Common Law doctrines create incentives for people to channel their transactions through the market (be it implicit—like the marriage market for example—or explicit). They do this by creating property rights (broadly defined) and protecting them through remedies designed to prevent coerced transfers—remedies such as injunctions, restitutions, punitive damages and criminal punishment. In settings in which the cost of allocating resources by voluntary transactions is prohibitively high—where, in other words, market transactions are not feasible—the Common Law prices on behaviour in such a way as to mimic the market. For example, the tort system allocates liability for accidents between railroad and farmer, driver and pedestrian, doctor and patient (. . .) in such a way as to bring about the allocation of resources to safety that market would bring about if the market could me made to work. The law of contracts does the same thing in regard to unforeseen contingencies that may make it impossible to perform a contract: it places liability on the party better able either to prevent the contingency from occurring or to minimise the disutility of its occurrence by buying insurance or by self-insuring. The law of property does the same thing by limiting property rights in

nothing were done would be answered as follows: if the market were to function properly—that is, without externalities or transaction costs—the problems would tend to settle themselves and the intervention of the state with its laws would at best be redundant. In such cases, there is no point in intervention. However, when real markets generate externalities and trade has transaction costs above zero, the state must intervene, but only to reconstitute the market by precisely defining property rights, that are presented as a rigorous formula to internalise all external effects; facilitate the functioning of the market by regulating contract laws in such a way as to eliminate or reduce transaction costs; and imitate the market, acting as it would have done if it had been able to function efficiently, that is, assigning rights and obligations, respectively, to those who can benefit most from them and to those who can bear them at the lowest cost. Any regulatory intervention beyond these strict limits would lead the legislator to inefficient solutions which, for the most extreme opinions, would therefore be unfair.

For those who, like R. Posner, argue that the first and foremost option for public authorities is in the tools of private law, maximising wealth is synonymous with efficiency, and efficiency is a sufficient criterion of justice. By moving away from the Paretian concept of efficiency (only those changes that benefit someone without harming a third party are efficient) that would lead to paralysis in decision-making, they are satisfied with a concept of efficiency according to which a solution is efficient if those who would gain from it can compensate the hypothetical losers (see Coleman 1982). There is no need for such compensation to occur in reality, the possibility is enough. And as for possible reactions by potential losers, they can be silenced by reminding them of the principles of autonomy and consent. In other words, policy makers must remain firm on the criterion of maximising wealth, since this would have been the chosen criterion if, with the veil of ignorance over their eyes, they'd had to establish a general rule for the distribution of resources.[6]

But it is more than doubtful that citizens are willing to accept such a rule. Perhaps they prefer a distribution of resources according to need, or effort, or outcome; or they may find the Rawlsian criterion of justice more just. This does not mean that the value of efficiency can be ignored: avoiding waste is an important part of a common notion of justice. Still, we need a more robust concept of justice: efficiency is certainly a part of it, but not the only one (Calabresi 1984). There are good reasons to think that efficiency cannot be a final attribute, but a medial attribute; that it only makes sense as an appropriate means to achieve certain ends in society. What these ultimate aims are is something that no economic consideration of the normative decision process can resolve. As a medial asset, efficiency does indeed have a prominent role in this process, by indicating how to do whatever should be done.

situations where insistence on an absolute right would prevent a value-maximizing exchange (...)—all to the end of facilitating the operation of the free market, and where the free market is unworkable of simulating its results".

[6]For a critic of Posner's thesis on the matter, see Coleman (1984), Dworkin (1980, 1985), Kronman (1980). Cf. Richard Posner's reply in Posner (1990, p. 374).

But it doesn't tell us precisely *what* to do. The actions of public authorities are determined by a more robust theory of justice. And in our case, they must respond to a very specific institutional framework, where the higher values of the system and the guiding principles of social and economic policy are set out in the constitution.

That is why a political leader, in search of solutions to a particular social problem, can only try to answer the questions of what would happen if no action were taken, what risks would be taken and what is their importance, after careful consideration of the objectives that the constitutional text and society itself have established. Doing nothing is hardly the answer. And it is not easy to find that answer by making use of private law techniques alone. Especially if we do not want to end up in a situation where children return to the mines, workers have to pay their own work insurance, rivers become pestilent dumps, the air is unbreathable, rapid advances in technology threaten privacy, medicines are unsafe, and a long etcetera. In short, doing nothing would end up destroying the connective tissue provided by a regulation that not only aspires to build and maintain the market but also to sustain a certain lifestyle (Tolchin and Tolchin 1983, p. 257). And this is what regulatory policy based on pure market and private law techniques alone cannot guarantee.

5.3 A Well-Equipped Toolbox

Any regulatory policy implies specifying the objectives to be reached, the resources available and the tools to be used in its implementation. The fulfilment of the aims pursued by our model of life—which are those of the social state—demands the use of a wider range of tools. To think that public authorities can achieve these ends simply by prohibiting, ordering or allowing certain behaviours—that is, commanding and controlling—is somewhat primitive and out of touch. Karl Renner, polemicising with the Bolsheviks, described their fetishistic attitude towards this kind of social leadership strategy as decrepit. More sophisticated and effective instruments had to be found. And this is what political science has been doing with the study of the normative process. Mayntz (1983), for example, offers a panoply of instruments composed of regulatory norms, financial incentives, provision of public goods, regulation of procedures, and the use of persuasion. In turn, Daintith (1998, p. 349 ff), in his comparative study of the different regulatory systems from 1973 to 1982, offers the following typology of instruments to which governments normally resort for economic regulation: unilateral regulation, fiscal policy, negotiated restrictions (control of activity through contractual agreements and other negotiations with governments), elimination or relaxation of regulations, elimination or relaxation of fiscal policy, public benefits (subsidies and other financial instruments, provision of public services and other forms of aid in kind), public sector management and, finally, information.

The concern to broaden the range of tools available to public authorities to achieve maximum efficacy and efficiency in public policies has also led the OECD (1992) to investigate, since the early 1990s, what other intervention instruments exist alongside classic regulation. The survey carried out stated that public authorities have at their disposal a wide range of means of action which, in addition to regulation in its various forms. It considered that public authorities often opt too early for the exclusive use of interventionist regulation, whereas other instruments could make it possible to achieve the pursued goal more effectively or at a lower cost, and that tradition often prevails over innovation in the choice of means of action (OECD 1992, p. 31). Public authorities—the same survey insists—would be in a better position to define the best means of action if, at the beginning of the policy-making process, the question were raised as to which type or combination of instruments is best suited to each case. The OECD's (1994) survey of member countries provided a first provisional list of formulas, including disclosure of information, economic incentives, commercialisation of property rights, risk and liability insurance, voluntary agreements, self-regulation and methods based on persuasion. We will talk about all of them in the next chapters.

As far as the tool of regulation in the strict sense is concerned, scholars of public policy have also analysed its different types. Such is the case of Mitnick (1989, p. 29 [9]), who starts off from the concept of regulation as a process that intentionally restricts a subject's choice of activity, established by an entity that is not involved in that activity. It is not relevant at this time to determine which instrument is used, whether it is an administrative intervention (regulations, orders, authorisations, etc.) or whether such a restriction is expressed in a law drawn up by parliament.[7] The key idea behind the concept of regulation is the external interference in the course of individual elections through the use of two mechanisms such as incentives and directives.

We are faced with regulation by directives when individual choice is limited by reducing options or by directing choice in a particular direction through rules that operate as behavioural guides (Mitnick 1989, p. 29 [9]). Directives include all kinds of devices called rules, regulations, standards, permits, prohibitions, orders, direct regulation, etc. The term directive is also strongly connected to the idea of negative incentives or sanctions. On the other hand, regulation by incentives occurs when public authorities change the perception of the nature of the options faced by the regulated party. A certain behaviour is neither ordered nor prohibited, some of the options are simply made more attractive.[8] Thus, if regulation is a social control technique consisting of interfering with the course of human behaviour through positive and negative incentives, there are two types of regulation: regulation by

[7]For a distinction between reglamentation and regulation, see Bustamante (1993).

[8]For Mitnick (1989), a basic relation of incentives implies a whole series of operations and premises: the establishment of stimuli that are sent and received by the regulator and the regulated; the sent stimuli promise the recipient a reward; the stimuli are connected to the behaviour of the recipient; the recipient in fact behaves in response to the stimulation and finally, if the recipient is a rational entity that will seek to avoid the negative and embrace the positive stimuli.

directives and regulation by incentives. As for the object of regulation, it can be both economic and social activity.[9]

It appears therefore that the *command and control* technique alone is not sufficient and that the strength of a regulatory policy depends to a large extent on the ability to open up the full range of available tools.[10] Among the nuts and bolts that a norm drafter can use to solve a particular problem—leaving aside for the moment the possibility of doing nothing—there is at least the use of private law, regulation by directives (self-regulation, obligation to inform, establishment of standards of conduct, or recourse to authorisation), regulation by incentives (persuasion, tax policy, subsidies), market substitution (provision of public services and price control) and, overflying them all, sanctioning power.

In other words, the question *what can public authorities do about a particular social problem?* can be answered at least in one of these five ways.[11] First, public authorities may allow market logic to prevail as a resource allocation mechanism. To this end, the state will limit itself to establishing those institutions that have an instrumental value for the efficient functioning of the market, such as property rights, liability regime and contract law. This involves the use of "facilitative" techniques that do not order nor prohibit any type of behaviour but rather constitute the social order.

Second, the State can replace the function of the market as a resource allocation mechanism by providing certain services and benefits to citizens, either offering such public services directly (through administrative management or through public enterprises) or managing them indirectly (through concessions). This type of functions, which the social rule of law has promoted, involve the use of we call public service.

---

[9]Ogus (1994) understands by reglamentation the regulation of a variety of industrial and nonindustrial activities that take a dual legal form: social regulation and economic regulation. Social regulation aims at making those market rectifications that are necessary to protect certain goods such as health, hygiene, safety and the environment. Its instruments include information, the establishment of standards, authorisations and licenses, economic instruments (canons and fees, subsidies, negotiable pollution rights) and private regulation (marketable rights, inalienable rights). The main purpose of economic regulation is to offer a substitute for competition in relation to natural monopolies and is expressed through three alternative formulas: public ownership, price and quality regulation, and administrative concessions.

[10]There are as many classifications of the tools available to public authorities as there are criteria to classify them; in turn, criteria and resulting classifications depend on the pursued objective. From what has been exposed so far, we see that, for some, the criterion is the type of instrument put into operation by the government (information, money, organisation or authority), whereas others classify the actions of public authorities according to the object of regulation (economic regulation or social regulation), and there are those who, like Summers, rearrange the instruments according to the legal techniques applied (reparation of damages, criminal, provider of benefits, regulator or facilitator of private agreements).

[11]Here I will not deal with nudging (see Thaler and Sunstein 2009).

Third, public authorities can try to influence the behaviour of citizens by providing them with information that may be relevant when deciding on the best course of action.

Fourth, another mechanism allows public authorities to try to condition the behaviour of citizens by establishing guidelines to which they must compulsorily adapt their behaviour: we are talking about regulation by directives. The development of such directives can be carried out directly by the public authorities or be "privatised", as is the case with self-regulation and other techniques.

Fifth, and finally, public authorities may try to indirectly encourage or discourage citizens' behaviour by changing the framework of expectations offered by the market. This is what has been called regulation by incentives and, among them, taxes (rates, special contributions and other figures) and economic aid (subsidies, loans and guarantees) are the most common.

Clarifying and expanding the tools available to policy-makers and rule drafters means strengthening the social governance mechanisms available to public authorities. The theory of legislation could, and should, contribute its reflections to this important matter.

5.4 Legislative Policy

But the theory of legislation cannot be limited to describing the range of techniques and tools available to public authorities. In its prescriptive dimension, it must investigate whether there are existing canons on how to best use those tools, i.e. it must make it possible to articulate a good regulatory policy.

The dream of technocracy was to find pre-determined equivalences between functions and resources so that, once a specific objective was politically defined, solutions could be calculated automatically.[12] But such mechanical equivalences simply do not exist, since the range of tools and their applicability will depend on factors related to the country's constitution, which determines its system of legal sources and the territorial distribution of power. Moreover, different political cultures and styles in each society may favour or hinder the use of self-regulation or negotiated regulation; the greater or lesser power of the public sector broadens or restricts the possibility of direct government action; or economic development and the resources of public authorities may encourage or restrict the use of incentives. However, even if it is not possible to obtain final criteria for the automatic application of the range of tools available to public authorities, it is possible to increase the accuracy of this kind of decisions by studying on a case-by-case basis the

[12] A first attempt to correlate the regulatory technique to be chosen with the regulatory problem at hand was offered by Summers (1971, p. 736), who discussed five major techniques, namely: damage reparation techniques, criminal law techniques; administrative-regulatory techniques; benefits-granting techniques; and private agreement techniques.

circumstances that make it advisable or appropriate to use one or the other technique. It is a question of adjusting the instruments available and the function they are applied to as much as possible, and this requires a regulatory strategy. This articulation of the regulatory policy is not only demanded by the economic and social sectors which, at European level, have been asking the EU for a declaration of regulatory policy and the appointment of a new European Union Commissioner to ensure its application (Unice 1995), but also by the right of each citizen to know not only the objectives pursued by the government but—which is also important—the means by which it will preferably implement its policies.

A sound regulatory policy could be structured around the following canons (Hood 1983, p. 133 ff). First, the instrument or combination of instruments to be used must be selected after an examination of the most important alternative tools. Unfolding the full range of solutions available to the political decision-maker is therefore a requisite of rationality. Analysts and institutions[13] are endeavouring to offer, as we have seen, the fullest possible taxonomy of the instruments with which public authorities can intervene. It is clear that a list of instruments at the disposal of the public authorities cannot be offered in the abstract: the constitution of each country, its history and culture, the political forces present and their relative importance determine the specificity of any list of instruments. Furthermore, the increasing internationalisation of economic and political life and the affiliation to inter-state and supra-state organisations offer states new opportunities to expand or restrict the range of instruments of intervention. But, in any case, it is possible to conclude that a good regulatory policy implies knowing how to deploy the widest range of instruments possible, ordered from greater to lesser intensity, like a regulatory pyramid.

Secondly, it should be kept in mind that the broader the list of instruments, the greater the capacity and efficacy of public decision-making. In designing a deterrent policy, one can fall into the trap of considering only passive deterrence. Using a warlike analogy, Ayres and Braithwaite (1992, p. 39) point out that one can have the atomic bomb and be weak for lack of conventional weapons: the design of regulatory deterrence tends to fall into the trap of considering only passive deterrence options, meaning that deterrent credibility is determined mainly by the scale of the sanctions to be applied. On the other hand, the design of deterrence in war has long since shown the importance of active staggering, and this active staggering will be all the more effective the greater the number of steps there are in the regulatory pyramid. Ayres and Braithwaite offer their regulatory pyramid: ideology has a lot to say here and therefore every significant political force should offer public opinion its own.

Thirdly, the instrument used must be adjusted as much as possible to the intended function. Although there are no ad hoc instruments that can be used effectively in all

---

[13]For the sake of illustration, see e.g., in the UK, *Thinking about Regulation. A Guide to Good Regulation*; in the U.S, *Alternative Regulatory Approach: an Overview*; in Australia (Queensland), *Business Regulation Review Unit. Training Module on Best Practice and Alternatives to Regulation* (Department of Business, Industry and Regional Development 1994); or, in Canada, *Evaluations des solutions de rechange à la reglementation. Guide des Affaires Reglementaires* (1994).

situations, governments need to understand the circumstances and criteria that favour the use of each of the intervention instruments. Careful analysis of when it is best to leave the solution to the market, or to regulate by directives, to opt for one kind or the other of incentives, or to resort to self-regulation, requires in turn, the establishment of certain parameters that allow for comparisons. Mitnick (1989, p. 295 ff [281 ff]) refers to this type of parameters or criteria, which he calls intermediate goals and which can be used to decide when one or the other instrument is appropriate: such parameters can refer to efficiency (quality in the performance of the activity), stability (maintenance or support of the activity), innovation (evolution or development of the activity) or the security generated by the application of this tool. Surely there are more criteria (also political and moral) and that is why it is useful to study such intermediate goals, their advantages and disadvantages or whether there are indications and contraindications in the use of each of the intervention instruments. Of course these—efficiency, stability, innovation, security—will not be the only decision-making criteria, especially when they clash head-on with higher values of justice. But, prima facie, they will have to be considered.

Fourth, the desired effects must be achieved with the least possible expenditure of the resources available to the public authorities. This means minimising human resource efforts, using scarce and depletable public resources with care, minimising constraints and obligations on citizens, and favouring those instruments that can best focus on the problem and are susceptible to graduation.

Fifth, preference should be given to those instruments that prove to be less coercive: it seems indisputable—as Eduardo García de Enterría (1991, p. 16) says—that, in the event of doubt as to the technique of intervention that can be used in practice, the one that involves the least restriction of freedom should be chosen. *In dubio pro libertate* is an inexcusable principle in this matter. Freedom is the rule, limitation is the exception. And this is not only—and it would be enough now—because it is a constitutional imperative but also for reasons of effectiveness and efficacy. Regulatory objectives are more likely to be achieved when stakeholders are informed that the first choice of public authorities is to take their criteria and interests into account. This may be so in some cases with self-regulation (Ayres and Braithwaite 1992; Braithwaite 1985), which, when functioning properly, is the least costly approach from the point of view of the taxpayer and the regulated activity. When the state negotiates substantive regulatory objectives with the industry, conceding a certain discretion and responsibility regarding how to achieve such objectives, we are operating with the best possible strategy since we have the opportunity to achieve the objective at the lowest possible cost on productive efficiency. Involving citizens through consultation and negotiation of objectives, and putting trust in them through self-regulatory policies, can result in a more participative and sometimes even more effective social management process.

Finally, in order to avoid the naivety of relying on self-regulation only, the regulated sector or group must be clearly aware that if the softer instruments fail, the regulators are prepared to continue climbing the pyramid, using ever tougher instruments of intervention. This is, in short, the old carrot and stick policy. If the regulated are tempted to take advantage of the privilege of soft self-regulation through a sub-optimal execution of regulatory objectives, the state must make it explicit, that it will use the more rigorous instruments if necessary: “Command regulation with non discretionary punishment has its military analogue in the burning bridges. If the bridges that are an army’s only route of retreat are burned, the enemy knows that its must fight a bloody battle if it advances beyond a certain point. Burning bridges and enacting a policy of non discretionary punishment both have the effect of demonstrating commitment—or communicating to an adversary an intention never to give in” (Ayres and Braithwaite 1992, p. 38).

It is evident that, with these proposals for regulatory policy, we enter the most ambitious field of the theory of legislation. And it is no less obvious that, besides this proposal to stagger resources by gradually increasing the intensity of the intervention, other regulatory policies can and must be considered. The political game in open societies is, to a large extent, not only a debate about the objectives to pursue but also, and sometimes primarily, about the means employed to solve the social problems commonly identified as such. The importance of studying the means of intervention is that it can help raise awareness about the variety of instruments of public action available to our societies and about the obligation of public authorities to seek the most suitable instrument for each case. This type of research can not only improve the efficacy of public administration, but also fortify the right of citizens to know both the objectives and the instruments of intervention chosen by each political player. This is what a good regulatory policy is all about.

References

Ayres I, Braithwaite J (1992) Responsive regulation. Transcending the deregulation debate. Oxford University Press, Oxford

Braithwaite J (1985) To punish or persuade: enforcement of coal mine safety. State University of New York Press, Albany

Buchanan A (1985) Ethics, efficiency and the market. Clarendon, Oxford

Bustamante JE (1993) Desregulación. Entre el derecho y la economía. Abeledo Perrot, Buenos Aires

Calabresi G (1984) First party, third party and product liability systems: can economic análisis of law tell us anithing about them? Iowa Law Rev 69:833–851

Coleman JL (1982) The normative basis of economic analysis. Stanford Law Rev 34:1105–1131

Coleman JL (1984) Economics and the law: a critical review of the foundations of the economic approach to law. Ethics 94:661–691

Croizier M (1991) Etat modeste, Etat moderne. Stratégies pour une autre Changement. Points, Essais, Paris

Daintith T (1998) Legal measures and their analysis. In: A reader on regulation (Oxford readings in socio-legal studies). Oxford University Press, Oxford

de Lucas J (1994) Introducción a la teoría del derecho. Tirant lo Blanch, Valencia

Dworkin RD (1991 [1980]) Is welth a value? J Leg Stud 9:191–226

Dworkin RD (1985) Why efficiency? In: A matter of principle. Harvard University Press, Cambridge

García de Enterría E (1991) Curso de Derecho Administrativo, vol II. Civitas, Madrid

GRETEL (Grupo de Estudios de Técnica Legislativa) (1989) Curso de técnica legislativa. Centro de Estudios Constitucionales, Madrid
Gustavsson S (1980) Types of policy and types of politics. Scand Polit Stud 3(2):123–142
Hood C (1983) The tools of government. Macmillan, London
Kronman AT (1980) Wealth maximization as a normative principle. J Leg Stud 9:227–242
Lessig L (1998) The new Chicago School. J Leg Stud 27:662–691
Llewellyn K (1940) The normative, the legal and the law-jobs: the problem of the juristic method. Yale Law J 49:1355–1400
Lowi T (1968) American business. Public policy, case- studies and political theory. World Polit 16:677–715
Lowi T (1970) Decission vs. policy making: toward an antidote for tecnocracy. Public Adm Rev 30:314–325
Lowi T (1972) Four systems of policy, politics and choice. Public Adm Rev 32:298–310
Lowi T (2001) Our millennium: political science confronts the global corporate economy. Int Polit Sci Rev 22(2):131–150
Mayntz R (1983) The condicions of effective public policy: a new challenge for policy analysis. Policy Polit 11:123–143
Mitnick BM (1989) La economía política de la regulación. FCE, México [The political economy of regulation. Creating, designing, and removing regulatory forms. Columbia University Press, New York, 1989]
Nozick R (1988) Anarquía, Estado y Utopía. FCE, México
OECD (1992) Gestion et reforme de la reglementation: sujets de reflexion dans les pays Membres de l'OCDE. OECD, Paris
OECD (1994) Liste provisoire de formules réglementaires et non réglementaires. Note du Secretariat, Reunion sur l'utilization d'autres instruments reglementaires, PUMA REG (94) 1. OECD, Paris
Ogus AI (1994) Regulation. Legal form and economic theory. Clarendon Press, Oxford
Paz-Ares C (1981) La economía política como jurisprudencia racional. Anuario de Derecho Civil 12:601–708
Polinsky AM (1989) An introduction to law and economics. Little Brown, Boston
Posner R (1990) The problems of jurisprudence. Harvard University Press, Cambridge
Posner R (2003) Economic analysis of law, 6th edn. Aspen, New York
Sabatier P, Mazmanian D (1979) The implementation of public policy. A framework of analysis. Institute of Governmental Affaires, Davis
Seidman A, Seidman RB (1996) Drafting legislation for development: lessons from a Chinese project. Am J Comp Law 44:1–44
Self PJ (1993) Government by the market? Mac Millan, Basingstoke
Shearing CD (1992) A constitutive conception of regulation. In: Gravbosky P, Braithwaite J (eds) Business regulation and Australia's future. Australian Institute of Criminology, Canberra, pp 67–79
Stone J (1966) Social dimensions of law and justice. Maitland Publications, Sydney
Summers RS (1971) The technique element in law. Calif Law Rev 59:733–751
Thaler RH, Sunstein CR (2009) Nudge. Improving decisions about health, wealth and happiness, rev edn. Penguin Books, London
Tolchin SJ, Tolchin M (1983) Dismantling America. The rush to deregulate. Houston Miflin Company, Boston
UK Government (1993) The deregulation iniciative. Thinking about regulation. A guide to good regulation. UK Government, London
Unice (1995) Releasing Europe's potencial through targeted regulatory reform, the Unice regulatory reform

Chapter 6
A Soft Law

6.1 New Paths

For some time now there has been a sense that there are more laws than we need in our societies. Legal tide, inflation of norms, explosion of Law, legislative motorisation... are some of the terms with which we usually refer to this increase in the number of rules in contemporary legal systems. This phenomenon is not caused by malformations, deviations or perversions of the regulatory system or its operators but, fundamentally, by the often unavoidable effect of functions performed by social states. This socio-political model has brought a transition from formal rationality to material rationality, from a formal law that was legitimised by the establishment of the order and the procedures that allow citizens to pursue their own fortune, to a materialised law, which assumes the commitment of the state to satisfy strong social and political demands and which is legitimised by the achievement of social and economic objectives such as decent housing, health for all, universal and quality education, care for the environment, the promotion of research... Law is now charged with economic and social purposes that go beyond the original function of the state as mere formal and general regulator of social relations. The social state simply needs more laws than a state limited to *laissez-faire, laissez-passer*.

But... is there a limit to this growing state interventionism and this increasing appeal to law as an instrument of social direction? Those who, like Hayek (1988: chapters 1–2; 1945), openly opposed state interventionism did not hesitate to disqualify what they called rationalist constructivism, i.e. the conviction that there is no human and social problem that laws can or should not solve. Because, it is argued, whoever attempts to artificially construct a social order is doomed to fail given the inevitable limitation of human knowledge, the necessary and hopeless ignorance to which we are subject in relation to most of the particular events that determine the behaviour of those who make up society or the synoptic illusion of believing that a single mind can come to know the many factors that determine a specific situation. Opposing the idea of a *created order*, the excellence of the

V. Zapatero Gómez, *The Art of Legislating*, Legisprudence Library 6,
https://doi.org/10.1007/978-3-030-23388-4_6

spontaneous order is proclaimed, a natural, self-regulating order that is easily disrupted by external intervention. The paradigm of this spontaneous order is the market, to which the human being must consciously provide only a formal, general and abstract regulation, without content or material purposes (Hayek 1988: II, p. 189 ff). All the rest is superfluous, therefore the recommended medicine is pure regulatory abstinence and, if necessary, a good slimming diet.

This idea of a spontaneous and self-regulating order, which has constituted the intellectual background of deregulation policies, and Hayek's criticism of social engineering has been taken up in a certain sense by N. Luhmann in his theory of autopoietic systems to explain the strict limitations that law faces as an instrument of social direction. Based on the theses of Maturana and Varela (1980; Varela 1979), a machine can be said to be autopoietic when it is organised as a network of production processes that continuously regenerate through interaction and transformation, thereby updating the same network of processes that define the machine as a concrete unity in space. Autonomy, unity, identity, circular completeness and self-reproduction are the elements that Luhmann integrates into the idea of self-referentiality. A self-referential system is therefore a system that produces and reproduces by itself the elements of which it is composed (Luhmann 1981, p. 66 ff), that functions by means of self-contact, i.e. in tune with other operations of the system itself; the system does not operate on a direct stimulus-response relationship with its environment, but is determined by factors that are inside the very system (Luhmann 1995, p. 21 ff; Luhmann 1983). It is in this sense that law—like politics and economics—can be defined as an autopoietic system.[1]

As such an autopoietic system, law has become an autonomous, positive, highly formalised and professionalized system that has its own internal logic (legality); a logic that is distinct and sometimes contradictory to the logic that flows from the political (the logic of power) and economic (the logic of money) subsystems. And it is this growing formalisation of the legal system that brings it into conflict with the economic and political demands of the social state. The challenge is to bring together the logic of three subsystems—law, politics and economics—that operate autonomously. But to what extent can law be sensitive to the logics of economics and/or politics, and to what extent can law affect the functioning of politics and economics?

Following Luhmann's theses, Teubner (1987, p. 421 ff) observes that the capacity of a subsystem to influence the spheres of the other subsystems is limited: social and political pressures or demands only have an effect on the legal order to the extent that they can be translated into the categories of legal constructs. Conversely, the ability of law to influence the progress of the economy is rather limited. Regulation, for instance, only serves to set in motion the process of self-regulation of the social or the economic systems but is unable to predict either the direction or the results of this process: it is a challenge for autopoietic adaptation. Teubner's diagnosis of the regulatory crisis is that the social system is now truly immune to policy interventions. Politics, economics and law operate according to their respective and different

[1]On the theses of Luhmann, Teubner and Wilke as applied to law, see further García Amado (1988).

internal logic which cannot be easily harmonised with the logic of the other systems. Each of these subsystems has its own operating modes, rationality criteria and organisational patterns. Neither the state nor the law can now fulfil the task of harmoniously integrating economic, legal and political rationality. And it is this limitation of reciprocal influence that leads Teubner to formulate his "regulatory trilemma": any regulatory intervention is either irrelevant or generates negative effects on society or produces the disintegration of law itself—a trilemma that, by the way, recalls the rhetoric of intransigence that Hirschman spoke of. Law in our social state has therefore reached its limits in terms of the effectiveness and timeliness of its normative interventions: it cannot adequately respond to the demands of politics and economics, nor can it in turn effectively influence them. It will therefore be necessary to seek new paths. And while some recommend pure and simple deregulation, others invite us to look for more indirect and abstract forms of social regulation.

Instead of resorting to direct regulation of social behaviour, a so-called *reflexive law* is proposed a law that is limited to regulating the organisation and the procedures of each subsystem and to redistributing competences. We must return to formal law; we must dematerialise law by eliminating from it the purpose of striving for social or economic goals. Instead of rigidly fixing the content of the law, legislation will regulate the framework within which the social actors must seek to resolve their differences "under the shadow of the law", a law that is limited to determining who the parties are, to compensating for the relative strength of each of them so there is equity, to setting the negotiation procedures. . ., but without establishing in advance what the outcome of the negotiation should be. The state—as Schmitter's (1977, 1982) procedural neo-corporativism suggests—maintains its capacity to design, monitor and rebalance the new system of self-regulation. The traditional field for self'regulation (no en el original) was labour relations, but little by little the state has withdrawn to this role in the industrial sector, in the regulation of corporate law and in the fields of advertising or consumer law. These are new forms of state intervention: an indirect, *softer* form of intervention which is allegedly not intended to replace regulation but to complement it with new paths that can eventually be effective and alleviate the congestion of the regulatory system.[2] We will now deal with some of these routes, starting with a curious kind of norms, namely: type-approval or homologation norms.

6.2 Companies to Develop Norms

Austin's definition of norms as general commands issued by a sovereign and reinforced by the threat of sanction was sharply criticised by Hart and replaced by a definition of law as a set of rules that either create models of conduct (primary

[2]For a critique of Luhmann's and Teubner's theses on this subject, see Zolo (1995, p. 203 ff).

norms) or establish bodies and procedures to create norms and enforce them (secondary norms). But it is clear that not all rules of conduct are produced by official bodies. And perhaps, in contradiction with a well-known Dworkinian thesis, a gradation or scale of normativity can be found not only in principles but also in *rules* themselves—which has led some scholars to differentiate between a *soft-law* and a *hard-law* (Timsit 1991). In any case, norms such as the ones we are talking about—homologation norms—can be an indication of the evolution we were talking about, which goes from a material law attached to the social state to a reflexive law of Luhmanian matrix (Teubner 1983).

The Report of the Canadian Parliament on *Réglémentation et Competitivité* (House of Commons 1993) accepted that the fact that norms play an important role in the economy does not mean that they must necessarily be established by the state; that there are other ways of creating norms and that, in fact, most of the existing norms have been created by the private sector. The technique of delegating regulatory powers to private bodies for this purpose began internationally in 1947 with the creation of the International Organisation for Standardisation (ISO), with the corresponding private national normative organisations such as ANSI (United States), AFNOR (France), DIN (Germany) or BSI (United Kingdom). These bodies are responsible for drawing up a type of norm containing technical specifications for the production and distribution of specific goods and services, which are produced not by the state but by the interested parties. These are groups or companies that are involved in the sector or activity regulated by the norm, with the help of certain technical committees. These rules are aimed at facilitating the exchange of goods and services by regulating either the results or the procedures for the production and distribution of those goods in such a way as to remove technical and commercial barriers. Their growth in Europe, driven by the development of the single market, has been spectacular in the most diverse sectors, from transport to information, including consume, energy, environment, medical care, chemicals, civil and mechanical engineering and others (see CEN 2006).

Also in Spain, this task of standardising the production and distribution of goods and services was completed in order to advance the national economy, improve health, safety and welfare of the public, help and protect consumers, facilitate domestic and foreign trade and develop international cooperation. According to Spanish regulations, the Ministry of Industry and Energy designates, from among the applicant associations or entities, the ones that will carry out standardisation and certification tasks. The designation implies the authorisation for them to carry out a double operation: to draw up technical specifications, on the one hand, and to issue "certificates of conformity" for products that will be thus recognised as valid by the administration. The administration has empowered the Spanish Association for Standardisation and Certification (AENOR) for this regulatory operation. AENOR draws up preliminary draft norms through committees of experts, in which the various stakeholders and interested economic agents participate. These preliminary drafts are published, for prior information and consultation, in the official gazette (BOE), so that all interested parties can make the appropriate allegations. Finally, the project is published "by the Association" in the BOE, after which, according to the decree, "it becomes Spanish law".

These norms are voluntary as long as they are not declared official.[3] but they have a strong appeal that guarantees their high degree of effectiveness: products manufactured according to harmonised standards guarantee that they comply with the various EU directives and will therefore be accepted in all the member states of the European Union. The new approach based on the Single European Act of 1986 led to a revitalisation of the Community's standardisation bodies (CEN, created in March 1961, and CENELEC, created in December 1972), which aim to facilitate the exchange of goods and/or products by eliminating all kinds of technical barriers. To this end, they have long been entrusted with the following missions: (a) to harmonise the rules laid down by the member states and create European standards, where appropriate standards do not exist; (b) to provide the Commission of the European Union, the European Free Trade Association and other intergovernmental organisations with European standards which can be referred to in legislative texts or other official documents; (c) to cooperate with governmental, economic and scientific organisations on standardisation and certification issues; (d) to support global normalisation within the International Organisation for Standardisation (ISO) and the International Electrotechnical Commission (IEC) by working together for the uniform application in Europe of the international ISO and IEC standards, in addition to other international standards or recommendations; and (e) to provide certification services on the basis of European standards.

This is how the needs of trade and the resulting international cooperation have led to the production of norms (sometimes they are referred to as *technical specifications*) by private or semi-private bodies. These norms are more than mere social practices and somewhat less than the norms set by governments in the exercise of their regulatory powers. In other words, they are of greater importance than social practices but it is debatable whether they can be considered as legal norms, in accordance with the positivist criterion of their *pedigree*. But until we discover their nature (whether they are norms or the components of norms Bentham talked about[4]), this type of regulation is here, displaying good health and constantly expanding the regulated areas.

[3]Of course, compliance with these norms is not mandatory. But they can become "official" when so advised by "a) the rationalization and ordering of public purchases; b) the need to formalize test or measurement procedures, in order to rationalise sectors and facilitate administrative inspection; and c) sanitary or environmental requirements in terms of procedures to determine compositions or percentages of elements, substances or products" (Art. 9 of the Royal Decree 1614/85 of 1 August 1985).

[4]Alongside simple imperatives and punitive laws there is, Bentham said, another type of legal reality which consists of neither coercive nor discoercive norms) and he called expository matter: "most laws— Bentham (1981, p. 433) wrote—contain complex terms that can only be understood after many explanations and definitions. It is not enough to prohibit theft in general, it is also necessary to explain what property is, and what theft is". The technical specifications or standards of homologation thus complement the state or community regulations.

Table 6.1 Regulatory recommendations of the Canadian House of Commons (1993)

Without regulation	With regulation
Finished product	Product can be exchanged
Low price	High price
Frequent renovation	Infrequent purchase
Information available at low cost	Information expensive or inaccessible
Low incidence on health, environment	Negative consequences to health and others
New and evolving technology	Relatively static technology

It is therefore a new and more indirect form of regulation that broadens yet again the range of tools available for social direction and that raises the need to consider whether there is any indication of when this type of para-regulatory technique can and/or should be used. We can find some guidance in specialised literature. Particularly interesting, for present purposes, are the recommendations of the Canadian Parliament (House of Commons 1993, p. 73). It outlines a model that can eventually serve to determine the requisite intensity of normative intervention. The model describes an ascending process that starts with the absence of norms, goes through the establishment of guidelines and the development of voluntary norms, and culminates in regulation (House of Commons 1993, p. 81).

Roughly, the Canadian Parliament's suggestion can be summarised with the help of the above table: when all the factors in the left column are present, the conclusion that normally prevails is to allow market forces to intervene, whether on a voluntary or statutory basis. When all the factors are intermingled, it will be necessary to intervene with some intermediate formula, between both poles (Table 6.1). This approach ends with the following recommendation (House of Commons 1993, p. XV ff): where the enactment of norms is deemed necessary, governments should do their utmost to coordinate normalisation obligations and activities by demanding more frequent reference to the norms that have been developed in the framework of the National System of Norms. More precisely, regulatory authorities should be obliged, when investigating and evaluating their options in the regulatory mechanism, to first consult the available lists of norms (in Canada, in other countries, or on the international level) to see if there are any norm that must be adopted.

The new problems created by this type of regulatory production are not small. First, norm-making companies are guided by commercial criteria. To meet the costs of producing regulation—which can be considerable—companies need to obtain revenues from their "customers", whether these are private companies or public bodies themselves. This makes the regulatory process itself fall under the influence of the principle of supply and demand: the pursuit of profit can lead, among other consequences, to loopholes in the regulation of certain sectors or to normative inflation—too many norms—in others. Second, governments are increasingly turning to this mode of regulatory production either by declaring specific regulation created by these companies to be "official" or by referring to them in their own body of laws and regulations. However, rules established in this way do not always represent the public interest. Moreover, they sometimes take too long to be adopted and the delegation of responsibilities that they often entail can raise legal issues. And third, the drafting procedure may not be fair: in a global economy, it will be necessary to decide who is involved in the drafting of norms and which bodies centralise normative activity. Participation costs are higher in the international arena than at national level. As the amount of norms set by international bodies increases many associations defending the public interest, as well as small businesses, will no longer be able to participate in policy making.

The same problems that affect laws produced by states are therefore also beginning to create concern for private regulation as regards the equitable participation of stakeholders, access for citizens, the costs they impose and their control by parliaments. How far can this private system of normative production go? It is difficult to make predictions today, but public powers are, to some extent, losing control of the development of this type of indirect regulation—a type of regulation that poses major problems, both theoretical (especially for political theory and legal science) and non-theoretical.

6.3 Self-Regulation

But the regulatory form that has attracted the most attention from theorists and experts lately has been a low-intensity law known as self-regulation. It has been presented by some as proof of the progress of the corporate state,[5] and by others as one of the proceedings with which to fill in the gaps that state regulation inevitably leaves behind. By self-regulation we understand the institutional arrangement by which an organisation regulates the norms of conduct of its members (Baggot 1989, p. 436). It is a tool which, despite the criticism it arouses, is increasingly being used to organise a wide range of activities, including health, advertising, financial services, consumer goods and the activity of certain qualified professions.

The reasons for this growing recourse to self-regulation are varied. Sometimes, for example, organisations protect their own interests by establishing certain barriers to the exercise of a profession or to the free movement of goods and services, in the form of codes of conduct. It can also happen—and indeed it has happened in advertising, in media and other sectors—that a certain sector seeks to clean up its image or gain credibility in the eyes of the public, disappointed by cases of malpractice that are difficult to prosecute criminally. Self-regulation can also be

---

[5]The so-called "voluntary agreements" as an alternative solution to regulation are different from self-regulation. They are voluntary and non-binding agreements between certain groups of companies or social entities and the state itself, whereby incentives for action are determined by mutual interest rather than fear of sanctions. Thus, the Government can reach an agreement with companies to withdraw certain goods from the market or establish a specific policy on televisions with the aim of protecting minors. These agreements have the advantage of avoiding conflicts, involving companies in political decisions, avoiding regulations, sharing responsibilities, etc. See Mannix (1994).

chosen by the government as a way of avoiding regulation. For example, governments can threaten to regulate advertising if agencies and broadcasters do not impose certain limits on themselves. And finally, it could be that governments themselves are driving self-regulation, especially when it comes to issues that are difficult to normalise centrally. This is the case, for example, in bioethical research.[6] The progress of science in the field of health, the concern generated by the use and manipulation of the body or the unpredictable repercussions that new technological developments can have in the long term, place societies before a dilemma: to regulate processes that are little known, or to run the risk that the lack of control leads to a real nightmare. Is law the best or the only answer to these problems? As pointed out before, the least possible volume of laws is desirable, but the fluctuating and always singular nature of these matters do not allow uniform treatment (Quéré 1991). Still, action can and should be taken without delay where the current legal vacuum is creating clear abuses. For this reason, together with some important national and international normative actions, *ethical committees* are created to advise public authorities and the scientific community on the possibilities and limits of research, while at the same time drawing up codes of conduct that operate as an alternative to state regulation—which is objectively limited, when not impeded in these fields.[7]

However, despite increasing recourse to this technique, and due to the great diversity of instruments that can be included in it, there is little clarity around its nature, its binding force or even the agents who are to participate in self-regulation (Ogus 1995, p. 374 ff). First of all, if we look at the nature of self-regulating bodies, they can show greater or lesser degree of formalisation. At the lowest level would be a system in which a specific company develops a code of ethics. A higher degree of formalisation would be a self-regulating body such as an association representing a group of companies or an industrial sector (the case of the Spanish Banking Association, for instance). An even higher level of self-regulation would be carried out by corporations with legal powers to issue regulations (such as professional associations). Secondly, taking its legal status into account, self-regulation may simply be optional for a specific sector, with no intervention by the government, or with governments reserving for themselves certain rights for intervention (Baggott 1986). Self-regulation may even be a substitute for regulation or complementary to state norms (such as the codes of ethics for securities firms). Thirdly, if we consider the participation of third parties, self-regulation might be done with or without the presence and participation of third parties (rules on laundering of money derived from drug trafficking). As we can see, self-regulation has become a

[6]See further Martín Mateo (1987), Conseil de l'Europe (1993, 1990), Etchegoyen (1991), Balandier (1990), Byk (1990), Commission de réforme du droit du Canada (1990), Conseil d'État (1988), Comité consultatif nacional d'Ethique pour les Sciencies de la Vie et de la Santé (1988); as well as the Council of Europe's Recommendation 1.160.

[7]A survey carried out by the Council of Europe (1993) showed how a good number of countries have set up Ethics Committees whose functions are to advise public authorities and the scientific community, inform, educate, and evaluate biomedical research.

mishmash that includes any piece of legislation not drawn up directly by the parliament or the government but by the parties concerned themselves. The norms produced in this way can be diverse in nature, have different degrees of binding force and allow different levels of intervention by public authorities.

The heterogeneity of forms in which self-regulation[8] is present in society requires a certain caution before making it the alternative that will resolve or even alleviate the burden of over-regulation of our states. The different formulas implemented so far have their advantages and disadvantages when compared to direct regulation by public authorities. Among the advantages, it should be pointed out that self-regulation would make it possible to regulate problems arising from the exercise of certain professions by going into a level of detail that no state regulation can deal with. Secondly, self-regulation is a procedure which is not subject to the limits of competence that bind the powers of public authorities, and therefore its personal and spatial scope of application may be much broader. Thirdly, self-regulation supports the confidence of consumers of goods and services and considerably reduces the volume of information and evaluation needed to make certain decisions. And finally, it is a much cheaper regulatory procedure since the costs of formulating and interpreting rules are lower: stakeholders have more knowledge and experience in the regulated field and the costs of enforcing the rules are attributed to the stakeholders themselves (Ogus 1995, pp. 374–375).

But this is perhaps all too abstract when it comes to deciding whether or not to opt for the tool of self-regulation. What is important is to assess whether self-regulation can be a better remedy than regulation by public authorities in a specific context. Comparative experience (see Gouvernement du Canada 1994, p. 57 ff) suggests that self-regulation may be an alternative solution in the following circumstances: (a) there is information asymmetry, i.e. consumers and potential buyers cannot know the characteristics of products and services; (b) the industry or sector is sufficiently organised for its members to ensure that norms are respected; (c) the sector is small enough to allow and facilitate the implementation and enforcement of norms; (d) there is an entitiy or body representing the sector that can assume the role of promoting norms; (e) all stakeholders are involved in the elaborarion of norms; (f) stakeholders are aware of the risks they face (health, liability, etc..) if they do not observe the norms; (g) stakeholders are convinced that if they don't do something, the government will take action; (h) industry members can identify free-riders; and (i) competitors and consumers can apply "sanctions" against free-riders. Opting a priori for self-regulation—or rejecting it from the outset—is therefore meaningless; what seems more appropriate is to see whether this tool is appropriate, or not, in each specific case.

Self-regulation may well have many virtues, but we must also recall what its disadvantages and shortcomings are—in comparison to regulation. And there is

[8]This diversity can be observed even in the most varied denominations such as codes of conduct, codes of good practice, guidelines, non-binding standards, etc., which reflect how difficult it is still today to profile such different instruments within public policies.

already enough experience to know that, as noted earlier, self-regulation can be used to strengthen competition-restricting practices—as the Spanish Tribunal for Defence of Competition (now integrated into the National Commission on Markets and Competition) has sometimes pointed out with regard to professional associations *(colegios profesionales)*. Self-regulation can easily be established and controlled by the strongest party and it is not easy to go after free-riders. Above all, however, there is no guarantee that self-regulation will be respected or that, in the event of a breach the codes, the pertinent penalties will be applied. In view of the real action of some groups that claim to be committed to self-regulation but do not care about their disciplinary regime, the effectiveness of this type of regulation can be sometimes compared to the effect of shooting with blank bullets. Therefore, recourse to self-regulation is not a good solution when: (a) the sector is not organised and cannot guarantee respect for the agreed normative; (b) the group is so numerous that it is difficult to ensure compliance; (c) there is nobody in charge of monitoring it; (d) it has been drawn up by a minority that has "captured" the process; (e) it is not possible to detect and control free-riders and (f) there is no awareness in the group about the fact that, unless they comply to the self-imposed rules, public authorities will intervene with their own official regulation. When these conditions are met, reliance on self-regulation to solve problems seems meaningless.

6.4 Reinforced Self-Regulation

The drawbacks and contraindications pointed out here, on the one hand, and the lack of proven effectiveness of some self-regulation methods put in place, on the other, have made it necessary to rethink the role of public authorities in this field. Mechanisms exist to ensure that compliance with this kind of rules is not at the mercy of the good or bad will of the self-regulated. In practice, what we find is not a substitution of the traditional regulatory technique for the new one, but the use of one or the other and even the complementary use of both methods depending on the case (Cafaggi 2004, pp. 23–36).

In this connection, the U.S. offers some interesting experiences. As a result of pressure from consumer organisations, the Consumer Products Safety Commission was set up in 1972 to lay down all the rules needed to ensure consumer safety. But the regulatory process did not live up to the expectations because of the slow procedures the Commission had to follow. Dissatisfaction led to a change in the approach to consumer protection in 1981, with a three-step procedure based on the carrot and stick policy: (a) once a safety problem has been identified in a given consumer product, the Commission launches the regulatory procedure; (b) the announcement of the development of a new norm by the Federal Administration typically prompts companies in the sector to develop a professional norm or to amend the existing one; and (c) if the professional norm finally agreed by the sector is considered satisfactory by the Commission, the regulatory process is interrupted. When assessing the new professional norm, the Commission often relies on "third-party approval", that is, the certification of independent laboratories. In Dawson's (1994) opinion, these professional norms seem no less effective than state norms and this is due, among other reasons, to the fact that third-party certification appears to have worked, the civil liability regime is particularly severe and the Commission has reserved for itself regulatory powers which it exercises whenever it considers that professional standards are ineffective or insufficient. This self-regulatory mechanism has been working acceptably well, which in 1990 led to a significant step forward in its institutionalisation: Congress has "completed" the current law in the light of the experience of past years. Under the latest reform, companies are required to inform the Commission of any product that does not comply with the professional standards trusted by the Commission. Failure to comply with this obligation entails heavy penalties.

Another interesting case is the attempt to solve the problem of safety on Canada's railways (McChesney 1994). Traditionally, safety issues in rail transport had been the responsibility of the government, which had to issue the appropriate regulations, monitor compliance with them and exert its power to impose penalties. Faced with the dissatisfaction generated by this procedure (which failed to reduce the number of accidents and entailed increasing costs for companies), in 1986 the Ministry of Transport summoned the companies in the sector, the trade unions and the administration departments involved in the problem, to study the regulatory approach to railway safety. The conclusion was that many regulatory texts hampered technological innovation in the sector without really improving safety. It seemed therefore necessary to investigate new methods. To this end, a new law on railway safety was adopted in 1989, inaugurating a new approach. The new strategy relied less on public authorities to set standards and monitor compliance. The railway companies were now empowered to issue safety regulations; these regulations were sent to the Ministry of Transport, which could approve the text or suggest any changes it deemed appropriate. Once the regulation had been approved by the Ministry of Transport, it was published by the railway company and from that moment on was considered compulsory. In this new approach, the initiative and development of policy was the responsibility of the companies themselves. The government reserved for itself wide powers, the two most important being the authority to endorse the new rules and to dictate for itself as many other rules as it would deem necessary. The experience gained in the years since the implementation of this new strategy seems to be positive from the point of view of safety effectiveness. It is also efficient in terms of administrative costs. On the basis of a high degree of consensus among the political forces regarding this new method, it seemed that only the trade unions raised concerns because some of the new rules could lead to a reduction in the number of jobs. Excepting such cases though, the system has not been questioned since.

Finally, Spain can provide a further example of the combined use of regulatory and self-regulatory techniques. Such is the case of ethical codes of conduct in the securities market. Developed societies are a complex clockwork mechanism that, in order to properly function, needs to maintain a balanced environment that depends as much on the reality of the system as on the appearance of seriousness and trust that the system is able to generate (Shearing 1993). As we saw with the 2008 sub-prime mortgage crisis, markets are fragile environments that depend on a sustained will on the part of market stakeholders to trust each other. In fact, trust is at the heart of market regulation. This need to sustain trust has led to a growing demand for financial ethics, business ethics, more stringent codes of conduct, etc.[9] The demand for more business ethics may not be completely altruistic (Daigne 1991), and it is sometimes suggested only for commercial purposes. In any case, in Spain two norms were enacted in this regard which fell in line with European legislation (Recommendation of 25 July 1977 approving a Code of Conduct on securities transactions) and the conclusions of the 15th Annual Conference of the International Organisation of Securities Commision (IOSCO) held in 1991 (which approved international rules of conduct for financial service providers): the Act 24/1988 on the Securities Market, and the Royal Decree 620/1993 on norms of conduct in the securities markets.[10] In accordance with the Spanish legislation, the deontological rules in the securities market consist of: (a) the *Rules of Conduct* contained in Title VII of the Act 24/1988 and which, in spite of their name, are genuine regulations, since failure to comply with them leads to the imposition of administrative sanctions; (b) the G*eneral Code of Conduct* drawn up by the Ministry of Economy and Finance and contained in the annex to the Royal Decree 620/1993; (c) the *internal codes of conduct* of financial mediators[11]; and (d) the *rules of conduct* applicable to members of governing bodies in secondary markets, which are a possibility opened by Art. 3.2 of the Royal Decree 620/1993. What we have here is therefore the imposition of rules of conduct laid down by law, to which a code of conduct drawn up by the Ministry is added, together with the obligation imposed on security-trading companies and agencies to draw up their own rules of conduct and the possibility for professional associations to do so as well.

These examples, and many more that could be mentioned, show the different techniques that can be used and their combinations, as well as the different degree of intervention that public authorities can assume. We are therefore witnessing a new regulatory strategy here, which Ayres and Braithwaite (1992, p. 101) call *enhanced* or *reinforced self-regulation*. This is an idea that is being advanced with the aim of tackling the slowness of public authorities when it comes to exercising their

[9]In the UK, e.g., the *Cadbury Report* has been an important mechanism of self-regulation: Ferry (1994).

[10]*Ley 24/1988, de 28 de julio, del mercado de valores*, and *Real Decreto 620/1993, de 3 de mayo, sobre normas de actuación en los mercados de valores y registros obligatorios.*

[11]According to Art. 3 of the aforementioned Royal Decree, all companies and securities agencies must draw up an internal code of conduct that regulates the actions of their governing bodies, employees and representatives. At the same time, the professional associations that group together the aforementioned persons and entities may draw up such internal regulations to which securities companies and agencies may adhere. Such regulations are drawn up through negotiations with the heads of the National Securities Market Commission (*Comisión Nacional del Mercado de Valores*, CNMV), who may make objections, recommendations and oblige them to make "the necessary modifications to ensure compliance". Approved regulations must be submitted to the National Securities Market Commission.

regulatory powers, the excessive formalism and the obstacles to innovation that regulation often entails. Reinforced self-regulation—also in line with G. Teubner's proposals—would involve the following steps: (a) individual companies draw up their own codes of conduct; (b) such codes must establish certain internal bodies responsible for inspecting and monitoring compliance. These internal control bodies must have some degree of independence and autonomy from the low and medium echelons of the company, which guarantees the possibility of exercising their powers of recommendation and sanction; and (c) the state reserves itself the right to approve the aforementioned codes or to suggest changes (the case of the Canadian railways), to supervise the operation of the internal control bodies, to sanction compliance with internal codes when the system of inspection and sanction provided for does not work effectively (the case of ethical codes in the Spanish securities market) and to promulgate the corresponding regulations in the sector that will operate as a minimum to be respected by the internal codes or as a supplementary law for those companies that do not resort to self-regulation.

According to Ayres and Braithwaite (1992, p. 110 ff), reinforced self-regulation has its advantages and disadvantages. Regarding its advantages, we can list the following: (a) the design of such norms can be much better adapted to the specific reality of companies. This means that rules can be much simpler and more specific. The risks of complexity, of too many rules stems from the need to provide answers for all the assumed cases that may arise in an entire sector. Through enhanced self-regulation, rules are aimed at a limited and known set of circumstances and not at an unlimited set of economic activities; (b) rules can be adjusted much more quickly to changes in the environment, without necessarily depending on the slow process of public production of rules; (c) such norms can encourage regulatory innovation by allowing companies to seek cheaper and more effective mechanisms to deal with problems; (d) these norms would be more comprehensive in their coverage of industrial risks and corporate abuse than the ones dictated by governments; (e) companies would be more committed to respecting rules that they themselves have established; (f) companies would not have to bear the confusion and the costs of having two types of regulation (official and company regulation); (g) companies bear the cost of producing their own regulation; (h) it would be easier and quicker to detect breaches; (i) a greater number or proportion of offenders found to be in breach could be punished than under the traditional system of public regulation; (j) it would be much easier for prosecutors to obtain evidence of breach with the cooperation of internal control bodies; and (k) there would be less resistance to comply with the norms in general.

But it is also true that reinforced self-regulation has its weaknesses, the most important of which are: (a) ministerial departments would have to bear the cost of regularly reviewing a huge number of codes of conduct; (b) public control can sometimes be more effective than private oversight; (c) the problem of the regulatory process being "captured" could worsen; (d) companies could see how time and paperwork increase the costs of getting internal codes approved; (e) the constitutionality of such procedures is not always clear; (f) the specificity of this kind of rules could weaken the moral force of a law that must be general; (g) companies can word their codes in a way that would allow them to evade the spirit of the regulation; (h) companies cannot enforce rules as effectively as governments; and (i) the independence of internal control bodies may never be fully guaranteed.

These weaknesses, in addition to the practical experiences we know of so far, lead to the conclusion that reinforced self-regulation cannot be presented as a universal remedy. There are countries more prone to self-regulation, such as Great Britain (Baggott and Harrison 1986), while in other countries this strategy will probably meet with more resistance. Cultural, historical, ideological or constitutional considerations might make the use of this instrument viable or useless. It's an idea that, when offered without great pretensions, can provide one more instrument to be considered in the regulatory strategy; this instrument, be it alone or in combination with other traditional regulatory instruments, can cover many policy needs. At first glance, there is no reason neither to reject nor to be naively dazzled by what would be considered the highest level of *soft law* we have referred to in this chapter. Anyhow, if self-regulation was initially seen as a feasible solution to the problem of norm overload in modern social states, by now those hopes have been corrected by experience.

6.5 Indirect Self-Regulation

The search for regulatory tools more adapted to the new times and needs has prompted the rediscovery of different formulas for social regulation. Perhaps the vision we have sketched here would be incomplete if we did not refer, albeit briefly, to the new proposals for indirect regulation into which the theory of Public Choice has led.

As discussed in the previous chapter (Sect. 5.2), for the early Chicago School human activity is regulated by four types of constraints. The law is one of them; it guides human activity by establishing patterns of behaviour. Social norms—the huge variety of norms that ranges from courtesy rules to the customs and habits of normality—constitute a second set of restrictions that guide us in the most diverse aspects of our lives. Nature itself also limits or facilitates the realisation of our desires. And, fourthly, markets make it easier or harder for us to carry out certain actions. Laws condition our behaviour through the threat of institutionalised sanctions, that is, sanctions that are regulated as to who imposes them, how, when and how much the sanction implies. Social norms also operate through threats, but they are not institutionalised. Physical and biological characteristics are natural limitations. The market uses the price system as an incentive or deterrence of behaviour. These four constraints, or modes of regulation,[12] constitute the sum of the forces that guide human behaviour, even if they do not guide it to the same degree and with the

[12]Of course, we cannot forget religion and morality as other powerful restrictors of human behavior; but its treatment is not relevant now.

same intensity. What the old Chicago School was telling us is that, among these four regulators, legislation is the least effective: its prescriptions are crude, its response to social problems slow and its results inefficient. Any of the other three regulators do much better than laws, especially the market.

Now, the orientation of the new Chicago School (Lessig 1998, p. 661 ff) is also interested in the study of the different regulatory mechanisms and also adopts the perspective of rational choice; but, unlike the old School, it doesn't share that clear-cut contempt for law. Quite on the contrary, the new Chicago School believes that these three regulatory modes are, or can be, precisely regulated by law. Thus, instead of diminishing the role of law, this new conception broadens its scope of intervention, since law governs human behaviour not only directly but also indirectly, i.e. by regulating the other regulators (social norms, market and nature). Regulation is a combination of these four regulators and the problem to be considered—regulatory policy—is to find out in each case or need (reducing tobacco use, increasing seat belt use, discrimination against people with disabilities, drug use, abortion, etc.) which tool, or combination of tools, is most appropriate. A combination of direct and indirect regulation is a typical feature of any modern normative regime.

In the new Chicago School, one of the most studied regulatory formulas is the one related to (social) norms or *norm management*. It is based on the premise that changing social norms, social meaning and roles can be the best way to improve social welfare, and governments would have an important role to play in this task (Sunstein 1995). Many of the decisions (individual choices) we make are guided by certain social norms, or by the role that society has assigned to us, or by the social significance that they have. Social norms (such as voting in elections, recycling garbage, greetings, keeping promises, or answering letters) tell us how to behave without further discussion; they make our lives easier. The same is true of social roles (father, mother, judge, husband, wife, teacher, etc.) which sometimes facilitate our decisions and guide us when certain behaviour is required and other times (in the case of women, for example) represent a limitation for our own individual autonomy and social advancement. The same happens with the meaning that society ascribes to the specific behaviour we show: raising our hand (with a closed fist or open palm), dressing formally or informally, using certain expressions (mister, lady, your honor, etc.), lighting a cigarette, fastening the belt in the car, tipping the waiter... have a certain social meaning that goes beyond the words we use, our will or our intention. Changing this meaning is, in other words, out of our own individual reach: it is, so to speak, an objective meaning (Lessig 1995).

Although it is true that social life would be impossible without social norms, without the ascription of meanings to actions, or without social roles, there are times when it is necessary or convenient to change certain norms, meanings and roles. And it is also true that each of us individually can do little to modify a social norm that hinders the well-being of citizens (not to recycle garbage, for example), or to create a new social norm that improves our lives (to vote in elections). There is little we can do individually to modify the behaviour that society demands from individuals depending on the social role they play (be it a politician, a lawyer or a banker). There is also not much we can do individually to change what the use of certain terms ("immigrant", "populist", etc.), wearing certain clothes (tie, or shorts), burning a flag or showing certain symbols actually mean in society. The individual citizen (Sunstein 1995, pp. 46–47) has little control over all of this: maybe it would be preferable to have other social norms, with other roles and other meanings, but it is not entirely up to each one of us to change them. This attempt might result in severe limits to the well-being of citizens. There is certainly a problem with existing rules when a large part of society would rather have rules, roles and meanings change, so people need a third party—governments—to take on the role of solving this problem of collective action in order to improve their lives. And that is the new mission assigned to law: not only to regulate directly what we should or should not do but also to modify certain social norms, to change roles and to construct or reconstruct the meanings that directly regulate our behaviour.

This new approach within the Chicago School—a school scarcely deferential towards law as a mechanism of social regulation—has led to a revaluation of the symbolic or expressive function of law. Until now, it was thought that legal norms were intended to modify social reality, the world around us and to do so in such a way that the degree of efficacy, effectiveness and efficiency of the norm could be evaluated. But there has always been a type of legislation that can be described as symbolic,[13] which has mainly two different objectives: sometimes public authorities announce promises of future goods, and sometimes they seek purely emotional benefits (Goodin 1977, p. 386 ff).[14]

Indeed, there are times when law pursues objectives that cannot be weighed, measured and counted but rather produce intangible effects such as changes in values, customs and other social norms (Sunstein 1996, p. 2021 ff). There are times when laws are used to make a certain statement instead of directly controlling the behaviour of citizens. Yet these statements are intended to change social norms. Debates on the death penalty, flag-burning and sexist language are good examples in this regard. Laws of this kind may seek to change social norms by stigmatising certain behaviours that are considered particularly hateful in the hope that they will be diminished or eradicated (terrorist crimes, flag burning, gender violence). This is indirectly a consequentialist approach: the laws in question are justified by their results, that is, whether and to what extent they succeed in reducing this type of crimes.

Symbolic legislation including purely emotional contents (in Spain, for instance, the legal self-definition of some autonomous regions as "nations") does not promise

[13]For Edelman (1964, p. 206), the anticipation of a future welfare or a danger is critical in the political language, for this language largely consists of promises about the benefits that will alleguedly follow from any political cause or candidate supported by the speaker. In this regard, ambiguous phrases reflect the lack of consensus within a society in which values are unevenly distributed: distressed people want promises of a future in which the pathologies of the present have been eliminated, and, when a promise is ambiguous, different groups can read different meanings in it.

[14]On symbolic legislation, see recently van Klink (2016).

anything particular but is used, rather, to reinforce the logic of identity,[15] or to proclaim and strengthen the values of certain social groups (be it a given conception of life or a moral stance with regard to abortion or euthanasia). There are even times when symbolic laws are proposed (criminalisation of the burning of flags or portraits of the head of state) even if it is clearly demonstrated that they are not only uncapable of reducing the specific type of behaviour they try to curb, but can even worsen it, precisely as a result of its persecution—the proposal of such laws is not uncommon, despite the empirical data speaking against them. This type of law, which is strictly expressive or symbolic and does not seek to change anything but to make certain statements, raises the most serious doubts for any open society that is not committed to the values and interests of one particular social group.

References

Ayres I, Braithwaite J (1992) Responsive regulation. Transcending the deregulation debate. Oxford University Press, Oxford

Baggot R (1989) Regulatory reform in Britain: the changing face of self-regulation. Public Adm 67 (4):435–454

Baggott R (1986) By voluntary agreement: the politics of instrument selection. Public Adm 64 (1):51–67

Baggott R, Harrison L (1986) The politics of self-regulation: the case of advertising control. Policy Polit 14(2):143–159

Balandier G (1990) La demande d'Ethique. Cahiers Internationaux de Sociologie 88:5–12

Bentham J (1981) Idea general de un cuerpo completo de legislación. In: Principios de legislación. Editora Nacional, Madrid

Byk C (1990) Les instances de l'Ethique en droit comparé (Actes du 1er Symposium du Conseil de l'Europe sur la bioethique). Cahiers Internationaux de Sociologie 88:215–230

Cafaggi F (2004) Le rôle des acteurs privés dans les processus de régulation: participation, autorregulation et régulation privée. Revue Française d'Administration Publique 109:23–36

CEN (European Committee for Standardisation) (2006) Rapport Annuel. CEN, Brussels

Comité Consultatif National d'Ethique pour les Sciencies de la Vie et de la Santé (1988) Recherche biomedicale et respect de la personne humaine. La Documentation Française, Paris

Commission de réforme du droit du Canada (1990) In: Commission de réforme du droit du Canada (ed) Por un conseil consultatif canadien d'ethique médicale, Ottawa

Conseil d'État (1988) De l'Ethique au droit. Rapports et Documents. La Documentation Française, Paris

Conseil de l'Europe (1990) L'Europe Et La Bioethique: Actes du 1er Symposium du Conseil de l'Europe sur la Bioethique. Conseil de l'Europe, Strasbourg

Conseil de l'Europe (1993) Les instances nacionales d'ethique. Les éditions du Conseil de l'Europe, Strasbourg

Daigne JF (1991) L'Ethique financière. PUF, Paris

[15]As Edelman (1964, p. 40) notes, a large number of people in our society tend to think in the form of stereotypes, personalization or hypersimplification because they cannot recognize or tolerate ambiguous or complex situations—accordingly, they respond to symbols that hypersimplify and distort.

Dawson CG (1994) Le recours aux accords volontaires pour la sécurité des produits de consummation aux Etats-Unis durant la période 1981-1993. Etude des cas des Etats-Unis. OECD, Paris
Edelman M (1964) The symbolic uses of politics. University of Illinois, Chicago
Etchegoyen A (1991) La valse des Ethiques. F. Bourin, Paris
Ferry H (1994) Self-regulation and informations disclosure: The cadbury report on financial aspects of corporate governance. A case study from the United Kingdom. OECD, Paris
García Amado JA (1988) Sociología sistémica y política legislativa. Anuario de Filosofía del Derecho 5:243–278
Goodin RE (1977) Symbolic rewards: being bougth off cheaply. Polit Stud 25(3):383–396
Gouvernement du Canada (1994) Evaluation des solutions de rechange à la réglementation. Ottawa
Hayek FA (1945) The use of knowledge in society. Am Econ Rev 35(4):519–530
Hayek FA (1988) Derecho, legislación y libertad, vol I–II, 2nd edn. Unión Editorial, Madrid
House of Commons (Canada) (1993) Reglémentation et compétitivité. Premier Rapport du Sous-Comité de la Réglementation et de la Competitivité. Ottawa
Lessig L (1995) The regulation of social meaning. Univ Chicago Law Rev 62(3):943–1045
Lessig L (1998) The New Chicago School. J Leg Stud 27:661–691
Luhmann N (1981) Teoria politica nello Stato del Benessere. Franco Agnelli, Milano
Luhmann N (1983) Sistema jurídico y dogmática jurídica. Centro de Estudios Constitucionales, Madrid
Luhmann N (1995) La autopoiesis de los sistemas sociales. Zona Abierta 70/71:21–52
Mannix B (1994) Améliorer le rapport cout-efficacité de la gestion gouvernamentale: formules proposées pour remplacer les réglementations visant "imponer et contrôler". OCDE, Paris
Martín Mateo R (1987) Bioética y derecho. Ariel, Barcelona
Maturana HR, Varela FJ (1980) Autopoiesis and cognition. The realization of the living. Springer, Dordrecht
McChesney A (1994) L'Utilisation d'autres instruments réglementaires au Canada: Une approche nouvelle de la securité ferroviaire. Etude de cas du Canada. OCDE, Paris
Ogus A (1995) Rethinking self-regulation. Oxford J Leg Stud 15(1):97–108. Published also in A Reader on Regulation, Baldwin R, Scout C, Hood Ch (eds) Oxford University Press, Oxford, 1998
Quéré F (1991) L'Ethique et la vie. Odile-Jacob, Paris
Schmitter PC (1977) Modes of interest intermediation and models of societal change in Westen Europe. Comp Polit Stud 10:7–38
Schmitter PC (1982) Organizzatione degli interessi e rendimento politico. In: La società complesse. Il Mulino, Bologna
Shearing CA (1993) A constitutive conception of business regulation. In: Grabosky P, Braithwaite J (eds) Business regulation and Australia's future. Australian Institute of Criminology, Canberra, pp 67–79
Sunstein CR (1995) Social norms and social rules. The coase lecture, John M. Olim Law and Economics Working Paper no. 36. University of Chicago, Chicago
Sunstein CR (1996) On the expresive function of law. Univ Pa Law Rev 144:2021–2053
Teubner G (1983) Substantive and reflexive elements in modern law. Law Soc Rev 17(2):239–285
Teubner G (1987) Juridification: concepts, aspects, limits, solutions. In: Teubner G (ed) Juridification of social spheres. A comparative analysis in the areas of labor, corporate, antitrust and social welfare law. Walter de Gruyter, Berlin, pp 3–48
Timsit G (1991) Les noms de la Loi. PUF, Paris
van Klink B (2016) Symbolic legislation. A political concept. In: van Klink B, van Beers B, Poort L (eds) Symbolic legislation theory and developments in biolaw. Springer, Cham, pp 19–35
Varela FJ (1979) Principles of biological autonomy. Holland, New York
Zolo D (1995) Autopoiesis: crítica de un paradigma posmoderno. Zona Abierta 70/71:203–262

Chapter 7
The Art of Regulating

7.1 Reward and Punishment

Nature, Bentham (1988) recalled, has placed human beings under the rule of two powerful sovereigns: pleasure and pain. And it is these sovereigns who tell us what is right and what is wrong, what we must do and what we must avoid: we can do nothing to escape from such an absolute dominance. That is why any legislator who wants to master the art of legislating must be an expert in *felicific calculus* and know precisely the intensity, the duration, the certainty or uncertainty, the closeness or distance, as well as the fecundity and the purity of the pleasure, or pain, caused by each measure he takes. It is therefore by seeking in his laboratory the convenient dose of pleasure or pain to be applied that the ruler achieves the fulfilment of his mandates and prohibitions (Bentham 1981a, p. 430).

But Bentham was well aware of the fact that commands and prohibitions—what is now known as "command-and-control"—were insufficient and that the art of legislating needed to be more refined, to investigate new techniques and mechanisms of social direction. And so, he insisted on his suggestion that the legislator, instead of directly prohibiting the production and marketing of certain products or services, could first try to correct the information deficit that afflicts consumers by forcing producers to report on the price, quantity and quality of their products (Bentham 1981b, p. 370 ff). He even went so far as to propose more sophisticated regulatory techniques such as the establishment of so-called *appellations d'origine*, the use of the media and the use of citizen education. Legislating was, and still is, more complicated than issuing, as Bentham's disciple Austin (2002) believed, general commands or orders backed by sanctions. However, what ended up prevailing in the legal discourse was not Bentham's more nuanced version but Austin's coercive and imperative conception that gives the legislator the dual task of giving orders and monitoring their implementation, nothing more.

Life has always been ahead of legal constructions, and legal constructions have not always allowed us to account for the legislator's use of prizes and incentives

V. Zapatero Gómez, *The Art of Legislating*, Legisprudence Library 6,
https://doi.org/10.1007/978-3-030-23388-4_7

instead of sanctions. That is what happened historically: the exercise of power has sometimes consisted in prohibiting and punishing unwanted behaviour, and other times—certainly less—in rewarding the desired behaviour. Power, in general terms, is the ability to attain the desired goals, and these can be achieved through coercion, through incentives or rewards, and also—and this should not be forgotten—through persuasion.[1] Let us move from the softest to the hardest of these solutions.

7.2 Information and Persuasion

Information is one of the most powerful tools. To decide without information is to put too much trust in chance, and can lead to making the kind of choice that we never would have made had we known all the relevant data. Now, one of the main assets of any government is the information it has at its disposal thanks to its strategic position, which makes it the connecting point of countless information channels. Disseminating certain information available to the government can correct information deficits for citizens: public information on road conditions or weather forecasts can be more effective in terms of road safety than detailed road traffic regulation. Public information on the price index can affect citizens' decisions on saving or spending. A public disclosure of the financial problems of the social insurance system may lead to an increase or decrease in private retirement plans. It is in this way that information can become a powerful instrument of social direction, an alternative solution to pure regulation.

Hood (1983, pp. 21–40) has looked at the different methods governments can use to inform citizens. The government can provide information by answering questions (the open line of the Moncloa Palace,[2] for example), making its archives and documentation available to citizens, providing information to individuals on its own initiative (such as census cards during the electoral period); it can direct information to certain groups on matters of interest to them (increase in pensions) or it can provide information to anyone who wants to listen (official statements, press realeases and the like). The effectiveness of information as a social management tool depends on several factors. Firstly, the size of the target population, because it determines the cost of information mechanisms. The degree of attention or interest of the addressees, in second place, also conditions the effort required. Thirdly, the more or less technical nature of the information to be provided bears on the applicability or inapplicability of this tool when it is intended for a broad spectrum of citizens. And, finally, the greater or lesser credibility of a government can turn the most reliable and important information into wastepaper. It is clear nevertheless that, where feasible, this alternative to pure regulation—ordering or prohibiting certain types of behaviour—should be the preferred solution because it respects personal

[1]As for nudging, see Thaler and Sunstein (2009), and Zorzetto and Ferraro (2019).

[2]Moncloa Palace is the residence of the Spanish prime minister.

autonomy and, by relying on the freedom and wilfulness of people, ensures greater effectiveness when it comes to reaching the desired objective.

Very close to information as a social management mechanism (sometimes even intertwined with it) are the persuasion techniques with which authorities try to achieve certain social effects by convincing citizens of voluntarily changing their behaviour. When resorting to information, public authorities normally do not reveal what the desired policy result is. By contrast, when persuasion is used, the pursued objective is openly established, and authorities prefer to convince rather than to prescribe. The premise here is that the "deviant" behaviour of many citizens is not based on the perversity of the individual—the *bad man* who worried Justice Holmes (1975, p. 15) so much—but often on ignorance of what is expected from him, or of the reasons for the effort required from him. If citizens were aware of the risks to their own health and the health of others caused by alcohol excess, there might be no need for rules to regulate its consumption in detail. Or, for example, if citizens knew exactly how much damage is being inflicted on our planet, they would be more careful when consuming finite resources without the need to limit water consumption or car use by regulation. Advertising and education campaigns against alcohol or drug abuse, for gender equality, against domestic violence, etc. can be more effective than the most precise, detailed and rigorous norms developed by public authorities.

The term institutional advertising is applied to a form of social communication in which authorities try to provide the public with information considered to be of general interest, influencing the behaviour of citizens, especially in the areas of consume, health, education, environment or fulfilment of civic duties such as tax-paying and other similar activities. Examples of institutional advertising include, among many others, ministerial campaigns to promote electoral participation; to improve road safety; to inform taxpayers about tax returns; to advise or to warn about the consumption of certain food products, etc. The health ministries' or departments' information campaigns on condom use are also institutional publicity. The increasing use of institutional advertising highlights—leaving aside for a moment the biased use of it—the progressive confidence of public authorities in this instrument of social management, especially when public opinion is not aware of the need for stronger measures or regulation may not be sufficient to change citizens' behaviour.[3]

---

[3]The use of information therefore has its indications and contraindications. The use of this instrument may be indicated, for example, when (a) behaviour is determined fundamentally by social and psychological factors; (b) knowledge, attitudes and the general way of dealing with the problem is more important when modifying behaviour than the strict imposition of rules (use of condoms, treatment of different people, etc.); (c) it is impossible to establish precise rules for every conceivable harm or for every possible problem (driving with prudence); (d) opinion leaders can favour change and are willing to participate (fight against drug use); or (d) the media have an interest in the campaign and its objectives. However, recourse to this technique may be contraindicated when (a) behaviour is determined for economic reasons (truckers' day); (b) those concerned prefer regulation (free-rider problems); (c) certain behaviour is absolutely necessary and may be required by law; and (d) resources are scarce for a good campaign.

Like any other social direction tool, advertising has its advantages and disadvantages (Gouvernement du Canada 1994). Advertising can have a faster impact on the behaviour that needs to be altered; it allows greater flexibility when dealing with changing situations; it is a less costly tool for governments and eludes the problems associated with centralised decision-making. But it may also be slower to bring about behavioural change; it may be more costly to assess the impact of a particular policy (advertising does not provide the information that taxes, for example, provide); and it may be seen by some people as an undesirable tool (as happened with the 1980s condom campaigns in Spain, which certain societal groups criticised for inducing sexual activity). But more importantly, advertising can also involve dangerous manipulation of public opinion.

If information makes it possible for citizens to decide what benefits them more, and publicity can convince citizens of the course of action that public authorities desire, it is not difficult to agree that, morally, the most exemplary form of power is persuasion—provided that it serves a legitimate purpose and legitimate means are used (Grant 2006, pp. 29–39). That is why it is common to think that persuasion is preferable to coercion, even though it is not so clear. Just as coercion can take different shapes—ranging from tyrannical power, brute force or threat, to the coercion entailed by the laws of a democratic society—, so can persuasion be based on deception and manipulation, or on rational deliberation among free beings. There are many forms of persuasion that are clearly more objectionable than the coercion or force of the laws enacted by democratically elected powers. But it is nevertheless true that persuasion—understood as a fair, non-manipulated debate among free citizens—is a morally sounder and even more effective option. In any case, as Socrates reminded Gorgias, one should never forget the enormous manipulative capacity of a rhetoric based on feelings and beliefs (see Plato 1992).

7.3 Incentive-Based Regulation

Traditionally the most emblematic legal instrument of social control has been to enact rules of behaviour and to monitor their observance: the threat of appropriate sanctions was thought to have a deterrent effect on unwanted behaviour. But a less Hobbesian and more realistic conception of human nature, and the limitations historically detected in this traditional form of social control, have encouraged the study of alternative regulatory solutions. And so it has been proven that the use of economic incentives—applied through instruments such as taxes, subsidies or public fees—is often a more effective and efficient form of social management.[4] These incentives can bring about profound changes, without imposing a particular

[4]On the promotional function of law, see Bobbio (1984). For his part, Pérez Lledó (2000, pp. 665–687) offers an interesting picture of the different promotional techniques that he classifies into pure prizes, promises of prizes, pure incentives and facilitations.

behaviour but by changing the costs and benefits attached to that behaviour. At the same time they offer greater flexibility to the legislator as they allow him to gauge the dose of benefit or cost needed to achieve the desired behaviour. From the citizens' perspective, this mechanism leaves more freedom to decide on the most advantageous behaviour; and as far as companies are concerned, it encourages them to seek the most innovative solutions in the long term. These are often the reasons why, in general terms, public opinion prefers this type of mechanism to giving orders and monitoring compliance.[5]

Perhaps the economic incentives with the most direct effects as a social steering mechanism are public subsidies. A subsidy is first and foremost a non-refundable asset allocation made by public authorities for the benefit of an individual or company (Parada 1995, p. 455 ff), which is normally attached to the development of a specific activity that is to be promoted as a means of achieving a social goal (see Fernández Farreres 1983, 1993). Subsidies have been used to implement industrial restructuring policies, to combat pollution, to maintain certain types of transport and to support a wide range of social and cultural activities. The logic underlying subsidies therefore is the reverse of that underlying public fees and prices. Whereas public fees and prices must cover the cost of certain services provided by the administration, in the case of subsidies the cost of the behavioural change required from individuals or companies is paid by the public purse—usually with the aim of eliminating externalities (water purification, avoiding atmospheric pollution, etc.). The key issue, therefore, is the precise assessment of the costs of the activities to be encouraged (Ogus 1994, pp. 248–249). If the cost is undervalued, the subsidy will not be an effective mechanism for achieving the desired goal. If the cost is overvalued, we will be faced with an inefficient mechanism that will in turn generate additional costs that affect taxpayers.

In recent years this social management mechanism has gradually lost significance, either because subsidies have to be charged on exhausted budgets, or because organisations such as the European Union have adopted a clearly unfavourable position with regard to this instrument, for it can impinge on the principle of free competition. Nonetheless, as we have recently experienced, subsidising actions may well be adopted, in periods of severe economic crisis, for the benefit of the market itself.

---

[5]Advocates of the use of incentive regulation believe that incentives address many of the shortcomings of traditional regulation. First, while the latter often gives rise to a complex and detailed set of centrally developed standards, economic incentives can operate on the basis of broader objectives, with reduced information and administrative costs for both regulators and regulated parties. Secondly, the greater freedom granted by economic incentives to companies encourages technological development. Thirdly, while the application of regulation by directives is subject to considerable uncertainty as regards detection of breaches, prosecution and level of sanctions, economic incentives are limited to the actual payment of specific sums. Fourthly, negative incentives generate revenue for the public purse that can be used to compensate victims for any externalities generated by such activity while the system of directives rarely makes it possible to compensate victims (see Ogus 1994, p. 246).

In any case, once subsidies are discarded—or reduced to a minimum—as an instrument of social management, the most powerful form of incentive based regulation is currently the use that public authorities make of their fiscal powers to reduce or increase the cost of certain behaviours or practices. The most important tool in this regard is taxation, where the taxable event is defined not by reference to services provided by the state but to the activities of the citizens themselves. Although it is accepted that the main objective of taxes is to provide the resources that are necessary to finance the general functioning of the state, on occasions they can also be used as instruments of political direction: taxing an activity—alcohol consumption, for example—can discourage or reduce its exercise; establishing a tax benefit—e.g. for hiring people with disabilities—can encourage it. The volume of economic resources being mobilised this way is considerable, and it was thought until recently that their diffuse costs and concentrated benefits meant that they were easier to establish than to remove. The current reality has changed the situation and for the public opinion—or at least the opinion of those who have influence—the costs are now concentrated and the benefits diffuse or long term. Perhaps this explains the race to reduce taxes in present times.[6]

A third incentive-based regulatory instrument are fees or taxes levied on the provision of certain services by the public administration, which can include, for instance, surface mining fees, fees for issuing academic titles, for the registration of pharmaceutical products, or for the licensing of betting games—or any other

[6]See Gouvernement du Canada (1994, p. 27 ff). In general terms, the following advantages of acting or intervening through tax policy can be cited: (a) it has the potential to greatly reduce the overall economic costs of achieving a particular regulatory objective; (b) it may be less costly to administer, if it connects to existing tax systems; (c) it has the capacity to incentivise innovation and competition, reduce government administrative burdens, and allow for aggregate flexibility in policymaking; (d) it generates revenue for the government; (e) it can be more effective than regulation since it gives free rein to market processes by depending on them; (f) it is less annoying since it gives more freedom of choice than traditional command and control regulation; (g) it is more transparent: the cost of the benefits of regulation (e.g. cleaner air) is directly reflected in product prices; (h) it allows flexibility and adaptation of affected behaviours; (i) it makes it possible to avoid the problems of centralised discretionary decision-making; (j) it allows all efforts to be directed at the economic determinants of behaviour; and (k) it can compensate for the lack of resources needed to enable stakeholders to adopt the behaviour in question. With regard to the drawbacks of taxes, the following should be mentioned: (a) taxes may be a relatively sophisticated mechanism in an already complex system; (b) eventual beneficiaries of fiscal measures may not be aware of its existence; (c) regulations governing liability and admissibility may be complex and (d) tax-based interventions may be difficult to apply with precision and (e) may require stronger vigilance than traditional and detailed regulation; (f) it may be difficult to determine the extent of the tax or fiscal stimulus needed to change behaviour; (g) habitual beneficiaries of a fiscal stimulus may come to believe that they are entitled to it, making it difficult later to reduce or eliminate it; (h) an indirect method used to influence behaviour may not be considered correct by the public; (i) administration may be relatively costly depending on the number of the affected and the need to establish a new tax system; (j) if recipients have very different economic capacities, it may be unfair that the more wealthy recipients benefit from tax reductions, or that the less wealthy have to cope with the complexities of the tax system; and (k) it may distort the competitive position of firms within the market.

instrument that may be established to provide a service to individuals. Next to fees are public prices, established as compensation for an exclusive use of the public domain or the provision of certain services. Clearly the most delicate problem with fees is the precise calculation of the cost of such services, because if this is valued under the real cost, fees will create externalities that will end up being paid for by the citizens in general. Meeting the costs of discharging water, emitting pollutants, treating or processing waste, etc. will not always be easy, especially when the effects can be spread over an indefinite time frame or area. On the other hand, although it is true that the application of this tool exempts the administration from knowing the cost of e.g. reducing pollution for individual companies, without this knowledge it will be difficult to predict how much pollution will actually be reduced. This means the public official will have to adjust by "trial and error" (see Pérez Royo 1995; García Añoveros et al. 1995).

These are the most common instruments of incentive regulation. But we must add to the list new formulas that are already being implemented in many countries, such as the Green Tax System in Denmark, or the tradable permits or negotiable licenses that were first applied in the United States for environmental matters—and have now extended to many other countries and activities.[7] These instruments are sometimes used to make beneficiaries internalise the social costs of their activities; sometimes to increase or reduce the cost of certain activities, and other times to ensure a price for certain services or goods, such as water or air quality, lower than real cost.

Of course, despite the theoretical advantages of all these economic incentives, they have not completely displaced regulation by directives. The preference of almost all governments for the technique of directives is due to the fact that the balance between advantages and disadvantages is not as clear in favour of incentives as their advocates claim—particularly when the costs and benefits of their establishment, change, execution and administration are considered (Mitnick 1989, p. 363 ff [346 ff]). Indeed, when it is not possible to know the inclinations of citizens or businesses (or when the costs of obtaining this information—in terms of time and resources—are very high), it is more difficult to opt for incentives than for directives. It may also be more difficult to change regulation by incentives than regulation by directives, for incentives have a tendency to be considered as consolidated rights which cannot be cut back. As far as the administration of either form of regulation is concerned, it should not be forgotten that incentives involve the use of limited public resources—whereas the costs of directives are borne by the citizens. On the other hand, in the case of incentives the costs of execution can be lower, as Mitnick

[7]These are licenses granted by the administration that holders can "sell" to third parties. Certain companies may be granted a "right" to emit a certain amount of pollution. If the holders of these "rights" do not exhaust the permitted quantity, they can "sell" this unused right to others. While respecting the objective of achieving a global reduction in emissions, this mechanism allows reductions to be made where they can be obtained in the most economic way and reduces the total economic cost of environmental protection. The same applies to airline slots, fishing quotas, milk quotas, taxi licenses, etc. This model also makes it possible to save the use of certain rights ("banking") in order to use them at another time or place.

reminds us, since the regulated groups are longing for them. The same applies to the costs of monitoring compliance, which may be higher for directives. Furthermore, reiterated application of directives does not necessarily diminish their effectiveness: incentives can be targeted at "saturated" recipients. Finally, directives can have in their execution phase the advantage of greater legitimacy, but incentives, in turn, have the advantage of being desired first and foremost by the recipients—who are obviously very interested in the execution of incentives, even when the administration does not apply them adequately.

It follows from this that any generic assertion about advantages and disadvantages of one or the other system of regulation must be replaced by a case-by-case examination of each of the possible incentives or directives to be applied and their comparison. And in this comparison the legislator, without prejudice towards one formula or the other—incentives or directives—, must take into account the costs, the benefits, the impact on the economy in general, the obligations assumed by public authorities and, of course, how the costs and benefits are spread among the citizens (OECD 2005).

7.4 Directive-Based Regulation

Among the instruments of social management available to public authorities, the most important is still the promulgation of norms, rules or directives that impose certain obligations on citizens and that are usually enforced through the threat of sanctions. Some call this social management mechanism "regulation by directives", or regulation by *command-and-control* or simply regulation.[8]

The reasons for the prevalence of this type of normative instrument is not well known. Possibly, as noted earlier, the expansion of regulatory activity is inseparable from the emergence of the administrative state, characterised by the increasingly detailed measures adopted by public authorities and the increasing bureaucratisation required by the multiplicity and complexity of modern life; regulatory interventionism is justified on the basis of the need to correct market failures (OECD 1992) or to achieve certain political and social goals. But it may also grow for the simple reason that it has been institutionalised—as Kahn (1990) points out, once regulation is in place it tends to be progressive and cumulative.

The Canadian House of Commons (1993) *Report on Regulation and Competitiveness* considers that governments' preference for this technique is not based on its superiority in terms of effectiveness or efficiency but on other reasons. First of all, its greater tangibility and visibility must be underlined: for example, setting a precise limit to the amount of pollution that companies can release into the atmosphere gives the impression that the government is getting involved in the issue and willing to intervene; on the contrary, explaining that the fight against pollution can be done by

[8]See OECD 1994: GD (94)59, *Improving the Quality of Laws and Regulations.*

Table 7.1 Types and degrees of regulatory intervention (Ogus 1994)

Degree of intervention		
Low	High	
Information	Directives	Authorisation
	Directives	
Goal directives	Result-oriented directives	Specification directives

more indirect and less coercive means can give the impression that the government is in doubt or, worse, has been captured by private interests. A second reason are the lower costs that regulation entails for governments, for most costs are borne by the citizens: since governments can offer solutions without having to find the financial means to meet the costs, the use of regulation becomes particularly attractive in times of scarcity of resources. Thirdly, we would point out that the attractiveness of regulation is all the greater because most of the costs are camouflaged: they are reflected in the higher prices of the products we buy, or in the weaker returns due to the lower productivity of labour or capital. Therefore, while the benefits of regulation are visible and known, the costs are often hidden and undervalued. These are some of the possible explanations for the preference for regulation.

The type of directives the legislator can use in this respect are different. Atienza and Ruiz Manero (1996, pp. 40–41) have distinguished, following von Wright, between rules of action and rules of purpose (*normas de acción* and *normas de fin*), whereas others suggest distinguishing between rules of action or omission, rules prescribing a state of affairs, rules of activity, and genuine rules of purpose (González Lagier 2007, p. 109 ff). But from a practical point of view, and within the framework of a theory of regulation, the distinction that Ogus (1994, pp. 150–151) makes is preferable (Table 7.1). For him, if we take into account the degree of regulatory intervention, a distinction should be made between a low level of intervention (rules requiring reporting about a particular activity) and a maximum level of intervention (the requirement of prior authorisation to carry out the activity). The intermediate zone would include the directives or norms that may set or require objectives, results or specifications.

As a regulatory technique, *information* consists in imposing, on the norm addressees, the obligation to disclose certain facts or data about their activity without adding further controls on their autonomy (a variation of this technique is e.g. be the imposition of an obligation to register a product). *Goal directives* or target standards allow the regulated parties freedom to pursue their activity but impose on them the obligation of achieving a certain objective (not to cause harm for example), making them accountable if the objective is not accomplished. *Result-oriented directives* or performance standards require that the final products or services have certain characteristics which are determined by the norm, but leave open what procedures and techniques are to be applied to achieve them. *Specification directives or standards*, or conception norms, determine that certain procedures must be followed in the production or distribution process, or that certain substances or materials must be used or avoided. Finally, *authorisation* is the technique that prevents the exercise of a particular activity without prior licensing by the relevant public body. Needless to say, the effectiveness of all these normative techniques—ordered here from lesser to greater coercive intensity—is backed by civil, administrative or criminal sanctions.

7.5 Norms Requiring the Provision of Information

The provision of appropriate information is an important regulatory tool (Majone 1993, p. 21). In certain cases, regulation by publication of facts can indeed be considered as an alternative to more conventional regulation. In this regard, public authorities may follow a twofold approach: on the one hand, they may try to influence citizens' behaviour by providing the information at their disposal, i.e. by disclosing public-held information; and, on the other, they may force those who possess certain relevant information to make it public, under the threat of applying sanctions if this information is not provided (Cranston 1993). The premise underlying both assumptions is the same: once certain data is made public and certain information gaps are corrected, citizens will know how to protect their interests without the need for further public directives.

As Ogus (1994) points out, the imposition of such obligations can be justified from different perspectives. For the public interest theory, the obligation to inform is justified by the need to correct information deficits: the market requires that citizens have sufficient information to make rational decisions. It is true that the dynamics of the market itself contains incentives for producers and suppliers of goods and services to inform their customers of the most relevant characteristics of their offers. The legitimate desire to increase sales and hence profit is a powerful incentive to provide information in a competitive economy. There are situations, tough, in which producers and suppliers do not have sufficient economic incentives to provide information: this occurs when the marginal cost of not providing information is equal to, or greater than, the marginal benefit that would be obtained with it. The efficiency criterion is an excellent justification for using this regulatory instrument.

Efficiency is not the only reason to increase the information made available to citizens: also the very functioning of democracy demands it. It is difficult for citizens and their representatives to make sensible decisions without the necessary information. Democracy requires debate, deliberation, the exchange of well-documented arguments on the different options in order to make the best choices, etc. Without information, there is neither deliberation nor democracy. That is why respect for the right of citizens to know, which is sometimes expressly provided for in constitutional or legal texts, is essential. This is the case of Art 51 of the Spanish Constitution,[9] of

[9] According to Art. 51 of the Spanish Constitution, "public authorities shall guarantee the protection of consumers and users and shall, by means of effective measures, safeguard their safety, health and legitimate financial interests" (Art. 51.1); "public authorities shall make means available to inform and educate consumers and users, shall foster their organisations, and shall provide hearings for such organisations on all matters affecting their members" (Art. 51.2).

Art. 18 of the Spanish Act on the protection of consumers and users,[10] or of Art. 129a of the Treaty on European Union.[11] In addition to the reasons related to efficiency and to the good functioning of the democratic system, information can be justified for reasons of distributive justice: it can be rightly assumed that citizens without sufficient economic means are usually less informed; so the obligation to give them information could increase their well-being in relation to those who are more prepared or do not mind paying for information. In any case, for one or the other reasons, whether based on the private or public interest, it is true that public authorities—instead of prohibiting certain conduct or products or regulating their content or forms of production—leave producers and suppliers free to make the offers they deem appropriate and simply oblige them to provide information on price, quantity, identity, quality, composition and/or designation, as well as warnings and instructions for use.[12]

[10]According to Art. 18.2 of the Legislative Royal Decree 1/2007, approving the consolidated text of the General Act on the protection of consumers and users and other complementary legislation, "all goods and services made available to consumers and users must include (. . .) clear, comprehensible, truthful, effective and sufficient information on their essential characteristics, and in particular on (a) the name and address of the producer; (b) the nature, composition and purpose [of the product or service]; (c) the quality, quantity, category and common designation and, where applicable, commercial designation; (d) the date of production or supply and the lot and, where required by law, the expiration date or the recommended date of consumption; (e) the instructions or indications for its proper use or consumption, warnings and previsible risks.

[11]The European Union Treaty, signed in Maastricht on 7 February 1992, considers specifically as European Community action its "contribution to strengthening consumer protection" (Art. 3.5 of the EC Treaty), which is developed in Art. 129a, which reads as follows: "The Community shall contribute to the attainment of a high level of consumer protection through (a) measures adopted pursuant to Art. 100a in the context of the competition of the internal market and (b) specific action which supports and supplements the policy pursued by the Member States to protect the health, safety and economic interests of consumers and to provide adequate information to consumers". Following the subsidiarity principle (EU action constitutes the lowest common denominator of protection), the Treaty does not prevent Member States "from maintaining or introducing more stringent protective measures", provided that these are "compatible with this Treaty" and the European Commission is "notified of them" (Art. 129a.3). According to Art. 169 of the Treaty on the Functioning of the European Union (consolidated version), "(1) In order to promote the interests of consumers and to ensure a high level of consumer protection, the Union shall contribute to protecting the health, safety and economic interests of consumers, as well as to promoting their right to information, education and to organise themselves in order to safeguard their interests; (2) The Union shall contribute to the attainment of the objectives referred to in paragraph 1 through: (a) measures adopted (. . .) in the context of the completion of the internal market; (b) measures which support, supplement and monitor the policy pursued by the Member States; (3) The European Parliament and the Council (. . .) shall adopt the measures referred to in paragraph 2(b); (4) Measures adopted pursuant to paragraph 3 shall not prevent any Member State from maintaining or introducing more stringent protective measures. Such measures must be compatible with the Treaties. The Commission shall be notified of them". With regard to the Spanish Constitution, it is worth recalling Art. 51, which refers to the protection of consumers and users.

[12]See Ogus (1994) for a detailed study on when and under what circumstances it is justified to impose such an information duty.

This kind of regulation promotes competitiveness and efficacy; preserves the stimulus for innovation; can contribute to improving the quality of products, services and practices; facilitates the rational choice of citizens; and allows the use of certain products which would otherwise be considered unsafe (cf. Gouvernement du Canada 1994). The costs of establishing these obligations (i.e. the costs for governments) and the costs of complying with them (i.e. the costs for citizens and businesses) are not very high. This technique can be really useful when there are information asymmetries and the lack of information is the cause of the behaviour that needs correcting; when the products or services are complex, relatively expensive and of infrequent use; or when there is an accelerated technological development in the regulated field, the risk levels are moderate or low, and no company is sufficiently motivated by the market to voluntarily disclose the necessary information.

However, this regulatory mechanism may be insufficient when citizens are not aware of the information deficit or when the information is complex or even unintelligible, or so voluminous that it cannot be processed; or in situations where, with or without information, citizens have no choice—for example, due to their limited economic capacity (see Cranston 1993; Sunstein 2004). This technique may also be insufficient if the health or safety risks associated with a given product are high—this may require a more rigorous intervention; or if there is a pressing or urgent need to bring about social or behavioural changes—if based on information alone, changes are slower or more unlikely. In a nutshell: while this instrument is definitely valuable in some scenarios, it may be indequate in many others, where public decision makers will have to explore more interventionist approaches.

7.6 Goal or Target Norms, Performance Norms, and Specification Norms

The imposition of information obligations is therefore not always an effective and sufficient social management mechanism. Sometimes other means are required. Perhaps one of the tools that leaves the greatest margin of autonomy to citizens is the use of *goal* or *target norms*.[13] A direction is set, a social goal—protecting the environment, public safety, food safety, ensuring health, etc.—, but no action is established that is causally linked to this objective (González Lagier 2007, p. 114). An example can be found in Art. 11 of the Spanish Act on Consumer and User Protection, which states that "products or services made available on the market must be safe", i.e. under normal circumstances "they shall not involve any risks to the health or safety of persons" except for "those minimal risks" that are "deemed admissible within a high level of health and safety protection". These are the genuine target norms: there is no indication of the procedures to be followed for the

[13]Goal norms have a certain similarity with what Hart and Sacks (1958, pp. 138–143) call "standards" viz. normative instruments pointing to a given direction. Cf. also Westerman (2007).

production of specific goods, or the characteristics they should have; they simply require that they do not cause any harm to consumers and users. It is an apparently attractive procedure (Ogus 1994, p. 163 ff) because it leaves citizens or companies autonomy to determine the best way to achieve the prescribed result, and public authorities do not have to worry about the causal links behind the intended goal. However, it is not always easy to determine where a particular problem originates and what needs to be done to prevent it. In addition, persons bound by this kind of rules may end up subject to a triple liability regime: administrative, civil and criminal. Anthony I. Ogus considers this type of regulation useful when the issue to be tackled affects many people but is small enough to make it impossible to rely simply on the civil liability regime, because the cost of the private claim would be higher in each individual case than the potential benefit that could be derived from it.

Among the various forms of what we have called regulation by directives, the second type of norms to be considered are *result* or *performance norms*. These norms require that the final output or product meets certain conditions or characteristics but leave it up to the regulated party to choose the most convenient way of achieving the requisite result. Consider, for example, the following provision, taken from a Spanish regulation on labelling and packaging: "foodstuffs produced exclusively for export to countries outside the European Economic Community which do not comply with the provisions in force for the internal market must be packaged and so labelled, that they are unambiguously identified as such in order to prevent their consumption on the national market".[14] The product must therefore be identifiable: how to achieve this is something that the rule leaves to the discretion of the interested party.

Specification norms are markedly different: instead of setting the objectives to be accomplished, they determine the procedures to follow, or the materials that can or must be used, in the production of certain goods—for this reason, they have been also called *technological* norms. Upon the assumption (or the certainty) that there is causal link between specific actions or specific technical patterns and the desired results, norm addresses are required to carry out such actions or respect such patterns. Art. 33 of the Spanish General Regulation on the Public Service of Combustible Gases offers us one of the many examples of this norms that can be found in any legal order: "The Ministry of Industry will indicate in the concession contract the quantitative composition and other characteristics of the gas, as well as the pressure inside the distribution network and at the user terminal. In any case, the permissible variation of the upper calorific value (HCV) shall be -2% of the value fixed as a basis, and its maximum spontaneous variation shall not exceed +/-5%". The complexity of certain products or services; their high cost, infrequent use or consumption; the relatively slow pace of certain technological changes; and the values and assets at stake (health and safety, for example) are often factors favouring the use of these norms.

[14] Art. 2 of the Royal Decree 1122/1988, of 23 September 1988.

It is true that these norms provide valuable information on when there is compliance and when there isn't, thus reducing uncertainty for producers and consumers or users. Resorting to these norms may also reduce the costs of inspection and control since these operations will be limited to verifying the presence or absence of certain elements or the follow-up of certain procedures. Against this kind of norms (OECD 1993), however, it can be said that they do not always take into account the diversity of situations and the different capacities of people; that they are too rigid to adapt to new situations and technologies, and thus may become obsolete very soon; that, since they focus on procedures instead of results, compliance with them may turn out to be merely ritual or "formalistic"; or that they can require the continuous production of new rules to fill in the gaps that social and economic dynamics can bring about, and may sometimes pose a real obstacle to technological competition and innovation.

Experts and analysts (OECD 1993) have been denouncing that public authorities generally tend to the use of specification norms rather than performance norms, and suggest that, where possible, this preference be reversed. The reasons for this is that performance norms have significant advantages over the rest of norms. For example, compared to norms that simply require the provision of information, performance norms offer a better response to the social demand for safety when it comes to the use or consumption of certain products: citizens may find it absolutely insufficient that public authorities simply supply or require the provision of information, and may call for a greater "commitment" to consumer protection on the part of governments. Performance standards, on the other hand, reduce the costs of information provision for businesses, and also reduce the need for citizens to process too much or complex information.

Compared now to specification standards, performance standards leave more room for citizens and entrepreneurs to develop innovative production methods, reduce the barriers to competition that overly detailed regulation can create, and enable significant savings to be made. It is also true, however, that it is sometimes the citizens and the companies who prefer specification norms because of the greater security they generate by allowing them to know precisely what can and should be done and what should not be done (Mannix 1994, p. 11). Certain companies cannot take this risk, particularly those whose commercial success depends on their public reputation. Technical specifications—because of their rigidity—allow these companies to know without any ambiguity that their products comply with the regulatory framework in force. In these cases, it is the need for certainty that matters, even if this regulatory approach proves more expensive and/or less effective. Yet, this is also a technique that can be very problematic for public authorities: although it is true that performance norms are less costly to draw up when compared to specification norms, their inspection and control costs are higher, because they require expert personnel to assess when the requisite yields have or have not been obtained.

It is therefore impossible to determine *a priori* when one or the other technique is advisable: each specific regulatory scenario must be examined carefully before taking a decision. And in many cases, a combination of techniques is likely to be the proper solution, i.e. both target, performance and specification standards will often have to coexist. Some scholars have proposed a two-pronged strategy: maintaining technical norms as a default or fallback technique, and setting performance norms for those companies that prefer higher degrees of autonomy. In the latter case, citizens or companies could prove that they have achieved the results demanded by the regulation, even if they have not followed the procedures laid down in technical or specification norms. And, of course, what is true for private companies can also be said of regional markets such as the EU: behind the discussions about harmonisation, standardisation and mutual recognition techniques within the EU stands a debate between performance norms and specification norms (Braithwaite 1993)—a debate which we have just outlined roughly.

7.7 Authorisations and Licences

A final regulatory technique to which we will refer, and which represents the maximum degree of interventionism, is the technique of authorisations and licences. This technique intervenes ex ante, trying to prevent what is considered undesirable from happening. To this end, it is established that a certain activity may not be carried out without prior permission from the administration. Such preliminary interventions are called by many different names: authorisations, permits, licenses, visas, registrations, etc. Whatever their name and nature might be according to the legal doctrine (García de Enterría 1991, p. 133 ff), for the Spanish legislator they refer to "those administrative acts, whatever their specific name, by which, in the exercise of a power of intervention legally attributed to the Administration, individuals are allowed to exercise an activity, subject to verification of their compliance with the legal system and assessment of the public interest concerned".[15]

There is scholarly debate over to the difference between authorisation and concession, a distinction that is not always easy to draw. It is claimed that, in the case of concessions, there is no prior right on the side of the beneficiary, whereas such a right does pre-exist in the case of authorisations. An operative criterion for distinguishing these two notions is the one offered by Parada (1995, p. 440), according to which the concept of authorisation must be applied to cases in which there is no limitation on the number of beneficiaries of the right, nor discretion in the granting of the authorisation (as occurs, for example, with driving licenses, hunting licenses, licenses to open educational establishments, urban planning licenses, etc.). The concession technique should be reserved to cases in which legislation clearly allows discretionality in the award of permits or limits the number of beneficiaries of the right according to legally defined conditions. The scope of authorisations is so wide that it is not quite clear whether a complete classification of them is useful or

[15]Art. 1 of the Royal Decree 1778/1994, of 5 August 1994, adapting the rules governing the procedures for granting, amending and terminating authorisations to the Act 30/1992 on Public Administrations and Common Administrative Procedure.

even possible: they range from the practice of certified professions to the manipulation of certain products or the exercise of property rights over land or subsoil.

Moreover, the justifications for the establishment of these limitations are different depending on the cases. In the case of the practice of certain qualified professions, public interest theory often bases such limitations of rights on the need to fill information gaps (Ogus 1994, p. 214 ff): in many cases a user cannot assess the quality of a professional service—e.g. a medical service—after it was provided, i.e. *a posteriori*. In such cases, the civil liability regime may be insufficient because the costs in money and time of bringing legal action are often high—e.g. it may be difficult to find a doctor willing to testify to the malpractice. Another justification for the use of the licensing technique is the existence of externalities, since the better or worse quality of the service can affect not only the customer but also third parties: think, for example, of the risks posed to third parties by a poorly designed building, a defective nuclear power plant, inadequate or lax audits, etc. Something similar may occur with other professions or activities or with the handling of certain products: in view of the legal goods at stake, it is assumed that it is better to authorise such activities on a case-by-case basis than to regulate their exercise through target, performance or specification norms.

Of course, such authorisations do not always easily pass the public interest test. Up to 400 activities have been counted in the USA that require a previous authorisation for their exercise: hunting, fishing, the use of firearms, opening of theaters, cinemas, bakeries or butcher shops, taxi driving, astrology, house-to-house mailing, funeral homes... We find similar results when we examine the European system. The problem here is to justify on a case-by-case basis the reasons for resorting to such an interventionist technique—which is not always applied to defend the public interest but is often intended to protect private interests, such as limiting competition of other professionals. Obviously, this is one of the most intrusive techniques and one against which there is a very strong push in our economic systems because they involve an unjustified alteration of the laws of the market, as has been denounced in Spain, among many others, by the Tribunal for Defence of Competition.[16]

[16]See the 1992 Report of the Tribunal for Defence of Competition on the free exercise of professions (*Informe sobre el libre ejercicio de las profesiones. Remedios politicos que pueden favorecer la libre competencia en los servicios públicos y atajar el daño causado por los monopolios*); and the National Commission on Competition's recommendations to the public administrations with regard to a more efficient and competition-fostering regulation (*Recomendaciones a las Administraciones Públicas para una regulación de los mercados más eficiente y favorecedora de la competencia*, 2008). Cf. also the Code of Conduct for the Members of the National Securities Market Commission (CNMV 2003) and the Good Governance Code for Securities Firms (CNMV 2015).

7.8 Commercialisation of Licences

A hybrid or mixed form of regulation is one that allows the sale and purchase of authorisations and licenses. Here, the idea is to combine the regulatory technique of licensing with market techniques: following the corresponding legal procedure, the administration assigns a licence or authorisation that becomes part of the holder's assets. Thus, this licence—provided that it was not granted because of the holder's particular and specific attributes— may be transferred to third parties, and it is the market that "controls" the practice of the activity or the use of the resources in question.

This kind of mechanism began to be applied in U.S. environmental policy. Between 1982 and 1987, the transferability of authorisations and licences was used as a strategy against pollution. The new approach was initiated by the conservative Bush Administration. For its promoters, before opting for one type of intervention or another, it was important to consider that, if they are properly structured, economic incentives offer two major advantages over command and control regulation. First, they enable companies and other stakeholders to meet the objectives of the regulation in the least costly way. Second, the market incentive-based approach benefits those who reduce costs or offer better levels of control through technological innovation (EPA 1992). And thus a program for the reduction of lead in petrol was established which operated as follows: the Environmental Protection Agency (EPA) established different levels of lead for refineries, not allowing the least flexibility with the overall goal of pollution reduction. The EPA established a uniform standard for lead content and authorised the negotiation of credits between refineries and importers: those who managed to reduce the level of lead below the established limit could "save" the difference for the future or sell it to those who had exceeded the limit. This scheme (not without criticism since it treats the environment as any other commodity) was extended to other sectors: "When governments around the world have begun to explore better ways to protect the environment, they have discovered that market mechanisms—pollution quotas, negotiated pollution systems, deposit systems—can be effective alternatives to regulation" (U.S. Government 1994, p. 62).

The exchange of such licences or authorisations serves two main purposes. On the one hand, it minimises the costs of pollution control by reducing major emissions where they are less costly, allowing for stronger emissions where the costs of depuration are higher. On the other hand, the aim is to reconcile economic development and environmental protection by allowing new firms to settle in a given area without increasing the total polluting emissions in that area. The new company may "buy" *pollution rights* from one or more other companies which will in turn have to reduce emissions by the same amount.

Today, these techniques are applied, depending on the country, to the control of air pollution, water pollution, fishing quotas, building permits, broadcast frequency allocation, mining, etc., sectors in which the aim is to create a market. The Kyoto Protocol itself, designed to reduce global warming, has created a whole series of mechanisms for the trading of emission rights in the hope that the reduction of the pollutant emissions will be carried out by those companies that can do so in the most efficient way—it is not yet clear if this hope is justified (Lomborg 2001, p. 303). One of the most emblematic and innovative mechanisms in the fight against climate change has been the commercialisation of emission rights and the creation of an international carbon market (United Nations 2007).

As an intervention mechanism, the market of licences or authorisations can be very useful for public authorities in terms of costs: public authorities do not need to have the detailed and complex information that would be necessary to draw up a regulatory framework. It can also be cheaper for companies, because they are not coerced into certifying their production processes; and it allows them greater autonomy, benefiting those companies that produce more efficiently and cleanly. Moreover, the economic stimulus is permanent so the incentive to reduce pollution will be constant, and this can lead to faster results. On the other hand, however, public opinion may not accept this regulatory mechanism, which turns certain particularly important public goods—such as air, water, forests, oceans, etc.—into commodities; and, as market failures may also occur, a strong system of monitoring and control seems to be necessary.

The point we are making here, however, is not so much the desirability of this technique—which is highly questioned in the field of environmental protection. The purpose of referring to it was to point to yet another instrument of intervention available to public authorities—whether it is implemented, or not, must be evaluated on a case-by-case basis. Anyway, the reference to this mechanism serves to emphasise once again that the important issue is how to combine the various regulatory instruments at hand. This is another of the challenges the social state faces today.

References

Atienza M, Ruiz Manero J (1996) Las piezas del Derecho. Ariel, Barcelona

Austin J (2002) El objeto de la Jurisprudencia. Centro de Estudios Constitucionales, Madrid

Bentham J (1981a) Idea general de un cuerpo completo de legislación. In: Tratado de Legislación Civil y Penal. Editora Nacional, Madrid

Bentham J (1981b) De los medios indirectos de prevenir los delitos. In: Tratado de Legislación Civil y Penal. Editora Nacional, Madrid

Bentham J (1988) The principles of morals and legislation. Prometheus Books, New York

Bobbio N (1984) La funzione promozionale del diritto rivisitata. Sociologia del Diritto 3:7–77

Braithwaite J (1993) Perspectives d'un rapprochement international des réglementations à cent pour cent de réussite. OECD, Paris

CNMV (National Securities Market Commission) (2003) Código general de conducta para los miembros de la Comisión Nacional de Valores. Comisión Nacional del Mercado de Valores (CNMV), Madrid

CNMV (National Securities Market Commission) (2015) Código de buen gobierno de las sociedades cotizadas. Comisión Nacional del Mercado de Valores (CNMV), Madrid

Cranston R (1993) Reform through legislation: the dimension of legislative technique. Northwest Univ Law Rev 73(5):873–875

EPA (Environment Protection Agency) (1992) Regulatory Program of the United States Government
Fernández Farreres G (1983) La subvención, concepto y régimen jurídico. Instituto de Estudios Fiscales, Madrid
Fernández Farreres G (1993) El régimen de las ayudas estatales en la Comunidad Europea. Fundación Universidad-Empresa, Madrid
García Añoveros J et al (1995) Manual del Sistema Tributario Español. Civitas, Madrid
García de Enterría E (1991) Curso de Derecho Administrativo, vol II. Civitas, Madrid
González Lagier D (2007) Algunas precisiones sobre la noción de contenido normativo en *Normative Systems*. In: Moreso JJ, Redondo C (eds) Un diálogo con la teoría del derecho de Eugenio Bulygin. Marcial Pons, Madrid, pp 109–116
Gouvernement du Canada (1994) Evaluation des solutions de rechange à la réglementation. Guide des Affaires Réglementaires, Ottawa
Grant RW (2006) Ethics and incentives: a political approach. Am Polit Sci Rev 100:29–39
Hart HM, Sacks AM (1958) The legal process. In: Tentative (ed) Basic problems in the making and application of law. Cambridge (MA) [Foundation Press, Westbury, 1994]
Holmes OW (1897) The path of the law. Harv Law Rev 10: 457–478 [La senda del Derecho, Abeledo-Perrot, Buenos Aires, 1975]
Hood C (1983) The tools of government. Macmillan, London
House of Commons (Canada) (1993) Reglémentation et compétitivité. Dix-septième Rapport du Commité Permanente des Finances de la Chambre des Communs. Premier Rapport du Sous-Comité de la Réglementation et de la Competitivité. Chambre del Communs, Ottawa
Kahn A (1990) Deregulation: looking backward and looking forward. Yale J Regul 7:325–354
Lomborg B (2001) The skeptical environmentalist. Cambridge University Press, Cambridge
Majone G (1993) Comparaison des stratégies de reprochement dans le domaine reglamentaire. OECD, Paris
Mannix B (1994) Améliorer le rapport cout-efficacité de la gestion gouvernamentale: formules proposées pour remplacer les réglementations visant "imponer et contrôler". OCDE, Paris
Mitnick BM (1989) La economía política de la regulación. FCE, México [The political economy of regulation. creating, designing, and removing regulatory forms. Columbia University Press, New York, 1989]
OECD (1992) Gestion et reforme de la réglementation: sujets de reflexion dans les pays membres de l'OCDE. OECD (Service de la Gestion Publique, Paris
OECD (1993) Liste provisoire de formules réglementaires et non réglementaires. OECD (Service de la Gestion Publique, Paris
OECD (1994) Improving the quality of laws and regulations: economic, legal and managerial techniques [OCDE/GD (94) 59]. OECD, Paris
OECD (2005) Guiding Principles for Regulatory Quality and Performance (adopted by the OECD Council on 28 April 2005). OECD, Paris
Ogus AI (1994) Regulation. Legal form and economic theory. Clarendon Press, Oxford
Parada R (1995) Derecho Administrativo. Parte General. Marcial Pons, Madrid
Pérez Lledó JA (2000) Sobre la función promocional del derecho. Doxa 23:665–687
Pérez Royo F (1995) Derecho Financiero y Tributario. Parte General, 5th edn. Civitas, Madrid
Plato (1992) Gorgias. In: Diálogos, vol II. Biblioteca Clásica Gredos, Madrid
Sunstein CR (2004) Risk and reason. Safety, law and the environment. Cambridge University Press, Cambridge [Riesgo y Razón. Seguridad, ley y medio ambiente. Katz, Buenos Aires, 2006]
Thaler RH, Sunstein CR (2009) Nudge. Improving decisions about health, wealth and happiness, rev edn. Penguin Books, London
U.S. Government (1994) Creating a Government that works better and costs less. Report of the National Performance Review. U.S. Government Printing Office, Washington DC
United Nations (2007) Unidos por el Clima. Guía de la Convención sobre Cambio Climático y el Protocolo de Kyoto. Climate Change Secretariat (UNFCCC), Bonn
Westerman P (2007) Governing by goals: governance as a legal style. Legisprudence 1(1):51–73
Zorzetto S, Ferraro F (2019) Legislation and nudging: towards a suitable definition. In: Oliver-Lalana AD (ed) Conceptions and misconceptions of legislation. Springer, Cham

Chapter 8
Models of Legislative Drafting

If every norm is the expression of, or the instrument for, the implementation of a public policy, its elaboration usually involves a process—sometimes a highly complex one—where a number of agents at different levels participate, with each of them performing differentiated functions. In view of this plurality of agents involved in their elaboration, Karl Olivecrona (1980, p. 127) was right to describe laws as impersonal imperatives. One of the professional groups that have an important role to play in any normative system are jurists. It may well happen that public policy experts—whose mission would be to identify problems, to analyse their causes, to look for possible solutions and to evaluate their advantages and disadvantages—are not called upon to participate (Meny and Thoenig 1992, p. 136); but it is very difficult to imagine this process without the involvement of a jurist in charge of preparing the draft norm.[1] Of course, the draft does not become valid law until the competent legal body or organ touches it with "the sceptre of its authority", but it is no less true that the persons who finally decide upon a legislative draft often confine themselves to ratify it; hence the importance of the role of jurists as drafters. It is therefore surprising how little attention is paid to their work, to their procedures, skills, abilities and—given the political, economic and social repercussions of their work—to the codes of conduct they follow. Some reflection on these points is certainly worth the while.

[1]Lord Renton (1990, pp. 13 ff) distinguishes the following four phases in the elaboration of a law: elaboration of the policy, preparation by the ministerial officers of the instructions for the drafters, the actual drafting of the bill, and the examination of the bill in both Houses.

V. Zapatero Gómez, *The Art of Legislating*, Legisprudence Library 6,
https://doi.org/10.1007/978-3-030-23388-4_8

Table 8.1 Legislative activity (1978–1982)

	Government bills		Private members' bills	
	Submitted	Passed	Submitted	Passed
Germany	396	400	139	80
Australia	1025	917	46	2
Austria	370	355	200	100
Belgium	276	380	934	66
Canada	222	133	838	18
Denmark	855	757	444	25
Spain	400	323	286	38
France	467	384	1638	57
Greece	639	491	94	0
Ireland	209	188	20	2
Italy	1672	858	4021	371
Holand	1690	1431	25	4
Luxemburg	317	320	25	5
Portugal	630	86	273	130
England	287	265	502	49
Sweden	1000	1000	12,000	1

8.1 The Protagonism of Governments

That governments must play a leading role in regulatory production is obvious—in the Spanish Constitution, for instance, the government is explicitly accorded "the regulatory power", i.e., the function of issuing regulations to implement and develop parliamentary legislation (Art. 97 CE).[2] What may be somewhat paradoxical, however, is that even in parliamentary systems—or in most of them—, it is also the government that normally elaborates and drafts the laws (Table 8.1).

Leaning on the data provided by the Inter-Parliamentary Union,[3] one might draw at least three provisional conclusions. First, it is clear that the so-called legislative initiative is usually exercised by the executive branch: in parliamentary democracies, most of the texts submitted to parliament are draft laws prepared by the government. This is highlighted by the Inter-Parliamentary Union's review of the work of 69 parliaments (IPU 1987): in 33 of the world's major parliaments, between 90% and 100% of the projects originate from the cabinet (government bills). Secondly, the vast majority of the projects presented by governments are usually approved by parliaments. Indeed, after examining the activity of 60 parliaments (IPU 1987, p. 1047), we can see that in 42 of them the parliament approved between 90% and 100% of the projects submitted by the government. And thirdly, the information

[2]Now I leave aside issues like the weakening of the regulatory force of legislation, or its increasingly limited capacity to govern society—what some call "legislative hypostenia" (Pérez Luño 1993, pp. 80 ff).

[3]Table 8.1 (legislative activity 1978–1982): origin of the legislative (government vs. MPs or parliamentary groups) and result of the legislative procedure (submitted vs. passed).

provided by the Inter-Parliamentary Union shows that few legislative initiatives coming from parliamentary groups (i.e., non-governmental, private member bills) are in fact approved: if we limit ourselves to considering how the impulse to legislate has been distributed in Spain in the decade 1982–1992, the data are equally eloquent.[4] In addition, it should be noted that in parliamentary systems most of the proposals approved by the parliament are either drafted by the executive services,[5] or are commissioned by the parliamentary majority that supports the government, or are approved after consultation between parliamentarians and the government.

The above data confirm that governments play a leading role in the drafting of laws. This is not only because the regulatory authority resides mainly in the executive, but also because, even with legislative projects that are shared with parliament, the drafting of bills falls mainly on the administration services. The only exceptions to this rule are presidentialist systems, such as the United States, where the separation of powers and their institutional configuration make the executive's role in the drafting of laws much less relevant, even practically non-existent.

And thus, three models can be clearly distinguished in terms of where the initiative of drafting laws resides: the governmental model,[6] which can in turn be split into the *Anglo-Saxon model* (that has extended its influence to the regulatory systems of the Commonwealth) and the *European continental model*, and the *presidentialist model*. In the first typical model, the Anglo-Saxon model, the drafting of bills is entrusted to and concentrated in a specialised body within the administration which acts on the basis of preexisting instructions. The approval of the text, on the other hand, is the responsibility of a political body such as the Cabinet. This system clearly separates the technical instance of drafting a law and the political instance of deciding on its approval. It is therefore a concentrated model of drafting legal texts. For its part, in the European model, which—in the absence of a better name—we will call continental, each ministerial department is normally responsible for drafting bills on matters of its competence: it is a governmental and distributed or "deconcentrated" drafting system. As far as the presidentialist model is concerned, the drafting of bills is not carried out in the government headquarters but in the Houses. However, in all three systems, including the presidentialist model, the role of jurists, whether as civil servants or as recruited staff, is crucial in the drafting of both regulations and bills.

---

[4]See further Zapatero (1996).

[5]Even in China the Bureau of Legislative Affairs was created as an advisory body to the State Council. In 1990, the Bureau of Legislative Affairs employed 260 people, including 164 draftmen. In addition, a Legal Affairs Department was created in each ministry, employing both jurists and non-jurists (with a total of ca. 1200 people working in all departments) who are responsible not only for drafting and formal issues but also for the content of laws (see Seidman and Seidman 1996).

[6]The main norms regulating this process in Europe can be found in Pagano (1988) and Santaolalla (2008).

8.2 The Continental European Drafting System

We find a first example[7] of governmental and distributed drafting of bills in the Republic of Germany, where the drafting phase of laws has been carefully regulated in the Joint Rules of Procedure of the Federal Ministries (*Gemeinsame Geschäftsordnung der Bundesministerien*), which are supplemented by the recommendations of the Federal Ministry of Justice and the principles established by the Federal Department of Justice and the Ministry of Interior to facilitate the unification of criteria in the field of legal drafting.

In the process preceding the bill's submission to the parliament, three phases are distinguished: the section draft, the department draft, and the government draft. The first draft, or section draft, is prepared by the section responsible for the subject matter within each ministry. It is therefore drafted by ministry officials, even though the work is sometimes entrusted to a commission. These are drafters who, as civil servants, have a legal background and who, when drafting projects, are subject to the existing regulations on the form and structure of laws.[8] These regulations indicate in detail the matters on which the various ministerial departments and other public and private organisations must necessarily be consulted; when the Chancellery's prior authorisation or notice of the content of the project is required; or in which cases the ministers of the *Länder* must be informed and consulted. Once this procedure has been completed, the draft is put through a questionnaire on the necessity, effectiveness and intelligibility of federal draft legislation,[9] being eventually approved by the competent minister, who will forward it to the Ministry of Justice—which is entrusted with the technical and legal revision of the text (this is done by lawyers who are specialised in revising legislative projects coming from each of the different departments).

The text thus drafted is sent to the Head of the Office of the Federal Chancellor. According to the Joint Rules of Procedure, the referral statement will specify whether the draft has been examined from the point of view of its legal form, whether and to what extent the ministries concerned agree with the draft and, where appropriate, whether the draft is urgent. The statement shall also indicate the effects on budgetary revenue and expenditure and in particular the foreseeable costs of implementing the law, highlighting expected increases or decreases in revenue and multi-annual budgetary costs. Once these requirements have been met, the project will be included in the agenda of the Council of Ministers, which will convert it, eventually, into a government project, and will send it to the chambers. In sum, the German model is a "deconcentrated" drafting model, in which the draft is prepared mainly by legal officers in each ministry, while its

[7]See Curcuruto (1985); Dale (1991, 1977); and Olivier (1993).

[8]See the Ministry of Justice's *Handbuch der Rechtsförmlichkeit* (Bundesministerium der Justiz 2008) at: http://hdr.bmj.de/.

[9]*Prüffragen für Rechtsvorschriften des Bundes* (11 December 1984).

legal form is examined and reviewed by the Ministry of Justice, which assumes a great deal of responsibility for the technical correction of laws.

A similar procedure is followed in France (Meny 1986). Bills are drafted within the competent ministries by the legal services of each department; these services are especially well endowed in ministries with a large regulatory output, such as the Ministry of Finance and the Ministry of Justice. Circulars drawn up by the government regulate in detail the procedures, legal form guidelines, and linguistic rules, as well as the consultations to be made and the Council of State's opinions to be taken into account by the officials responsible for writing up the projects.

Particularly relevant at this stage is the work carried out by the Council of State, whose participation in the pre-legislative phase is mandatory. As is well known (Plantey 2005, pp. 55 ff), the Council of State is one of the most important bodies in France's institutional system.[10] And it has, among many other tasks, the function of examining, prior to their discussion in the Council of Ministers, draft bills written by the ministerial departments (Arts. 38 and 39 of the French Constitution). In this process, the Council of State is entrusted not so much with assessing the appropriateness of the bill as with evaluating its consistency with government objectives as well as its formal aspects and style. This procedure often ends with a new text, which is the result of meetings between the delegate appointed by the Council and the government representatives. The text offered by the Council is not binding for the government but, given the prestige of the Council and the quality of its work, it usually determines the final wording to be adopted by the Council of Ministers.

Also actively involved in the process, both before and after the opinion of the Council of State (Lasvignes 2005, pp. 49 ff), is the General Secretariat of the Government's "Service de la Législation et de la Qualitè du Droit". This important administrative unit is responsible for preparing interministerial meetings and for the arbitration between the various departments. Once agreement has been reached between the various ministries on a draft bill, the Secretary-General of the Government proposes the Prime Minister and the President of the Republic its inclusion on the agenda of the Council of Ministers. As we see, the procedure followed in France for drafting legislation is also non concentrated, that is, it is shared by the various ministries, entrusted to legal officers in each ministerial department and supervised by the Council of State, which performs similar functions to the Ministry of Justice in Germany.

A variant of this "continental" model was developed a few years ago in Italy: a 1988 law[11] established a centralised office for legislative coordination (*Ufficio per il coordinamento dell'iniziativa legislativa e dell'attività normativa del Governo*)[12] which may be seen as an attempt to convert the Italian legislative drafting model into

---

[10]See Costa (1993); Long (1992); Luchaire and Conac (1980); or Robineau and Truchet (1994).

[11]*Legge 23 agosto 1988, n. 400, Disciplina dell'attività di Governo e ordinamento della Presidenza del Consiglio dei Ministri.*

[12]For Cassese (1992, p. 414), the lenght of this office's name is directly proportional to its ineffecitivenes.

a mixed system.[13] On paper, this was a system of concentrated drafting for projects initiated by the President of the Council of Ministers, and of diffuse (non-concentrated) drafting for projects originated by ministerial initiative. The latter had to be prepared by the legislative drafting units (*uffici legislativi*) of each ministry, and sometimes by the minister's own office; sometimes external experts were also called upon. The *Ufficcio Centrale* played the role of interministerial coordination: Art. 3 of the Decree of 19 July 1989 (which implemented Art. 23 of the law of 23 August 1988) endowed this institution with a whole series of powers, including the power to request information and documentation on draft projects drawn up by each ministry, and the power to liaise with the units of the various ministries responsible for drafting regulations. Today these tasks are performed by a Unit for Simplification and Quality of Regulation attached to the Department of Legal and Legislative Affairs of the Presidency of the Council of Ministers.[14]

8.3 The Anglo-Saxon System

The Anglo-Saxon system is the alternative model to the drafting system usually followed in continental Europe, and deserves special consideration.[15]

Historically, in the common law tradition, the drafting of bills was a function entrusted to barristers. Practising lawyers therefore were responsible for elaborating draft norms on behalf of the various ministries. It was not until the middle of the nineteenth century that, under the influence of the theses of Bentham (1983)[16] and John Stuart Mill (1994, pp. 61 ff), the administration began to consider it more appropriate to have its own lawyers carry out such a delicate task. Finally, in 1869, the Office of Parliamentary Counsel was created—despite its name, it is formally attached to the Treasury and functionally dependent on the Prime Minister. This office was and remains the body of the executive in charge of drafting the bills included in the government's program. For almost 50 years the Parliamentary Counsel was composed of two advisers; in 1917 it was increased to three, and in 1930 to four advisers. It currently employs lawyers, some of whom are temporarily transferred to the Law Commission (mainly responsible for codification). Some specialised laws are entrusted to external jurists, bust most laws are drafted by the Office of Parliamentary Counsel.

[13]See Cheli and Caretti (1986); Cusmano (1985); Scoti (1985); Strano (1985); or Trocoli (1986). Cf. also Albanesi (2013).

[14]See further http://presidenza.governo.it/DAGL/uff_coordinamento/ufficio_coordinamento.html and http://www.funzionepubblica.gov.it/uffici/unita-la-semplificazione-e-la-qualita-della-regolazione.

[15]See Frosini (1988); Martin Casals and Viver Pi Suñer (1990); or Patchett (1991). Cf. recently Russell and Gover (2017).

[16]See especially Art. 9 ff of Bentham's *Constitutional Code*.

The first characteristic of the British system—that clearly differentiates it from what we have called the continental system—is that it concentrates the responsibility for drafting laws in a single, highly specialised body, the Office of Parliamentary Counsel. A second feature is the separation, or attempted separation, between the responsibility for planning legislation (a task for the cabinet) and the responsibility for drafting it (a task for specialist jurists). This differentiation between planning and drafting implies the need to articulate the connection between the two functions: the so-called *instructions* of the political bodies play a decisive role in this regard. It may be interesting to follow the path of a law, from the moment it appears as a simple idea to the instant it is presented as a bill to parliament.

In England, the birth of a bill always takes place in the autumn, when the Cabinet Office requests from the various departments the list of bills they intend to present to the House of Commons during the following year, which will be announced in the Crown Address. The suggestions of the various ministers are forwarded to the Future Legislation Committee, which includes the parliamentary leaders of both houses and the chief whip of the Commons. At the beginning of the year, the committee examines the proposals with the assistance of the ministers involved and the head of the Parliamentary Counsel. Once agreement has been reached on the list of future bills and their possible timetable, and depending on the progress in the chambers of the bills of the previous term, the new list of bills is passed to the cabinet, which will approve it, and include it in the Crown Address that opens the new parliamentary term. The cabinet will then formally instruct the Parliamentary Counsel on the content of each bill that must be drafted.

Numerous British drafters have explained, in their memoirs or at lectures or conferences, the working method of this elite group of jurists who make up the Office of Parliamentary Counsel. According to Sir Granville Ram (1951) (quoted in Zander 1994, pp. 11 ff), after receiving the instructions (which are usually written) from the cabinet, the task is assigned to a lawyer who contacts the proposing ministerial department and begins to write the draft. From that moment on, a good number of meetings and contacts may be necessary to clarify the government's aims regarding the project. The government, through the representative of the proposing department, is responsible for defining the policy; the drafter is ultimately responsible for the form and style of the bill. As soon as the drafter is confident about the objectives pursued by the government, he or she prepares a first draft, which is submitted to the proposing department for clarification and discussion—if necessary, further instructions may be requested from the cabinet. The draft is reviewed and commented by other lawyers from the Office of Parliamentary Counsel and, when a final text is available, the promoting ministerial department refers it to the Legislation Committee. This committee is chaired by the cabinet's senior minister, Lord Chancellor; and attended by the leaders of both houses, the law officers, the chief whip and any other minister who wishes to participate. Representatives of the Office of Parliamentary Counsel can also attend. If the Legislation Committee approves the proposed text, it shall refer it, with appropriate modifications, to one of the two houses where the bill's parliamentary proceedings begin.

However, the work of the Office of Parliamentary Counsel does not end with the submission of the bill to the houses. This office is also responsible for drafting the amendments presented by the government to its own bills—which make the most part of the amendments approved by the houses. Sometimes, the Office of Parliamentary Counsel also drafts amendments presented by majority parliamentarians with which the government agrees. In this sense, it can be said that the laws in Great Britain are drafted by a very small group of highly specialised and prestigious jurists.

This concentrated procedure for drafting bills has not been exempt from criticism. Sir William Dale (1977, 1991), for instance, has advocated a change in the legislative style, the establishment of a law council in imitation of the French Conseil d'Etat, a greater role for experts in substantive policies and a modification of the organisation and working methods of the chambers. The most significant proposals on the preparation of legislation were those contained in the Renton Report (1975). Anyway, Britain's drafting system is a very influential model, and has been largely followed by all Commonwealth countries.[17]

[17]In Australia, for example, we find a detailed regulation of the composition, the role and the procedures of the Office of Parliamentary Counsel. According to the Parliamentary Counsel Act of 1970 and the *Legislation Handbook* (Department of the Prime Minister and Cabinet, July 1988, updated in February 2017) the procedure is as follows: (a) the Cabinet refers instructions to the Parliamentary Counsel; (b) the Parliamentary Counsel, on the basis of the bills' date of entry into the Chamber assigns the task of drafting to one of the qualified jurists who is assisted by a young jurist; (c) there are as many meetings with the Ministry's policymakers as necessary to clarify and/or extend the instructions; (d) it is also the responsibility of the Parliamentary Counsel to study how the project affects current legislation, which sometimes raises controversial issues. In this regard, the Parliamentary Counsel must consult with the Government's Attorney-General and the Solicitor-General on proposals affecting existing constitutional relationships (e.g., involving prolonged delegation of parliamentary legislative powers to an executive body) or affecting fundamental rights; provisions affecting governmental prerogatives; retroactive provisions; proposals affecting international law or extraterritorial legislation, or which may impose unexpected obligations on the Government; (e) the Parliamentary Counsel's drafting group formulates a legislative plan for the bill which provides an overall structure within which detailed rules can logically be inserted; (f) the Office of Parliamentary Counsel will need to be sensitive to the Government's interests in the parliamentary handling of the Act—a bill is made to be approved; (g) the capacity to maintain a coherent order depends on the number and heterogeneity of subjects that a bill tries to cover; (h) the final wording of the bill: the final wording is increasingly inserted into a database, using a text processing program designed to produce and print the standardised articles of the bill; this practice allows a quick job, high quality, and the monitoring of the changes that are introduced in subsequent procedures; and (i) parliamentary processes. The finalisation of a bill requires an extensive series of consultations between the Parliamentary Counsel and the Department concerned with the exchange of numerous drafts in this regard. The final text will be approved by the Minister and the Legislative Commission. Obviously the drafting process continues in the parliamentary phase. The Office of Parliamentary Counsel monitors the parliamentary process and ensures that each amendment fits perfectly into the text and does not lead to incoherences. The Parliamentary Counsel follows the draft until it is sanctioned. It is an almost British-style procedure with a greater degree of formalisation and regulation.

8.4 The U.S. Drafting System

The American drafting system is radically different from both the continental (distributed) and the British (concentrated) systems (Dickerson 1959, p. 49). The difference between the British and the American systems is that in the former almost all bills passed by parliament are drafted by a small group of people, expert drafters from the Office of Parliamentary Counsel, while in Washington, where legislation is prepared by the Offices of the Legislative Counsel of the House and Senate, by members of the professional staff of the numerous permanent and special committees of Congress, and even by private individuals. Some American scholars argue that the cause of the higher quality of Britain's legislative production compared to the U.S.' is to be found in the fact that in Britain it is the government that controls the legislative program, while in the U.S. it is the Congress, and not the executive, that has the leading role in the production of laws. Similarly, upon studying the production of norms in the U.S., Robert Summers—perhaps somewhat hastily—blames this model of parliamentary initiative (with unprepared parliamentarians, an atomised House and the absence of group discipline) for the fact that American legislation is copious and of very poor quality (Atiyah and Summers 1987, pp. 315 ff).

Obviously, the procedure followed in the U.S. for drafting regulations is also different: since the Clinton's administration this procedure is decentralised in the agencies, but supervised by a centralised, specialised body, the Office of Information and Regulatory Affairs (OIRA), which is attached to the Office of Management and Budget (OMB). Pursuant to the Executive Order 12866 of 30 September 1993—and its subsequent developments—,[18] which set out the regulatory policy of the administration, the model of norm development in the various agencies was reorganised, and the Office of Management and Budget was entrusted with the task of reviewing and studying the "most significant" draft norms. These were understood to be norms which had an impact on any sector of the economy over 100 million dollars; norms which could interfere with the authority or the competences of other agencies; norms which might negatively affect the execution of the budget; and norms which might give rise to legal or political conflict. In this model, each agency has to draw up an annual regulatory plan[19] which the different projects proposed—including their

[18]See Executive Order 12866 (Regulatory Planning and Review) of 30 September 1993. Federal Register 4 October 1993, vol. 58, no. 190. Amended in 2002 and 2007.

[19]These plans have to contain at least the following items: (a) a statement of the department's policy objectives and priorities and their connection to the President's priorities; (b) a summary of the most significant norms being planned, including, as far as possible, alternatives to be considered and preliminary estimates of anticipated costs and benefits; (c) a summary of the legal basis on which the envisaged norm rests, including whether legal or regulatory changes will be required; (d) a justification of the need for regulatory action and, where applicable, of how this action will reduce public health and safety or environmental risks, as well as how severe these risks are compared to other risks which the department has a duty to solve; (e) the department's timeframe for regulatory action; and (f) the contact details of the person appointed to inform interested citizens about the upcoming regulation.

timetables, their costs and the justification of their need, as well as an explanation of the legal basis of the agency's regulatory intervention. These annual plans have to be submitted to the Office of Information and Regulatory Affairs each year in October, together with the text of the most significant drafts. The new regulation cannot be published in the Federal Register until the OIRA had completed the review of both its material and formal aspects.

Thus, the drafting of bills in the U.S.—in contrast to the European systems—follows a parliamentary model and is therefore diffuse, whereas the drafting of regulations is based on a decentralised model (distributed in the agencies) which incorporates centralised supervision by the OIRA; an office which, besides examining the formal quality of draft regulations, focuses mainly on their scope (to make sure that they do not interfere with the powers of other state or federal regulators), as well as on their economic[20] and political repercussions.

8.5 The Spanish System

Constitutional and administrative law experts have studied in detail the procedure followed in Spain for the approval of regulatory provisions by the government. However, the doctrine has left the study of the governmental phase of the production of bills in relative obscurity. It is understood—and rightly so from a formal perspective—that in general terms the drafting of bills by the government does not need to follow a very

[20]If the draft regulation has an economic impact of more than $100 million; if it may adversely affect the economy, employment, competitiveness, the environment, or public health and safety; or if interferes with other regulators' powers, the department in question must also submit the following additional information to OIRA: (a) an analysis and assessment of the benefits of the norm (inter alia, promotion of efficiency in the economy and in private markets; improvement of health and safety; protection of the environment; or elimination or reduction of discrimination or social prejudices), including, as far as possible, a quantification of such benefits; (b) an analysis and assessment of the costs to be incurred as a result of the application of the new norm (inter alia, direct costs for the government, enterprises and other recipients involved in its implementation, and any other adverse effects on the efficient functioning of the economy, private markets, productivity, employment, competitiveness, health, safety and environment), together with a quantification of such costs; (c) a cost-benefit analysis and assessment of the potentially effective and reasonably practicable alternatives to the proposed norm that have been identified by both the department and the public consulted; and (d) an explanation of why the proposed norm is preferable to the analysed alternatives.

different procedure from the one that applies to the drafting of other general provisions.[21] Broadly speaking, we can say that the Spanish system presents the following characteristics.[22]

First of all, in Spain the difference between a regulatory planning phase and a drafting phase is not as clearly marked as in the Anglo-Saxon system. In Great Britain, a bill cannot be drafted until the cabinet has taken the political decision to use such an instrument and has decided on its content, whereas in Spain the drafting of bills can start without any involvement of the Council of Ministers. Moreover, it is no exaggeration to say that in many cases projects are drafted not only without the formal authorisation but even without any prior knowledge of the competent minister. In absence of an explicit requirement of authorisation by the ministers or the Council of Ministers, General Directorates have a great deal of autonomy in terms of initiating the process of drafting norms. Both formally and in practice, the reality corresponds perfectly with the legal framework: most of the bills, with the exception of those which have a certain political significance, are born from initiatives taken by those administration echelons (General Directorates) that are at the border between the political and the technical spheres—echelons that, at this stage, operate with an autonomy that would be unthinkable in the Anglo-Saxon system.

The political implications of this procedure are quite remarkable. First of all, it is clear that, once the mechanism for drafting a legislative text has been put in place, there is a certain probability that the draft law will be eventually approved by the government: thus, the risk that the political bodies are "captured" by the administration is mitigated by the fact—which can be verified—that the administrative bodies tend to propose only those texts that are likely to be accepted by their political superiors. There is a risk, however, that the political bodies are unaware of the dimension and the implications of the policy underpinning a specific regulatory text—such an awareness can only be taken for granted when the text is known by the potentially affected sectors or stakeholders, which may eventually give rise to public debates that make it politically difficult to withdraw the project. Furthermore, legislative drafts in Spain are rather "resistant to change": politicians who take the ultimate decision usually limit themselves to endorse the draft. On the one hand, as noted earlier, they lack the necessary time for a detailed study of the content of each legislative proposal. On the other, this way of proceeding contributes to reinforcing

---

[21]The legal framework applicable in this respect is basically as follows: Act on Public Administrations and Common Administrative Procedure (*Ley de Régimen Jurídico de las Administraciones Públicas del procedimiento administrativo común*); Agreement of the Council of Ministers of 29 December 1989; Agreement of the Council of Ministers of 26 January 1990; and Agreement of the Council of Ministers of 18 October 1991, replaced today by the Agreement of the Council of Ministers of 22 July 2005 (Ministerio de la Presidencia 2011). To this list we must add the sectoral legislation regulating the participation of certain bodies such as the General Council of the Judiciary, the Autonomous Regions, the Council of State, etc. In addition, some ministerial departments have regulated the internal procedure for drafting general provisions.

[22]See further the works of Joaquín Abajo Quintana (1995) and José María Jiménez Cruz (1991), who have worked in the Secretariat of Government and therefore have a profound knowledge of the real procedures that are followed in this phase.

mutual trust between the political and the bureaucratic bodies—a trust without which an administration cannot function properly. Still, a specific regulation in this respect would prevent or at least alleviate the risk that politicians adopt or pass norms, say, blindly.

Secondly, unlike most countries in the European continent, Spain lacks a centralised body to draft bills. The consequence is a decentralised or distributed system in which the various ministries—more exactly, their upper echelons, i.e., the General Directorates—are responsible for initiating the projects. Yet, a detailed regulation on how to proceed within the ministries is also lacking: they have a great autonomy regarding who can prepare or write the legislative draft. In some cases, the drafting task is assigned to a very proficient and technically specialised organ, namely the Codification Commission (*Comisión General de Codificación*); occasionally, specialists working outside the administration are hired to write the project; mostly, however, it is the officials of the General Directorate or of the General Technical Secretariat (*Secretaría General Técnica*) of each department who draft the norms, whether regulations or laws. Such officials are often very well trained jurists. But there is no rule that establishes criteria in this regard, and the decision of who will in fact write the bill is left to the good judgement of the heads of the administrative unit, who will assess the level of specialisation required for each draft and the human and financial resources available to them—as well as whether their budget allows them to hire external experts as drafters.

The only "centralised" stage in the review of norm projects (especially of draft regulations) are the mandatory reports and opinions that must be requested from, e.g., the General Technical Secretariat of each department, from the Ministry of Economy and Finance, from the Ministry of Public Administrations (in specific cases), or from the Council of State.[23] This latter body plays a key role in the lawmaking process. The Government must request the Council of State's opinion in the case of draft legislative decrees,[24] as well as of early drafts (*anteproyectos*) of legislation implementing or developing international treaties, covenants or agreements. In addition, the government must request the opinion of the Council prior to the adoption of regulations developing or implementing parliamentary laws. This is a second examination of the legality of draft texts—and it is a very important one.[25] Yet, for our purposes this second examination is important, above all, because the Council of State is staffed by personnel who is especially well trained and very prestigious: their comments on draft norms are usually accepted, and clearly improve

[23]The opinion of the Council of State must also be requested in case of draft bills or regulations affecting the organisation, powers or functioning of the Council of State itself; on early drafts (*anteproyectos*) of constitutional reform—unless such drafts have been prepared by the Council of State itself; or on the drafts of organic laws transferring or delegating state powers to the autonomous regions (Arts. 21 and 22 of the Organic Law 3/1980 of the Council of State).

[24]According to art. 85 of the Spanish Constitution, Government provisions containing delegated legislation are entitled "legislative decrees" (*decretos legislativos*).

[25]I leave aside the question of whether non-compliance with this requirement, as a procedural flaw, may or should lead courts to invalidate a regulation.

the quality of the texts finally approved by the government. The rest of mandatory opinions and reports, such as those issued by the Ministry for Public Administrations, the National School Council (*Consejo Escolar*), the Fiscal and Financial Policy Council, the National Defence Board, the Inter-territorial Council of the National Health System, etc., are less important in terms of legislative technique.[26]

A survey carried out in 1993 by the former Ministry of Relations with the Parliament (*Ministerio de Relaciones con las Cortes*) among the technical general secretariats (*secretarías generales técnicas*) offers a good critical summary of the procedure for the elaboration of norms in Spain. The conclusions of this survey included the following findings: (a) the lack of an specific regulation—or even of a set of general instructions—in this area leads to very different ways of applying and materialising the provisions of the law; (b) the legislative dossier or record should be configurated as a unitary set of documents which includes all the texts, reports, writings and other documents produced along the entire process of the elaboration of the norm, from its beginning until final approval—in the current situation, it is to be feared that the dossier is fragmented, with its different parts being held by or stored at different ministerial offices; (c) moreover, and as a consequence of the previous point, there is no clear assignment of the responsibility for the project dossier to a specific body; (d) neither is it established that, when referred to consultive bodies, drafts be accompanied by the studies and opinions already produced—this would obviously strengthen the assessment capacity of the requested body; (e) in absence of explicit rules, there is uncertainty as to which authority decides whether or not to modify the draft text according to the criteria, suggestions or comments included in the reports or opinions that have been requested, or resulting from hearings or public consultations; and the survey concludes by pointing out that, (f) with only a few exceptions, ministries do not hold a comprehensive norm register (*registro de disposiciones*) or anything comparable. Such a register could be a useful tool for *de lege ferenda* tasks, e.g., for the preparation of "validity and derogation tables", and also—together with the unification of legislative dossiers—when it comes to submitting legislative records to the courts.[27]

---

[26]There is a tendency among politicians to consider that all these procedures are obstacles that limit the effectiveness of the Administration's operation. An objective examination of them highlights their importance and the need to take them seriously. In some cases, because they are procedures that technically improve the text that will be submitted for approval by the responsible body. In other cases, because they make it possible to defend legitimate interests or promote the exercise of the right of participation enshrined in the Constitution. For this reason, at this stage of the procedure, the drafter of a rule has a special political responsibility: he has to guarantee that all the procedures foreseen have been completed so that the draft can be discussed and, if necessary, approved by the competent bodies, and the rule is valid.

[27]As for the other shortcomings identified by the 1993 survey, such as the absence of general instructions on normative technique and the absence of handbooks of administrative language, they have already been solved—in subsequent years, the Council of Ministers has taken several measures in this respect: see, e.g., the Legislative Technique Guidelines adopted in 2005 (*Resolución de 28 de julio de 2005, de la Subsecretaría, por la que se da publicidad al Acuerdo*

This is the general procedure followed in Spain for drawing up normative texts. It is a procedure that fits, generally speaking, into the continental European model: a distributed, non-concentrated procedure of drafting norms, with no organic differentiation between those entrusted with the task of planning regulatory intervention and those entrusted with drafting the norm. Should the model be changed?

8.6 A Comparison Between Systems

Those on the Anglo-Saxon side who suggest abandoning the concentrated system and assigning the function of drafting rules to the ministerial departments see in the formula of the French Council of State a model to follow: the Law Council suggested by Sir William Dale would have to review the drafts before their presentation to the houses. The Renton Report (1975, pp. 129 ff), however, is reluctant about the feasibility of such a proposal. According to this report, it is the members of the government and the Cabinet themselves who are responsible to Parliament for the quality of the bills, and it would not be possible to expect independent bodies to assume any responsibility for the drafting of the texts. In the same vein, Kolts (1980) has said that no government of the common law countries would accept the creation of such a new body, which would put an end to the confidentiality required for certain projects. Dale's proposal on the necessary changes in the parliamentary procedure for bills has suffered a similar fate.

There is no unanimity on the advantages and disadvantages of the centralised procedure when compared with the diffuse procedure. Sir William Dale had been proposing in the UK, among other ideas, to adopt the continental European procedure and to allow the ministerial departments themselves—rather than the Office of Parliamentary Counsel—to draft their own texts. But while Dale and others have considered the advantages of the European distributed or diffuse system, the vast majority of specialists do not see any fundamental reasons for rejecting the concentrated system followed in common law countries. Moreover, some consider that one of the reasons for the better quality of English laws, compared to that of the United States, is precisely the concentrated and specialised system of drafting (Dickerson 1959).

The question of which is the best system is not easy to answer. Keith Patchett (1991) has tried to list the advantages and disadvantages of the concentrated system which are, in turn, the disadvantages and advantages of the diffuse system. Among the advantages of the concentrated system are the following: (a) the service is provided by a highly cohesive group of very prestigious and experienced lawyers; (b) the service provides a pool of collective experience and legislative technique of

del Consejo de Ministros, de 22 de julio de 2005, por el que se aprueban las Directrices de técnica normativa) (Ministerio de la Presidencia 2011).

the highest level which are transmitted to the members who join it; (c) this system ensures that standard procedures will be followed as closely as possible in the preparation of legislation; (d) it leads to consistent levels of uniformity and well-tested drafting styles in legislation; (e) it gives governments the assurance that their interests and needs will be met and that their legislative program is properly implemented; and (f) since such a skilled staff is often scarce, limited resources are optimised.

As for the drawbacks of the concentrated system, Keith Patchett points out the following: (a) the drafting of laws is a highly specialised function requiring such qualifications that very few are attracted to it, causing a permanent shortage of drafters: the more competent these jurists are, the more difficult it will be to recruit them from the private sector; (b) collective techniques and experiences can only be transmitted if the drafters remain in their position for a significant period of time and there is a systematic training program in place, but this transmission fails if the pressure of work is high and the rotation of the drafters frequent; (c) there is always a tendency to elitism or corporatism among drafters, as well as a certain degree of opposition to innovation of methods and procedures; (d) the lack of expertise of drafters can be a frequent cause of complaints among the ministries; (e) the whole system depends on the quality of the ministerial instructions; (f) it is rare for a drafter to be involved in the political decision, and this is sometimes desirable in order to draft the text properly; and (g) drafters have little concern for the problems of legislative evaluation—a key ex post or retrospective function which is normally attributed to the respective ministerial departments.

It is not easy to decide which of the various systems of legislative drafting may be more convenient. Obviously, the option for one or the other is determined by factors such as the history and tradition of the different countries, as well as the constitutional design of the functions of the various authorities and their relations. In general terms, we can say that most of the specialists in the field are relatively dissatisfied with the system in place in their country and that they are all in favour of reforming it. In any case, all of the systems are based on the professionalism and excellence of the drafters, who in most countries are jurists. But... is it really so clear that the drafters of rules must be jurists?

Concerned about the general dissatisfaction with the quality and comprehensibility of legislation, the Standing Committee on Legal and Constitutional Affairs of the Australian House of Representatives delivered a documented report on the reform of draft legislation in the Commonwealth of Australia (Australian House of Representatives 1993). One of the first questions raised in this report was "who should draft legal texts?" Among the proposals that were analysed was the possibility of laws not being drafted by lawyers, since they are not necessarily the best users of the English language. The fact is that sometimes, without much basis, the task of the drafter is often considered a mere translation of the instructions given by the relevant political body into legal language. But to reduce the role of the drafter to this function means not understanding—as the First Parliamentary Counsel pointed out to the aforementioned Committee—that there are essential duties in the process of drafting a law which can only be carried out seriously by a lawyer: anticipating the effects of the law on the constitutional system, taking into account the legal framework in which the law is to be inserted, identifying the possible antinomies or gaps that the wording may generate or the practical problems that the application of the law may cause... These are just some of the many issues that a drafter has to deal with and for which legal training is required. This does not mean that non-lawyers cannot provide valuable assistance in the drafting of certain normative texts; moreover, it would be desirable to encourage closer cooperation with experts in substantive politics and linguistics, who could improve the quality of projects. In any case, it seems that the ultimate responsibility for the drafting of normative texts should be reserved to jurists.

A different question is whether these lawyers should belong to the administration or whether they can also work in the private sector. In both the Anglo-Saxon and the continental European systems, most of the rules are drafted by public officials. However, the volume of work (especially in concentrated systems) or the lack of expertise have sometimes led to entrust the task to lawyers from the private sector. The Renton Report insisted on the need to increase training in legislative technique in universities and wondered whether it would make sense to make use of services outside the administration. The Renton Report (1975, p. 49) was rather reluctant about this possibility and therefore limited itself to recommending to the administration that all available methods be used to recruit and train legal drafters. Usually, the reasons for not hiring external drafters have mainly to do with the due confidentiality required by the drafting tasks, or with eventual conflicts of interest—which can even result in influence peddling.

But apart from this reason, it must be borne in mind that normally the work of the drafter should not end with the delivery of the bill to the body or authority that entrusted the job but cover the entire parliamentary process, including the study of the amendments introduced by the parliamentary groups and the drafting of those amendments that need to be presented to improve the text or to achieve the necessary political consensus. This monitoring of the parliamentary processing of draft legislation is often much more rigorous when it is entrusted to the legal officers who wrote it in the first place. Finally, it should be noted that it is easier to standardise the drafting techniques of governmental services than to impose guides on the style, structure and form of laws on experts from the private sector—this does not mean, however, that it is not appropriate to resort to external lawyers either to draft or advise on a specific bill.

All systems of norm drafting—Anglo-Saxon, continental European or presidentialist—rely heavily, as we have seen, on the work of jurists as *drafters*. But... are the functions entrusted to them clear? And are their limits and codes of conduct equally clear?

References

Abajo Quintana J (1995) La implementación de las normas. La secuencia del proceso decisional. In: Figueroa A (ed) Los procesos de implementación de las normas jurídicas. IVAP, Bilbao, pp 29–92

Albanesi E (2013) Teoria e tecnica legislativa nel sistema costituzionale. Editoriale Scientifica, Napoli

Atiyah PS, Summers R (1987) Form and substance in Anglo-American law. A comparative study in legal reasoning, legal theory and legal institutions. Clarendon Press, Oxford

Australian Government (1988) Legislation handbook. Department of the Prime Minister and Cabinet, Canberra. updated February 2017

Australian House of Representatives (1993) Report of the inquiry into legislative drafting by the Commonwealth (Standing Committee on Legal and Constitutional Affairs). Australian Government Publishing Service, Canberra

Bentham J (1983) The collected works of Jeremy Bentham. Clarendon, Oxford

Bundesministerium der Justiz (2008) Handbuch der Rechtsförmlichkeit, 3rd. edn. Published in the Bundesanzeiger 60, no. 160a, 22 September 2008. http://hdr.bmj.de

Cassese S (1992) Introduzione allo studio della normazione. Rivista trimestrale di diritto pubblico 2:307–330

Costa J-P (1993) Le Conseil d'Etat dans la Société Comtemporaine. Economica, Paris

Curcuruto F (1985) La preparazione dei progetti di legge nella Repubblica Tedesca. Quaderni della Giustizia 47:119

Cusmano A (1985) Tecnica legislativa: experienze nazionali e regionali. Le Regioni XIII (2/3):254–269

Cheli E, Caretti P (1986) El proceso legislativo en Italia. Revista Española de Derecho Constitucional 16:203–222

Dale W (1977) Legislative drafting: a new approach. Butterworths, London

Dale W (1991) The European Legislative scene. Statute Law Rev 6:79–97

Dickerson R (1959) Legislative drafting in London and in Washington. Camb Law J 17(1):49–55

Frosini V (1988) Il messagio legislativo: tecnica e interpretazione. In: Pagano R (ed) Normative europee sulla tecnica legislativa. Camera dei Deputati, Roma

IPU (Interparliamentary Union) (1987) Les Parlements dans le monde, Recueil des donnés comparatives. IPU, Bruxelles

Jiménez Cruz JM (1991) El procedimiento de elaboración de normas, con especial referencia al derecho autonómico. In Técnica Normativa de las Comunidades Autónomas. Comunidad de Madrid, Madrid

Kolts G (1980) Observations on the proposed new approach to legislative drafting in common law countries. Statute Law Rev 1(3):144–148

Lasvignes S (2005) Le rôle du Secretariat Géneral du gouvernement dans la preparation des lois. In: Drago R (ed) La confection de la loi. PUF, Paris

Long M (1992) Le Conseil d'Etat et la fonction consultative. Revue Francaise de Droit Administratif 85:787

Luchaire F, Conac G (1980) La Constitution de la Republique Française. Economica, Paris

Martin Casals M, Suñer CVP (1990) ¿Quien redacta las leyes? Los modelos de redacción "concentrada" y de redacción "difusa" de los proyectos de ley. Revista de las Cortes Generales 21:7–34

Meny I (1986) El proceso legislativo en Francia. Revista Española de Derecho Constitucional 16:115–179

Meny I, Thoenig J-C (1992) Las políticas públicas. Ariel, Barcelona

Mill JS (1994) El gobierno representativo. Tecnos, Madrid

Ministerio de la Presidencia (2011) Directrices de Técnica Normativa. Catalogo de las publicaciones de la Administración General del Estado, Madrid

Olivecrona K (1980) El Derecho como hecho. La estructura del ordenamiento jurídico. Labor, Barcelona
Olivier J (1993) L'elaboration de la loi en la Republica Federale d'Allemagne. Pouvoirs 66:83–99
Pagano R (ed) (1988) Normative europee sulla tecnica legislativa. Camera dei Deputati, Roma
Patchett K (1991) Legislaçao e redacçao legislativa no Reino Unido. Legislaçao 2:29–69
Pérez Luño AE (1993) El desbordamiento de las fuentes del derecho. Real Academia Sevillana de Legislación y Jurisprudencia, Sevilla
Plantey A (2005) Le róle du Conseil d'État dans la confection de la loi. In: Drago R (ed) La confection de la loi. PUF, Paris
Ram SG (1951) The improvement of the statute law. J Soc Public Teachers Law (n.s.) 1:447–449
Renton Committee (1975) The preparation of legislation. Report of a Committee appointed by the Lord President of the Council. H.M. Stationery Office, London
Renton D (1990) Current drafting: practices and problems in the UK. Statute Law Rev 11:11–17
Robineau I, Truchet D (1994) Le Conseil d'État. PUF, Paris
Russell M, Gover D (2017) Legislation at Westminster. Parliamentary actors and influence in the making of British Law. OUP, Oxford
Santaolalla F (ed) (2008) Técnica Normativa en la Unión Europea, 2 vols. Senado de España, Madrid
Scoti L (1985) I piu ricenti indirizzi operativi per razionalizzare la legislazione: i lavori della Sotto-Commissione Cassese. Il Foro Italiano 108(5):248–275
Seidman A, Seidman RB (1996) Drafting legislation for development: lessons from a Chinese Project. Am J Comp Law 44:1–44
Strano M (1985) La nuova disciplina della pubblicazione delle leggi e degli atti normativi nella raccolta e nella gazzetta ufficiale. Rivista Trim di Diritto Pubblico 35:171–190
Trocoli G (1986) Un tentativo di coordinamento dell'attivita legislativa del Governo in Parlamento. Quaderni Costituzionali VI(3/4):576–582
Zander M (1994) The law-making process, 4th edn. Butterworths, London
Zapatero V (1996) Producción de normas. In: Ruiz Miguel A, Díaz E (eds) Enciclopedia Iberoamericana de Filosofía. Vol. 2: Filosofía política. Trotta/CSIC, Madrid, pp 161–186

Chapter 9
The Drafter's Tasks

9.1 First Steps

The drafter's function implies becoming the recipient of very different demands (Bennion 1978, p. 235; 1980, pp. 25 ff): effectiveness, procedural legitimacy, timeliness, certainty, comprehensibility, acceptability, brevity, debatability and legal compatibility; these demands can sometimes contradict each other. Governments expect from drafters that the draft—the output of the drafting work—will achieve the goals set out in the underlying policy, that it will comply with all legal formalities, that it will be submitted at the appropriate time and, if the draft is a bill, that it will have a high probability of being approved by parliament. Parliament, in turn, hopes that the bill will be presented in such a way that parliamentarians can understand it, discuss it, amend it and, if necessary, give their consent to it. Citizens, in turn expect the draft law to be understandable, to clearly define their rights and obligations and to be in line with their interests or ideology. And on the list of those who critically examine the work of the drafter are also the public officials who process it and the judges or magistrates who will apply the norm. Now, what is important for some—what constitutes the horizon to which the drafter, in their mind, should strive—, for others may often be a secondary issue. It is not easy to give satisfaction to so many, so important and sometimes so contradictory demands. The drafters themselves will not usually aspire to do so.

Indeed, if we were to look carefully at what drafters thinks of their work, what their role is, or to whom they owe allegiance in the event of conflicting demands, we would understand to what extent they feel that their "client" is the body that has entrusted them with the norm project: usually the government. This is not to say that drafters are not aware of the interpretative canons that will be used by the courts[1]: drafters are usually skilled jurists who are familiar with case law and legal doctrine. But while judges or magistrates privilege the virtues of clarity and technical

[1]See, however, Gluck and Schultz Bressman (2013, 2014), and cf. also Chap. 13 of this book.

V. Zapatero Gómez, *The Art of Legislating*, Legisprudence Library 6,
https://doi.org/10.1007/978-3-030-23388-4_9

perfection in legal texts, governments attach greater value and importance to the ability of a text to be approved by the houses: as the First Parliamentary Counsel, Lord Thring, once said, just as shaving blades are made for shaving, so bills are written to be approved (see Engle 1983).

The field study of how the drafters see themselves reveals two sets of skills that sometimes contradict each other: some authors have called them the *interpretative* and the *constitutive virtues* (Nourse and Schacter 2002, pp. 575 ff). The drafters' interpretative virtues are the virtues generally ascribed to judges: precision in the wording, adherence to the rules and canons of legal interpretation, discovery or construction of the meaning of legislation through impartial reflection on the language of legislative texts and in the light of the relevant case law, etc. On the other hand, constitutive virtues tend to privilege the institutional values of parliament: action and agreement, reconciliation of political interests, and attention to the pragmatic needs of the recipients of the norm. In the event of a contradiction between the two sets of virtues, interpretative and constitutive, drafters normally favours the latter. Perhaps because they see themselves more as technicians at the service of the government than as what they really are: "servants" of the norm-making process whose work inevitably has a political dimension, and who are therefore bound to a whole series of specific duties as state officials. Only if drafters are aware of their place in the legislative process can they strike a balance between the different and sometimes conflicting demands they are expected to satisfy. In this regard, we should realise that legislative drafting is at the very heart of the production of laws, and that drafters therefore must be provided with all the institutional guarantees that the adequate performance of their job requires. And this is also a political decision.

However, alongside the institutional recognition of the sensitivity of the role they play, a whole theory and technique is also needed to serve it: we worry about what judges do, but often forget what drafters do. Fortunately, this is no longer the case in most of the countries where the drafting of norms has been regulated—e.g. the UK, Canada, Australia, or the United States,[2] as well as most EU member states: as is highlighted in Pagano's (1988) or F. Santaolalla's (2008) compilations of European legislative technique.[3] Furthermore, legal and legislative drafting is studied in both universities (see e.g. Bartole 1988) and specialised research centres in different countries.[4]

[2]Consider e.g., in the UK, the Office of Parliamentary Counsel and the Renton Report (Renton Committe 1975), or the Guidance for Members of the Office of Parliamentary Counsel who are drafting bills to be considered in Parliament (UK Government 2010 [2018]); in Australia, the Legislation Handbook of the Australian Government (1988 [2017], pp. 1–81), the Plain English Manual (Australian Government 1993 [2016]), or the report on clearer Commonwealth law (Australian House of Representatives 1993); in Canada, the Uniform Acts Drafting Conventions (Uniform Law Conference of Canada 1989); in the U.S., the Guide to Legislation Drafting (U.S. House of Representatives 1997) and Legislative Drafting Manual (U.S. Senate 1997).

[3]Cf. also recently Xanthaki (2014), Uhlmann and Höfler (2016) and Karpen and Xanthaki (2017).

[4]Legal drafting does not only include the drafting of bills and regulations, or of other governmental or parliamentary documents: it also includes the drafting of legal texts such as contracts, wills, etc.

In Spain, for its part, the scholarly and political concern for the technique of legal text drafting is very recent. There is minimal regulation in place—several Council of Ministers' agreements on the evaluation questionnaires for bills and on the form and structure of laws.[5] And the literature on legislative technique, albeit rigorous, is still incipient.[6] It is to be hoped that these pioneering efforts will pave the way to new research on the subject and introduce this type of study into university curricula, as has long been customary in the Anglo-Saxon world. In this way, progress could be made towards institutionalising the figure of the drafter and providing him with the resources and skills required for such an important function.

What follows here is not intended to present a systematic model of legal drafting: rather, it is an attempt to streamline certain experiences looking at already well-established procedures of normative drafting, pointing out the problems that usually arise in each of the phases the draft text goes through. Professionals and theorists in the field of norm drafting often disaggregate the process into five distinct phases: setting objectives, analysis, text planning, drafting and revision of the draft. Such is the division suggested in Thornton's (1987) classic book—a division which, with minimal variations, can be found in any legislative drafting manual.

9.1.1 Goal-Setting

Possibly, for an experienced drafter the actual drafting of a normative text does not require as much time or effort as the preliminary tasks do. And among these, the determination of the desired objectives is the first and most important. This is true for the drafters themselves, who can hardly undertake the task of drawing up a draft without knowing exactly what is intended by it. But legislative objectives are likewise important for the parliamentarians who will discuss and eventually pass the bill, as well as for its addressees and for those who have to enforce it. As discussed in Chap. 4 (Sect. 4.3), when we talk about objectives we are not referring to the motives nor to the reasons: we are referring to the states of affairs that legislation is trying to materialise in the "environment", i.e. in society. The envisaged states of affairs, the objectives, must be expressed with sufficient precision as to make it possible to evaluate their achievement afterwards. Generic goal statements are nothing more than rhetoric unless their degree of achievement can be verified: declaring that the objective of a norm is "the protection of consumers", for example, is nothing more than a slogan—proper goal-setting would entail, rather, establishing

See, among many others, Martineau (1991), Rylance (1994), Holland and Webb (1994), or Costanzo (1994).

[5]See the Council of Ministers' Agreements of 29 December 1989, 26 January 1990 and 18 October 1991, as well as the Legislative Technique Guidelines (*Diretrices de Técnica Normativa*) adopted by the Council of Ministers on 22 July 2005 (Ministerio de la Presidencia 2011).

[6]In Spain, the pioneering works in this field were produced by the Group for Legislative Technique Studies (GRETEL 1986, 1989). See also García Escudero (2010).

precisely what relevant information ought to be on the label of a product (Rubin 1991/1992, pp. 283 ff).

Much has been discussed, and will continue to be discussed, about who should determine the objectives of norms and which organisational structure is best suited for this purpose. The Anglo-Saxon system—with its organic separation between the instruction and the drafting phase—is usually put forward as a model that respects the democratic principle while allowing for due deference to professionals and specialists in legal drafting: they cannot begin drafting if the cabinet has not previously approved instructions setting out the objectives and the basic content of the draft.[7] This is not some old legal procedure that is maintained as a tribute to tradition: modern approaches to this matter continue to insist on the need for the political authority to monopolise the determination of the objectives of new norms.[8] And in principle this would be the correct thing to do. But a permanent and fluid dialogue between politicians and technicians nevertheless is unavoidable when it comes to specifying the objectives of legislation. Normally what politicians know is that there is a problem to solve; what they don't know is how to exactly define the problem, what possible solutions exist or which of them, if any, is the right one. They still find themselves in what the Renton Report calls the "grey zone" of the normative production process—in which it is agreed that something has to be done but is not yet clear what precisely must be done. In both the Anglo-Saxon and continental European models, it is by means of fluid communication between politicians and technicians that the objective will emerge and will be profiled to a reasonable level of precision.

The role of the drafters—despite some claims (see e.g. Drieger 1953)—is not limited to giving legal form to the government's projects. Drafters also actively participate in the very definition of policies. They do so quite directly through their knowledge and experience, for example, by requesting further information or the clarification of obscure points in the draft; by highlighting possible outcomes unforeseen by the politician; by asking for new guidelines to face the difficulties that arise in the drafting process; by warning about eventual illegalities or unconstitutionalities hidden in the text, or about possible conflicts of competence that might lead to modify the initial objectives. All this implies the need for numerous dialogue sessions between the drafting technicians and the politicians, something that is often in contradiction with the urgency that pressures the latter. Obviously, all the time that is devoted to this task of precisely setting the objectives will greatly increase the quality and effectiveness of the final text (Dickerson 1986, p. 71).

In addition to this direct influence of the drafter, the application of legislative technique can in its own have an indirect (and often positive) influence on the

---

[7]See especially the Australian Government's *Legislation Handbook* (1988 [2017]), which includes quite detailed rules on when, how, and by whom such instructions must be provided.

[8]For instance, the Standing Committee on Legal and Constitutional Affairs of the Australian House of Representatives (1993) considers that government departments alone should be responsible for giving instructions to drafters.

establishment of the objectives of the norm. One of the technical contributions in this regard is the use of so-called directives or goal norms which, as an effect of the European Union's standardisation of regulatory methods, are being increasingly implemented in the Spanish legal system. Their use facilitates the clarification and formalisation of the objectives pursued by the new norm and thus a better parliamentary debate, its easier understanding by citizens and a more effective application both by the public administration and the courts.

9.1.2 Choossing the Appropriate Normative Tool

Having set the objective or, where necessary, multiple objectives of a text, the drafter also participates politically through the selection of the best normative instrument. The selection of the normative instrument is an eminently political decision (Marcello 1996). Once the coercive and imperative conception of law as an instrument of social direction has been surpassed (as discussed in Chap. 7), the drafter of norms is the one who best understands the wide range of intervention instruments available to politicians, as well as the cases in which these instruments are more or less indicated. It will normally be the specialist who helps the politician assess, in view of each specific case, whether it is more efficacious, more effective or more efficient to regulate by incentives or by directives. It will be up to the specialist to indicate whether the objective pursued can be better achieved by information, by fiscal policy, by applying target, performance or specification norms, or by introducing an entire system of authorisations or licenses. These are decisions that again require a fluid and loyal dialogue between technicians and politicians, without which the normative decision could not be said to be informed by experience and knowledge.

9.1.3 Inserting the Norm in the Existing Framework

Among the preliminary tasks of the drafter is also the exploration of the existing legal framework in order to understand how the projected norm will fit in it. There are no empty legal or juridical spaces: every new norm is in some way a reform of the preexisting law. Expressly or tacitly the new norm repeals the previous one—unless there is some distribution of competences between them. On this point, as Bennion (1980, pp. 35 and 36) said, drafters have an impressive power: the sovereignty of parliament grants them virtually the final word and hence the capacity of changing all previous laws. Drafters must therefore carefully examine the compatibility of the new norm with the whole *corpus iuris* if they do not want to take the risk of unwanted derogations or modifications.

In Spain, one of the tasks required of the drafter by the *evaluation questionnaire* approved by the Government consists in examining the repercussions of any norm project with regard to the legal framework in force, to EU law, to regional legislation, and to the competences of the state administration bodies. As concerns the European Union, the drafter must answer the question of whether the project has an impact on EU legislation, and/or whether it has been previously notified—if this is legally required—to the European Commission, and what, if any, has been the result of this consultation. As for the autonomous regions, the drafter must first clarify which "titles of competence" support (i.e. which the legal-constitutional basis is for) the state intervention and whether or not a "conflict of competences" is foreseeable.[9] The drafter must also examine how the project relates to other bodies of state administration and clarify, for example, whether the project attributes new powers to the Council of Ministers or—and this is often the cause of innumerable polemics and delays in the final approval—changes the current distribution of powers among the various ministerial departments. The drafter will also need to indicate beforehand which existing rules can be totally or partially repealed by the project, which opinions and reports are mandatory and whether all have been requested, as well as what other provisions would need to be dictated for the full effectiveness of the new normative text. As Reed Dickerson (1986, p. 58) points out, it would never occur to a skilled architect to remodel a house without first looking inside. Similarly, the drafter of a legal text must closely examine the relevant existing regulations in order to understand what needs to be preserved, what needs to be amended, what needs to be repealed and what needs to be supplemented. If this is not done, the result will be derogations, overlaps and terminological inconsistencies; in other words, confusion.

This phase is particularly important in the Spanish legal system, which is articulated through the delegation of competences or powers upwards (i.e. to the European Union) and downwards (to the autonomous regions). In this sense, the delimitation of competences is one of the first things to be examined by the drafter—actually, many legislative "shipwrecks" and failures are due to a defective examination of competence issues. The number of "conflicts of competence" or jurisdiction between the state and the autonomous regions heard before the Constitutional Court is quite illustrative of the need to take special care in this point.[10] If the government and the drafter do not want to waste time and resources and cause important political conflict, they must clarify if they have the constitutional capacity to dictate the proposed norm before going ahead with the project—much the same goes for the interaction between Spanish and European legislation. As María Jesús Montoro Chiner (1989, pp. 54 ff) has convincingly argued, however, the

---

[9]According to Art. 161 of the Spanish Constitution, "the Constitutional Court (...) is competent to hear: (...) conflicts of jurisdiction (*competencia*) between the State and the autonomous regions (*Comunidades Autónomas*) or amongst the autonomous regions themselves".

[10]According to official data on the conflictivity between the state and the autonomous regions, there were 554 such conflicts between 1981 and 1993; 52 between 1996 and 2000; and 71 between 2003 and 2007.

constitutionality test for draft norms cannot be limited to a mere examination of powers or competences: it must also comprise a formal check for the observance of the norm hierarchy established by the Constitution; and, as for the content, it is crucial to make sure that norms are substantially compatible with the constitutional order,[11] in particular with fundamental rights (proportionality) and with basic rule of law requirements (such as determinacy, clarity and legal certainty).

9.1.4 First Sketch and Structure of the Text

Once the objectives of the proposal have been set, the normative instrument has been chosen and the framework in which it will be inserted has been explored, the subsequent step will be to develop an organisational plan (Dickerson 1986, pp. 59 ff; Thornton 1987, pp. 120 ff), i.e. a sort of sketch of the project. This very provisional outline of the text has the main purpose of helping the drafter organise ideas around the projected norm, on the one hand, and, on the other, of facilitating the debate between the drafter and the politicians. As for the virtues of this first draft or sketch, professionals with long dedication to the subject often highlight how better planning inevitably leads to a better project: there is a close relationship between the clarity of ideas in the initial design of a legislative project and the clarity of the resulting text (cf. Australian Office of Parliamentary Counsel 1993 [2016]). If the outline is well thought out, if it is clear and simple, it will be easier to translate into a clear and orderly text. Contrarily, starting to write without a previous plan is like trying to build any kind of machinery without having idea of its general organisation. It is not a matter, at this stage, of distracting attention away from the specific details of the final text, but it is necessary to concentrate on the substance and leave the form for later.

In this connection, the recommendations of the Australian Office of Parliamentary Counsel (1993 [2016]) are very helpful: (a) identifying objectives: the usefulness of the planning phase will significantly increase if the main objectives and principles of the draft norm are determined from the outset; (b) reducing the number and complexity of concepts: complicated ideas lead to an equally complicated project—the final project will thus be better if the plan is conceived in few "pieces", i.e. in the smallest number of concepts which are necessary for the plan to fulfil its function; (c) concentrating on important principles: it is necessary to identify and emphasise the main points at the start, for later changes affecting central issues can cause serious drafting problems down the line (at this early stage, there is no point in wasting too much time with the detailed wording of items that do not affect the basic structure of the draft); (d) making sure that policy makers understand the plan: one of

[11]The number of cases brought before the Constitutional Court in 2007 was 9998—including actions of unconstitutionality, individual appeals for constitutional protection (*recursos de amparo*), and questions of unconstitutionality promoted by courts.

the most important functions of a plan is to highlight, before starting to write, the main obstacles the new policy faces; it is therefore crucial that those politically responsible are involved in the formulation of the plan and fully understand it; (e) explaining what will not be included in the project: it is necessary to agree from the outset on which particular items will not be included in the draft and will be set aside to be dealt with by other normative instruments; and (f) making use of all kinds of aids to facilitate the structuring and comprehension of the text: tables, diagrams, footnotes, etc.

Obviously enough, this sketch or first draft—that outlines in a text the most important issues the law deals with—will grow and purify itself throughout the subsequent phases of composition and critical revision of the text. Therefore, the drafter has to take into account what the final arrangement of the text should be, its form and ultimate structure. The strictest organisation possible of the normative text will not only facilitate the latter stages of drafting but will also improve its understanding and interpretation.

Much has been written about the interpretative and reconstructive functions fulfilled by the fiction of the "rational legislator".[12] The interpreters of law speak of the legislator as a single individual who dictates norms, who is imperishable, conscious, omniscient, just, coherent and precise. These characteristics—which are hardly to be found in any real legislator—define a model of rational legislator on whose "presumed rationality" the various interpretations of a law are based. The presumption of the legislator's rationality leads to affirm that he cannot dictate contradictory norms; that there cannot be gaps or loopholes in the legal framework he has established, no ambiguity or vagueness in his words. Also derived from the rational legislator fiction is the idea that there is no disorder in the normative text: the arrangement of the words in the legislator's discourse would be intentional and would have a meaning that the interpreter has to discover. Here lies one of the reasons for the importance of properly organising the draft text: regardless of how rationally or carefully real legislators have proceeded in this respect, most interpreters will consider that the actual position and order of the words and provisions in the normative text is deliberate and will construe their meaning in the light of their location in the text. In Spanish case-law, for instance, this is where the argumentation *a rubrica* and the arguments based on the so-called *sedes materiae* come to play. As Francisco Ezquiaga (1987, p. 119) observes in his research on the *sedes materiae* argument in constitutional case-law, the meaning ascribed to a general rule is often connected to the place it occupies within the legal text of which it is a part. Along with this pattern of interpretation, the Spanish Constitutional Court has also used the argument *a rubrica*, which implies that normative statements are interpreted according to the title or rubric that heads the group of articles in which they are found.

[12]See, among others, Nowak (1964, quoted in Nino 1993, pp. 328 ff), Nino (1989), Igartua (1990), Ezquiaga (1994), or, more recently, Wintgens (2013).

As we see, the systematisation of normative texts is therefore very important. The need to take care of their internal arrangement does not derive from an aesthetic pruritus, or from the mere need to facilitate the task of drafting. A focus on the systematics of draft legislation is needed, rather, in order to realise the constitutional principle of legal security,[13] and to improve the practices of interpretation and application of laws. To this end, in many legal systems we can find specific legistic guidelines and even "templates" that provide valuable guidance on how to organise, divide, classify and sequence the clauses and provisions of legislative texts (see Pagano 1988). Also in Spain, and partly as a result of the work of the GRETEL Group (1989), the government has issued specific guidelines on the form and structure of early draft laws (*anteproyectos de ley*), which has contributed to improving the clarity and order of laws. Such guidelines are not only an aid for the drafter: ultimately, they are also beneficial for the reader of legislative texts—and should probably play a greater role in their interpretation (see e.g. GRETEL 1989 or Sainz and Ochoa 1989).

9.2 Drafting the Text

After these preparatory tasks have been carried out,[14] it is time to draft the norm. In both concentrated and distributed systems of normative drafting, this is usually a task for legal experts. It is said that Gladstone wrote his projects hand in hand with Lord Thring, his first parliamentary adviser; and in Spain we can find a few legal texts that must be attributed to the imprudent pen of a minister. However, today it is unusual for political decision-makers to write laws themselves. But when this does happen, failure is the most probable outcome: power does not always go hand in hand with the preparation and specialisation required for drafting laws. For this reason, perhaps the best teaching that can be drawn from the study of norm production is that legal writing is a technique that requires specialised knowledge and sufficient experience. It is only by practicing an activity that we can acquire mastery over it (Oakeshott 1991, p. 101).

[13]According to Art. 9.3 of the Spanish Constitution, "the Constitution guarantees the principle of legality, the hierarchy of legal provisions (*jerarquía normativa*), the publicity of legal norms, the nonretroactivity of sanctioning measures (...) or of measures restricting individual rights, the certainty of law (*seguridad jurídica*), and the accountability of public authorities and the ban on arbitrary action on their part".

[14]As part of the preliminary works, the drafter must clarify certain legal or administrative implications and difficulties raised by the requested text before starting to draft it. The *Legislation Handbook* of the Australian Government, for example, states that the drafter of a bill should be instructed at least on issues bearing on the following matters: date of entry into force and (eventual) retroactivity of the piece of legislation; burden of proof; certificates; offences and penalties; official secrets; the granting of discretionary powers to the administration; review of administrative decisions; international law obligations and human rights; public aid for the exercise of judicial actions; mentions to other Departments and delegations to other bodies, etc.

9.2.1 *Mastery of Language*

The first thing a drafter has to master is the use of language. To legislate is, as John Langshaw Austin (2004) would say, to do things with words, it is to direct the behaviour of citizens through words. Nobody can ever be a good jurist, far less a good legislative drafter, unless she masters the language she uses. In Spain, Prieto de Pedro (1991) has justified the need for closer attention to the use of language by jurists, especially by legislative drafters, on constitutional grounds—such as the principle of the democratic state, the state's due commitment to culture (*Estado de Cultura*),[15] or the legal security principle. He aptly observes how the linguistic errors of drafters are most likely to consolidate and expand, as it were by osmosis, to the language of courts, legal scholars and legal practitioners. The language of legislation leaves its imprint on other variants of legal language, and influences their development: its accomplishments and defects extend over them like an oil stain. We must recognise this paradigmatic influence of legal language in the fate of the other languages of law—a decisive reason for demanding rigour in the practice of drafting laws.

Drafting a law correctly implies, in the first place, avoiding common orthographic vices related e.g. to the use of capital letters, abbreviations, acronyms, hyphens and parentheses, to the orthography of words belonging to foreign languages, to the writing of quantities, to the use of commas, to grammatical gender issues, etc.[16] But, above all, a drafter must have the necessary linguistic preparation to face awkward syntactic, logical (inconsistency, and redundancy) and semantic difficulties. And in this regard, legal theory has much to say (Ross 1963): its contributions to the field of interpretation must be poured into the problems of legislation. It is not an exaggeration to conclude that a good legal drafter must posses also a solid background in legal theory and methodology, and be well acquainted with legal interpretation techniques.

The drafter's linguistic ability, in turn, has important policy implications. As Reed Dickerson (1986) points out, there are three tenets or principles which, when properly applied, have an indirect influence on substantive policy: consistency,

[15] According to Art. 44 of the Spanish Constitution, "public authorities shall promote and watch over access to cultural opportunities, to which all are entitled"—and in the Constitution's preamble, the Spanish nation "proclaims its will to (...) promote the progress of culture".

[16] Jesús Prieto de Pedro (1989, 1991) warns jurists about the proliferation of capital letters for emphatic or empty purposes—which runs counter to the recommendations of the Royal Academy of the Spanish Language—; about the recurrent use of abbreviations and the excessive use of acronyms—which should be limited to those standing for widely known bodies—; and about the use of parentheses and stripes. Prieto de Pedro condems the use of such "aids", and recommends translating all the voices of other living languages into Spanish (or, if the use of untranslated terms is unavoidable, writing them in their own spelling); writing quantities in letters and not in numbers; and being particularly careful when it comes to the use of commas—"the most thorny punctuation sign, since its misuse can end in litigation" (Prieto de Pedro 1991, p. 162). See further the official Legislative Technique Guidelines adopted by the Spanish Government in 2005 (Ministerio de la Presidencia 2011).

correct design, and normal use of words and expressions. According to the principle of consistency—as is recalled e.g. in the Drafting Conventions of the Uniform Law Conference of Canada (1989)—, different terms are not to be used to express the same idea within the same law; and the same term is not to be used with different meanings within the same law, unless, within a given context, the intended specific meaning is perfectly clear and no other term is available. Second, the principle of correct design demands a rigorous and systematic structuring of the draft text: taking good care of the "architecture" of the text will probably improve the policy it serves. And the third most important formal principle of legal drafting is to make sure that words and phrases are used in their most usual and conventional sense[17]: for Dickerson (1986, pp. 8 ff), there is no surer trap for the unwary reader and even for the careful drafter of a norm than the use of a specific term in a sense that significantly strays away from the meaning generally attributed to it by the norm addressees. It is a matter of avoiding "humpty-dumptism", of being aware of the risk implied in fabricating words through legal language. By applying these basic linguistic techniques—and combining them with their knowledge and experience—, drafters can contribute, without usurping any political functions, to a better definition of the goals pursued by the government (Martín Casals 1989, pp. 240 ff).

9.2.2 Problems Arisen from Ambiguity

The best tool at the drafter's disposal is the mastery of his own language. As a tool, language holds great possibilities but also some natural limitations that must be confronted by anyone who wants to transmit patterns of behaviour through words. The main limitation of language is ambiguity and its main advantage is vagueness—sometimes called "open texture". These limitations can degenerate into hyper-elaboration and hyper-vagueness. Ambiguity, hyper-vagueness, hyper-precision and hyper-generality are the main diseases of legal language (Dickerson 1981, pp. 54 ff; 1986, pp. 31 ff).

Words are very often ambiguous, that is, they do not have a single semantic referent, but two or more. Syntactic ambiguity appears when there are several different meanings arising from the structure of the sentence itself, that is, from the order of the words and from the way in which they are connected. Alf Ross (1963, pp. 111 ff) points out how this type of ambiguity will create what he calls "syntactic problems of interpretation". The study of these syntactic problems is relevant to both the drafting and the interpretation of laws. Ambiguity-related difficulties are often caused by adjectives or adjectival phrases—particularly when it is unclear wether an adjective might relate to two or more words—, by careless use of demonstrative and relative pronouns, or by subordinate sentences introducing

[17]For the sake of simplicity, I will dispense with the distinction between sense and meaning, and will use both terms synonymously.

modifications, exceptions or conditions. To avoid or at least to minimise such difficulties, drafters must certainly have a good knowledge of the grammar and syntax of the language in which they write[18]; and it is also advisable that linguistic experts are called upon to help them during the drafting process.

Semantic ambiguity occurs when a specific word cannot be accorded a single precise meaning because it can possess several. When stressing that words should be always used with the same sense within a norm (ideal of consistency), drafting scholars often overlook that words in fact normally have different meanings. A dictionary is nothing more than a compilation of the different meanings that can be assigned to each word. Of course, this type of ambiguity can be relatively easy to clarify through context. But real ambiguities appear when the uncertainty is not solved by the context alone. This is why, given their potential for deception and confusion, ambiguous words should be avoided by the drafter if the context does not clearly determine their meaning.[19] He must therefore prevent the use of an ambiguous word whenever the appropriate meaning can be expressed by another term.

There are also contextual ambiguities. Sometimes, when neither words nor syntax generate ambiguity, the true meaning of a legal text can still be elusive, because the exact relation between a specific section or paragraph of a norm and other sections of the same norm (or other norms) is uncertain. We are now referring to inconsistencies and redundancies, two issues that have always concerned legal theorists (see Ross 1963, p. 124). Those ambiguities which are produced by "presuppositions" or "implications" are also particularly relevant here. Francis Bennion (1980, pp. 115–119) observes how the search for brevity leads the drafter to omit certain words—a normative text will be shorter if the obvious is omitted. But what is obvious to the writer may not be obvious to the reader: does the ancient rule *expressio unius est exclusion alterius* apply, or may legislative provisions be taken to have a non-stated content, so that something that has not been made explicit in the text is considered to be implicit in it? The context will not always provide the answer.

The natural ambiguity of language is a serious limitation for the drafter as it will be later for the interpreter (Eskridge 1994, p. 38). But it is not necessarily an inevitable problem. It is precisely at this point where the drafter can do more: he can take good care of spelling and syntax and when, despite the application of the

[18]See, for example, Prieto de Pedro (1991), for a number of very pertinent recommendations with regard to the most recurrent vices of legal language.

[19]For Reed Dickerson, context in turn contains two elements: the established model of ideas and values immediately underlying language and the collateral and usually tacit assumptions shared and taken into account by the majority of members of a given language community. The first element of context tells the writer how to select a particular kind of language; the second element is important because it tells him that this is what he can omit; it is the "silent language" of rules. That is why, for Reed Dickerson, it is clear that for communication purposes it is not enough for the writer and the audience to share the legal instrument. They must also share the relevant elements of the same general cultural environment and, within this environment, the same knowledge, values and objectives.

basic principles (consistency, correct design, and normal use of words) there is still a contextual or semantic ambiguity, he can modify the wording or use precise definitions to eliminate it. An ambiguous text is a defective text, a fault of its drafter—most often an avoidable fault. A more delicate problem occurs when ambiguity is intentional, when it conceals an attempt to obscure the text so that the reader or interpreter can find in it what suits their best interest (Grandfest and Pritchard 2002, pp. 666 ff). In this case, we are talking about a serious fraud.

9.2.3 *The Virtues of Vagueness*

If ambiguity in a normative text is a problem, vagueness can be an advantage. Unlike ambiguity, vagueness entails that uncertainty of meaning is produced, not by the semantic plurality of a term but because of its indefinition. Precisely this indefinite meaning can be an invaluable aid for the drafter. As Herbert Hart (1968, pp. 159–160 [127–128]) famously said, "whichever device, precedent or legislation, is chosen for the communication of standards of behaviour" these standards "will, at some point where their application is in question, prove indeterminate", i.e. they will have "an open texture". Indeed, any word in any language has a clear core of meaning and an area of indefinition around it. The lack of certainty in this marginal zone—as Hart recalled—is "the price to be paid for the use of general classifying terms in any form of communication concerning matters of fact". Natural language show an irreductible open texture, and this open texture or vagueness is what makes it possible to write general rules—and to write them with the desired degree of precision.

Vagueness, on the other hand, fulfils a precious function as a legislative technique when it comes to reaching certain political agreements that would be unthinkable without it. It is not uncommon for legal doctrine to consider as failures of the legislators or as simple political arrangements (Zagrebelsky 1992, pp. 37 ff) what is only the result of an objective limitation imposed by factual politics. In this regard, Pablo Salvador Coderch (1989a, p. 15) reminds us that the best technical solutions are often impossible due only to political limitations or urgencies; and in such cases the drafter has to assume the primacy of politics. Technique can and must cooperate with politics, but cannot replace it. That is why the drafter has to be ready to use formulas that, if not technically perfect, do satisfy certain political needs. The obscurity of certain texts is clearly intentional. It can be caused, for example (Bennion 1980, pp. 132 ff), when the parties involved desire a minimum agreement, but do not have the time to reach it. They then "pretend" an agreement that does not really exist but does allow them to approve the norm (Mermin 1982, pp. 223 ff). Vagueness can also occur when a normative proposal that faces strong political opposition is sweetened by the government with the use of less precise or "softer" terms. In such cases, the drafter will be forced to give way to the political need for a broader consensus (Schepsle 1972; see also Grandfest and Pritchard 2002, pp. 640 ff).

In any case, the vagueness of terms can be controlled by drafters, to some extent at least, through the use of definitions (Salvador Coderch 1989b). For example, it may be that the drafter is using a vague term that has already been defined by the courts' jurisprudence (Bennion 1980, pp. 177 ff), such as "good family father" (*le bon père de famille*), and therefore he must first consider whether the term in question has already been defined by the legislator or has been specified or clarified by case law. If the drafter does not agree with such pre-existing definitions, or if he prefers to reformulate any of them, he must explicitly define the term in the draft text. More importantly, he must be aware of the fact that if the new definition is not included in the draft norm or is not clear enough, he is delegating lawmaking powers to judges and courts (MacIntyre 1986, pp. 72–74), who will make their own interpretation of the term.

Vagueness is thus manageable, it can be adjusted by the drafter with the help of definitions—a legistic tool that is increasingly applied—, and through greater concretion and detail within the legislative text (Dickerson 1986, p. 41). Through the choice of terms, the use of definitions and a partial control of the context, drafters have a fairly ample control of the areas and degrees of vagueness. They may not be able to eliminate all trace of vagueness, but can significantly reduce it. Vagueness, that is, may well be a natural limitation but is not necessarily an intractable issue for drafters. Problems occur when they are unaware of vagueness and produce an unwanted normative "delegation" or when they fail to control the precise degree of vagueness. They might then end up falling into one of the two great traps of legal language: "hyper-vagueness" or "hyper-precision". These—along with "hyper-generality" (over-inclusiveness) or "hypo-generality" (under-inclusiveness)[20]—are the real diseases of legal language.

9.2.4 *Precision Versus Clarity*

It is not easy for legal drafters to satisfy all the demands that they are often expected to meet (Pagano 1988). In Austria, "the formulation of legal rules should be concise and simple and, as far as possible, expressed in the active voice". In Belgium, the regulation on drafting of legal texts states that "legal rules must be concise and exact. Imprecision, fantasy, superfluousness and ambiguities have no place in their formulation". In France, "the drafting of a legal project and its complementary documentation (explanatory memorandum and presentation report) must be clear, sober and grammatically correct". For the German government, "laws should be drafted, from a linguistic point of view, and as far as possible, in a way that is comprehensible to

[20]The question of "generalisation"—the definition of classes of individuals and objects—is a no less important subject of study for drafters: if badly constructed, generalisations give rise to normative texts whose personal or material scope is greater (hyper-generalisation or over-inclusiveness) or smaller (hypo-generalisation or under-inclusiveness) than desired or projected. On this point, see further Schauer (1991).

all". In Canada "a law must be drafted simply, clearly and concisely, with the necessary degree of precision and, as far as possible, in ordinary language". In Spain, the legislative technique guidelines require that legal provisions are addressed to the citizen, so they must be written in a cultured language register, but accessible to the average person, in a clear, precise and simple manner. Despite their different formulations, all these demands seem to agree on the same points: brevity, clarity and precision. But... are these requirements always compatible with each other? A short text may not be precise, a precise text may not be clear, a clear text may not be brief.

Perhaps the different users of norms do not expect the same things from drafters (Renton Committee 1975). The government that entrusts the drafter with a new norm wants the final text to achieve the intended objectives, so precision may be more important than clarity or brevity. The parliamentarians who have to give their final approval to a norm demand that the draft be debatable, that is, orderly and clear about the policy they are being asked to vote on. Citizens demand that laws be understandable and the same can be said of those who apply them. For some the ideal to strive for may be precision, for others it may be clarity. Given that different actors (Miers 1986, p. 93) pursue objectives that may be incompatible with their own priorities or with the priorities of others, it comes as no surprise that what is perceived by one group as a failure may not be considered as such by another. This is not always taken into account by jurists when assessing the quality of norms.

But who should the drafter primarily serve? It is a mistake to think—as Kelsen did, for example—that the addressees of norms are always the public officials who apply them, and it is likewise mistaken to consider that norms are always addressed to citizens. The reality is that sometimes norms are addressed to all citizens, on other occasions they have a more restricted audience, and in most cases different parts of the norms are addressed to different audiences. Legal norms therefore have a multiple audience. During the drafting process, politicians and technicians will have to specify who the primary and who the secondary norm users are. If there is no awareness of the nature of the target audience (Dickerson 1986, pp. 25 ff), there will be no effective legislative communication. The concepts used in the draft, its form and specific wording will be determined by the nature of the linguistic community the norm is addressed to: their level of education, their degree of knowledge of the problem at stake and their possible prejudices... In short, it is the type of audience that determines what needs to be said and what does not—because it is well known or taken for granted. The style, the precision and the detail with which the norm has to be written largely depends on the audience to which it is addressed as well as on the audience's context.[21] As Lord Renton (1990, p. 15) said,

---

[21]After investigating the issue of who should norms be drafted for, the Standing Committee on Legal and Constitucional Affairs of the Australian House of Representatives (1993, p. 95) has adopted the following criteria: (a) the Committee accepts that there are often many different groups of norm users, and considers that (b) the problem of having a multiple audience should be dealt with by keeping in mind, when drafting norms, who will actually be affected by them—this may be difficult, though, if the range of people affected is very broad, as is usual e.g. in the field of social

in most parliamentary democracies the drafter of laws is faced with a conflict between the need to be precise and accurate (with a view to accomplishing effectiveness), on the one hand, and the citizen's demand for the use of ordinary language in legislative texts, on the other. If accuracy is given priority, the risk is hyper-elaboration; if clarity is given priority, the risk is hyper-vagueness. In a manner, these two risks seem to correlate, respectively, with the British and the continental European style of drafting norms.

9.2.5 *Two Styles of Drafting: English and Continental-European*

For some time now, one of the most stimulating debates in legislative technique has revolved around the style of drafting laws (Aigler 1923).[22] Basically, there are two major traditions: the drafting by means of general norms and clauses—which is typical for the legal culture of continental Europe—, and the Anglo-Saxon "casuistic" approach. In continental Europe, the traditional approach has been to formulate the law through general principles (cf. Renton Committee 1975, p. 55), leaving it up to the executive branch or the courts to specify the details when it comes to applying general legislative provisions to particular cases—under consideration of the parliament's intent as stated in legislative preambles or elicited from legislative records and materials. This approach seems to lead to simpler and clearer legislation, since details are omitted, but this is done at the cost of reducing certainty—the certainty that a more detailed development of the general provisions could produce. By contrast, the approach in Britain has been to specify, within the laws themselves, the manner in which they should be applied to particular cases, thus taking this task—or at least a part of it—off the shoulders of courts. As the Renton Report concludes, this second approach leads to a more convoluted legislation that is less accessible to the reader.

The option for one or the other drafting style is explained by a whole series of factors that are deeply rooted in the history, culture and institutional system of each country. Patchett (1982, pp. 35 ff), for instance, has identified a number of factors that may be associated with the British drafting style. First, the relationship between

security; (c) the Committee recognises that different people may be interested in the same piece of legislation in different ways, i.e. that norm addresses may not constitute a homogeneous group, so that it may be necessary to draft the text in accordance with the various audiences it affects; (d) by contrast, there may be some cases where it is possible to identify a single audience, i.e. a homogeneous group with common interests; (e) the department or agency in charge of giving instructions to drafters will generally be in a better position than the drafters themselves to know what kind of training and knowledge the target audience is likely to have, so this department or agency should inform drafters of the composition and attributes of the target audience of the envisaged norm.

[22]Cf. also Voermans (2011, pp. 38 ff).

statutes and common law should be highlighted: written law—which has more weight in the Anglo-Saxon system as usually assumed—has been elaborated following common law parameters, i.e. paying careful attention to particular circumstances and details. The effort to prevent courts from obstructing the political and social reforms of nineteenth century parliamentary legislation also contributed to the detailed wording of laws. Secondly, the doctrine of the supremacy of parliament establishes that courts are constitutionally obliged to apply the laws voted by the House: they cannot invalidate them nor declare them void. Laws must reflect what the will of the legislator was through a text that is as clear and precise as necessary to tie the hands of judges and courts. As Lord Denning said,[23] the legislator must try to think of all the possibilities and, as far as possible, include them into the statutory text so that even those who do not want to understand it cannot find a loophole. Thirdly, Patchett highlights the rule of law principle—particularly important in Great Britain since there is no written constitution—, which requires that any limitation of rights be explicitly provided for. The fourth factor is the role of courts: mistrust of judges, who lack the power to inapplicate or invalidate laws, leads the legislator to try to foresee all conceivable cases. Fifth, as a result of the relevant role played by the drafter in the process of legislation, the value of certainty is accorded special significance. Sixth, given that laws are drafted on the basis of specific instructions, drafters do their best to conform exactly to these instructions. And finally, the very requirements of the parliamentary process force the drafter of laws to anticipate all the possible concerns of the parliamentarians who will approve the final text: MPs want simple texts that make legislative debate easier, but at the same time they want texts that respond to the interests of their constituents.

These are the factors that influence the style and manner in which bills are drafted in the UK. They are deeply rooted in the British tradition and constitutional system. It is quite possible that the UK's membership to the European Union has led to an exchange of influence, allowing for greater approximation in the way laws are drafted in the UK and in continental Europe.[24] Sir William Dale (1992), a staunch

---

[23]In *Bulmer Ltd and Bollinger SA* (1974) 3 WLR 202, at 215, on the Treaty.

[24]Initially, the European Community adopted the continental style: a structured and synthetic legislative composition and a relatively concise and abstract wording that opened up a wide margin for judicial interpretation. That is why Lord Denning, in *Bulmer Ltd and Bollinger SA* (1974), could say from England: "the draftsmen of our statutes have striven to express themselves with utmost exactness. They have tried to foresee all possible circumstances that may arise and to provide for them. They have sacrificed style and simplicity (. . .). How different is this Treaty! It lays down general principles. It express its aims and purpose. All in sentences of moderate length and commendable style. But it lacks precision. It uses word and phrases without defining what they mean". But it is also true that the British style has influenced EU law over time. Now it is the continental jurists who denounce the English influence on EU law—reflected in the use of preliminary definitions, long articles subdivided into multiple headings, provisions stating principles, and exceptions to principles, derogations from exceptions, etc. It is not for no reason that 2/3 of the documents on which the Commission, the Permanent Representatives Committee and the Council work are written in English in their original version. One of the clearest signs of penetration of English formulas into EU law and into the Spanish and other member states' legislation is the

defender of the continental approach as opposed to the detailed style practiced in the UK, compared the length and tidiness of British laws with the French: in England, in 1984 the three volumes of Public General Acts contained 62 laws with 978,520 words. In France, for the same year, a somewhat higher number of laws had been passed—exactly 69—with only 213,000 words. The same law, the Copyright Act, is five times longer in Britain than in Sweden, three and a half times longer than in France and about twice as long as in Germany. According to Dale (1977, p. 331), the extension of British laws, their level of detail, their internal disorganisation, their scarcity of general principles, and their system of amendments are characteristics of the British style that contrast with the sober, lucid and succinct continental style.

The British style has therefore opted for precision to the detriment, where necessary, of clarity and comprehensibility. For its part, the continental style—marked by the frequent use of vague terms, general concepts or declarations of principles—seems to favour clarity over precision. Legislation based on general principles, as is typical for the continent, has a great advantage: it is easy to read and its objectives are easy to understand. But it also has a great disadvantage: the precise meaning of the text is uncertain since it is the executive branch and ultimately the judiciary that, a posteriori, provide those general formulations with content and meaning. This being the case (Wassermann 1982, p. 98), the legislator should know that each time he uses these broad formulations he relinquishes control of the real facts and hands it over to the judiciary. In other words, he forsakes his own competences and powers to the judges—and it is quite difficult to predict how these will interpret the legislator's work.

Which style should be adopted and which level of detail or "penetration"[25] laws should have are, therefore, eminently political options—for both questions are of utmost importance. It is not something that must be decided by the drafter: the drafter's responsibility is to warn the politician of the effects of using general

recurrent use of legislative definitions—e.g. all EU directives are preceded by a series of definitions. A second sign of English influence, according to Conseil d'État. Rapport Public (1992, p. 46), is that "EU directives now seem to abound in recommendations which are obvious, and in indications given to the judge. Is it not a question of transposing into Community law the principle of 'literal interpretation' imposed on British judges?" Another sign of the Anglo-Saxon influence can be seen in the fact that "directives deal successively with a multitude of particular cases without trying to formulate any guiding principle and adopt an analytical structure dotted with references and referrals. Aren't these the characteristics of Anglo-Saxon law?" For Conseil d'État. Rapport Public (1992, p. 47) "this hybridization of national laws, this pairing of concepts, vocabulary and forms under the impulse of the Community, can also prove fruitful: European law selects, in short, what is best in each of the national systems".

[25]Maria Jesús Montoro Chiner (1989), following Böhret and Hugger (1980), distinguishes between the "intensity" of regulation (understood as the relationship between the regulated fields and the non-regulated fields) and the degree of "penetration" of a law (which describes the degree of detail of a given regulation). For Montoro (1989, p. 82), the current state of the discussion points towards the negative evaluation of both "imperative" and excessively detailed laws, since they produce effects contrary to those intended by inducing the bureaucratic structure to hide against them, to ignore them as annoying and casuistic.

clauses, principles or excessively vague terms in the draft.[26] In any case, the question of what degree of regulatory intensity is desirable does not seem a priori to have a single general answer. It is a quite complex question that calls, rather, for differentiated answers, depending on factors such as the domain of law (e.g. public, private, constitutional law, etc.) which is concerned, or the various functions that modern legislation can be enacted for (think e.g. of "liberal", non-interventionist legislation as contrasted to "promotional" legislation on social and public services).[27]

Civic culture in general, and the culture of judges in particular, is an element to consider when choosing between drafting styles. Justice Holmes said that the legislator must draft laws thinking only of the alleged offender, who will read and scrutinise them in order to find a loophole that will allow him to carry out his illegitimate intention. If this were always true, the only option for the drafter would seem to be the detailed style, the meticulousness that leads to obese norms. The same thing happens when the judiciary is reluctant to cooperate faithfully with the legislative bodies and intends to replace them. The effectiveness of the diffuse style, of making use of broad concepts, principles, and general clauses depends very much on the willingness of citizens and above all, of judges, to make the ideal of the rule of law come true. For this reason, as Reed Dickerson (1986, p. 45) says, drafters must do their best to eliminate or minimise uncertainty whenever there is a relevant possibility that the language of a norm might be misread by a typical reader. No rules or guidelines for this task can substitute for the better judgment of an experienced drafter who is sensitive to the nuances of the text and the context.

---

[26]In view of the respective advantages and disadvantages of the continental style and the English style, the Plain English Manual (Australian Government 1993 [2016]) recommends that, in the case of a less detailed style using general clauses, the drafter should: (a) inform the policy responsibles about how complex a casuistic wording might be and how the law could be drafted in a simpler way; (b) inform them of the areas of uncertainty that a simpler style will create; (c) make sure that they fully understand the likely effect of any uncertainty that may be created; (d) discuss with them the degree of generality to be used and (e) whether the details should be supplemented by delegated legislation or administrative rules, or be left for the tribunals to interpret; and (f) remind them that in some cases delegating to courts may have unacceptable consequences.

[27]As concerns the desirable normative intensity, i.e. casuism versus generality, Macheret (1982, pp. 135 and 136) summarised the 1982 European Law Colloquium in four major points. First, international law and especially Community law are leading to a progressive *rapprochement* in the way of legislating between common law and continental countries, although the former are not willing to give up their style. Second, generality and concision do not necessarily guarantee clarity; conversely, precision and detail do not always guarantee legal certainty. Third, the question of what degree of regulatory intensity is desirable merits a differentiated response, depending on whether we are dealing with private or with public law, with constitutional or with administrative law, with "police laws" or with "promotional" administrative legislation, etc. The circle of addressees can also be relevant here. And finally, the legist must have, from the outset, a clear idea of the powers he intends to confer on the norm applicators, i.e. on administrative authorities and judges.

9.2.6 Delegations

Another major decision that the drafter must make very carefully concerns delegations (Arandson et al. 1982). Some of the ambiguities and obscurities of legislative texts certainly originate in the incompetence or the mistakes of the drafter. However, there are often other explanations for the comprehension problems that legislative texts pose—for example, such problems may be due to the mere fact that a single text cannot say and decide everything (Bennion 1980, pp. 101 ff). In order to solve this difficulty, the drafter can resort, as in ordinary language, to ellipsis, and rely on the technique of delegation. As stressed in the recommendations of the Council of the OECD,[28] in addition to the question of legislative competence,[29] it must be decided whether or not delegation is appropriate.

The search for guiding criteria in this respect has already been the subject of important studies. For present purposes, it may be worthwhile taking into account the canons proposed by Barry M. Mitnick (1989, pp. 343 ff [327 ff]) in order to decide whether to regulate certain aspects of a norm, or to delegate their regulation. In parliament, delegation usually occurs due to the following reasons: (a) "inexpertness" or lack of experience in taking such a decision—this is usual in parliaments, and leads them to delegate the decision in specialised bodies of the administration; (b) slowness in the process of legislation: certain legislative decisions might be urgent, and urgency may be incompatible with regular, slow parliamentary procedures; (c) lacking continuity along the decision-making process: there might be a problem that requires successive decisions over a period of time that is longer than the parliamentary cycle; (d) the impossibility of permanent oversight: legislators cannot monitor and control specific policies and must therefore often delegate these functions; (e) the convenience of avoiding undesired partisan interference: rigid fidelity to party interests may lead to entrusting a specific decision to another body in which partisan influence is less pronounced; (f) the need to promote a certain consensus for constitutional or strictly political reasons: in this case, it is the parliament that provides for the broad formulation of the goals of legislation, while their specification and concretisation is delegated to another organ; (g) the need to offer single rationales, which must often be phrased in broad or vague terms; (h) the desire of the delegatees to expand their powers: it is often the case that the administration, with the strategic aim of maximising resources, presses for a delegation that gives it more powers; (i) the search for mechanisms to resolve the dilemma of collective decision making: finding a third party to resolve such a dilemma is another powerful incentive for delegation; (j) lack of capacity to deal with change and uncertainty: parliaments may be aware of their inability to foresee all future contingencies and to respond quickly to changes in the environment, and may therefore choose to delegate to bodies that are closer to the specific problems

[28] See *Recommandation du Conseil de l'OCDE concernant L'Amélioration de la Qualité de la Réglementation Officielle* (9 March 1995).

[29] In this regard, see EC Commission (1993).

and can operate more swiftly. And finally, we could add to the previous list the desire not to decide, that is, not to take effective action on a specific matter—an objective that is sometimes achieved by delegating the decision to bodies that are under-resourced or particularly prone to inactivity.

The role of the drafter on this particular point is not to replace politicians or policymakers in determining whether or not one of these reasons justify the delegation of a specific decision. This is a highly political issue that should be neither hidden nor manipulated (Marcello 1996, p. 2446). The drafter's mission here is to warn about the possible consequences, to draw attention to the political effects of any delegation, to regulate the limits and guarantees to be applied in each case and, above all, to prevent delegation when it might involve fraud in the democratic process.

9.3 The Critical Review of Drafts

The drafter of a norm has to be willing to revise the initial draft as many times as the difficulty and complexity of the text requires. He must be prepared to make numerous consultations with political leaders and experts involved in the process in order to shape—on this basis—what will be the definitive text. The redefinition and precision of the objectives by the political leaders will cause the drafter to introduce successive variations in the text. But there is a moment when this continuous redefinition process reaches an end (Engle 1983, pp. 10 ff) and the text of the last draft must be submitted for critical review.

The first review is made by the drafter himself though an overall examination of all the terms and concepts used in the text, as well as of the coherence of the definitions provided. The article-by-article drafting of a norm may have generated gaps, antinomies, or inconsistencies between different sections or parts of the text. The text has to speak with one voice throughout all its articles (Dickerson 1986, pp. 64 ff), and this is why Thornton (1987, p. 133) recommends the drafter the tedious routine of checking: the consistency of language; all references to other norms, as well as all internal cross-references within the text; the use of definitions; numbering and tabulation; the use of paragraphs, capital letters, orthography, punctuation; the coherence and proportionality of sanctions; the proper location of each article in its corresponding section; introductory formulas; geographical references; references to departments; correction of the headers and margin notes; and adequacy of the title.

Yet, whatever the level of professionalism and seriousness of the drafter is, the best review always comes from another professional. In this regard, normative drafting is not very different from any other intellectual task that requires external criticism. For this reason, the most unanimous advice that can be found in legal drafting studies is the submission of the final text to the consideration and objections of other professionals who can detect the faults that the drafter is unable to discover no matter how much he continues to revise the text.

Particularly important in this last phase of drafting is the comprehensibility of the text. Legal or legislative language cannot be reduced to common language, as Camilo José Cela claimed in the Spanish Constitutional Assembly (*Cortes Constituyentes*)[30]; but the technical—both legal and non-legal—components of legislative language do not imply that the comprehensibility of legal texts cannot be significantly improved. In many legal systems, there is a clear aim to improve the comprehensibility of legislative texts through the training of drafters, the issuing of norms or guidelines on the use of language, or the implementation of readability and comprehension tests. This latter approach to improving comprehensibility was pioneered by the Australian parliament, which carefully studied in which particular cases it is advisable to utilise this type of test. If legislation is ineffective when it cannot be understood, a good way to assess its comprehensibility is to submit the draft to a reading test by the addressees. We can thus join the Australian House of Representatives' Committee on Legal and Constitutional Affairs in saying that testing the understanding of a norm by those who will be its users has considerable advantages not only in ensuring that the piece of legislation in question is as clear as possible, but also in identifying what plain language techniques are effective. For reasons of confidentiality of because of time or resource constraints, among other factors, it is not always possible to conduct such a test and check for the comprehensibility of all norms. However, the benefits of establishing an ambitious program in this regard cannot be overstated (cf. Australian House of Representatives 1993, pp. 96 ff). Of course, for this approach to succeed, it is necessary to define the potential primary users of a normative text, and this, as mentioned, is not always easy.[31] But the suggestion of having legislative texts tested for comprehensibility by its potential users should be taken very seriously.

References

Aigler W (1923) Legislation in vague or general terms. Mich Law Rev 21:831–851

Arandson PH et al (1982) A theory of legislative delegation. Cornell Law Rev 68:1–67

Austin JL (2004) Cómo hacer cosas con palabras, 4th edn. Paidós, Barcelona

Australian Government (1988 [2017]) Legislation handbook (updated in February 2017). Department of the Prime Minister and Cabinet, Canberra

Australian Government (1993 [2016]) Plain English manual (updated in August 2016). Office of Parliamentary Counsel, Canberra

Australian House of Representatives (1993) Clearer Commonwealth law: report of the inquiry into legislative drafting by the Commonwealth. House of Representatives Standing Committee on Legal and Constitutional Affairs. Australian Government Publication Service, Canberra

---

[30]The literature Nobel Prize holder Camilo José Cela was a Senator, appointed by the king, in the 1977 Constitutional Assembly, where he presented a whole package of amendments to the Draft Constitution to improve the use of Spanish language in the constitutional text. See Gregorio Peces-Barba's (1996, pp. 195 ff) comments on the subject.

[31]See however Xanthaki (2019).

Bartole S (ed) (1988) Lezioni di Tecnica Legislativa. CEDAM, Padova
Bennion F (1978) Statute law obscurity and the drafting parameters. Br J Law Soc 5(2):235–245
Bennion F (1980) Statute law. Oyez Publishing, London
Böhret C, Hugger W (1980) Entburokratisierung durch Vollzugsfreundlichere und Wirksame Gesetz. (Speyerer Arbeitshefte 35). Deutsche Hochschule für Verwaltungswissenschaften, Speyer
Conseil d'État. Rapport Public (1992) La Semaine Juridique. Edition Générale, N.23, 9 juin 1993
Costanzo M (1994) Legal writing. Cavendish Publishing, London
Dale W (1977) Legislative drafting: a new approach. Butterworths, London
Dale W (1992) The European legislative scene. Statute Law Rev 13(2):79–96
Dickerson R (1981) Materials on legal drafting. American casebook series. West Publishing, St. Paul, MN
Dickerson R (1986) The fundamentals of legal drafting, 2nd edn. Little Brown & Co., Toronto
Drieger EA (1953) The preparation of legislation. Can Bar Rev 31:33–39
EC Commission (1993) Report to the European Council on the adaptation of existing legislation to the subsidiarity principle. EC Commission, Edinburgh
Engle G (1983) Bills are made to pass as razors are made to shave: practical constrains in the preparation of legislation. Statute Law Rev 4(2):7–23
Eskridge WN Jr (1994) Dynamic statutory interpretation. Harvard University Press, Cambridge
Ezquiaga FJ (1987) La argumentación en la justicia constitucional española. HAAE/IVAP, Oñati
Ezquiaga FJ (1994) Argumentos interpretativos y postulado del legislador racional. Isonomía 1:69–98
García-Escudero P (2010) Técnica legislativa y seguridad jurídica: ¿hacia el control constitucional de la calidad de las leyes? Thomson-Civitas, Madrid
Gluck AR, Schultz Bressman L (2013) Statutory interpretation from the inside—an empirical study of congressional drafting, delegation, and the canons: part I. Stanford Law Rev 65(5):901–1026
Gluck AR, Schultz Bressman L (2014) Statutory interpretation from the inside—an empirical study of congressional drafting, delegation, and the canons: part II. Stanford Law Rev 66(4):725–802
Grandfest JA, Pritchard C (2002) Statutes with multiple personality disorders: the value of ambiguity in statutory design and interpretation. Stanford Law Rev 54:666–736
GRETEL (Grupo de Estudios de Técnica Legislativa) (1986) La forma de las leyes. Centro de Estudios Constitucionales, Madrid
GRETEL (Grupo de Estudios de Técnica Legislativa) (1989) Curso de técnica legislativa. Centro de Estudios Constitucionales, Madrid
Hart HLA (1968) El concepto del derecho. Abeledo Perrot, Buenos Aires. [The concept of law. Oxford: Clarendon Press, 1961]
Holland JA, Webb J (1994) Learning legal rules. Blackstone Press, London
Igartua J (1990) El postulado del legislador racional (entre metodología y mitología). Revista Vasca de Administración Pública 28:113–126
Karpen U, Xanthaki H (2017) Legislation in Europe. A comprehensive guide for scholars and practitioners. Hart (Bloomsbury), Oxford
Macheret A (1982) Rapport general. In: Principes et méthodes d'élaboration des normes juridiques. Actes du douzième Colloque de Droit Européen (Friburg, 13–15 octobre 1982). Conseil de l'Europe, Strasbourg, pp 131–139
MacIntyre A (1986) The multiple sources of legislative ambiguity: tracing the legislative origins of administrative discretion. In: Avon DS, Hibben HK (eds) Administrative discretion and the implementation of public policy. Praeger, Santa Barbara, pp 67–88
Marcello DA (1996) The ethics and politics of legislative drafting. Tulane Law Rev 70:2437–2465
Martín Casals M (1989) Planificación de la intervención legislativa. In: GRETEL (ed) Curso de Técnica Legislativa. Centro de Estudios Constitucionales, Madrid, pp 231–251
Martineau R (1991) Drafting legislation and rules in plain English. West, New York
Mermin S (1982) Law and the legal system, 2nd edn. Little Brown & Co., Boston
Miers D (1986) Legislation, linguistic adequacy and public policy. Statute Law Rev 7(2):90–113

Ministerio de la Presidencia (2011) Directrices de Técnica Normativa. Catalogo de las publicaciones de la Administración General del Estado, Madrid
Mitnick BM (1989) La economía política de la regulación. FCE, México. [The political economy of regulation. Creating, designing, and removing regulatory forms. Columbia University Press, New York, 1989]
Montoro MJ (1989) Adecuación al ordenamiento y factibilidad. Presupuestos de calidad de las normas. Centro de Estudios Constitucionales, Madrid
Nino CS (1989) Consideraciones sobre la dogmática jurídica (con referencia particular a la dogmática penal). México, UNAM (Instituto de Investigaciones Jurídicas)
Nino CS (1993) Introducción al análisis del Derecho. Astrea, Buenos Aires
Nourse VF, Schacter JS (2002) The politics of legislative drafting: a Congressional Case Study. N Y Univ Law Rev 77:575–624
Nowak L (1964) De la rationalité du legislateur comme élément de l'interpretation juridique. Logique et Analyse 12:45–65
Oakeshott M (1991) Rationalism in politics and others essays. Liberty Press, Indianapolis
Pagano R (ed) (1988) Normative europee sulla tecnica legislativa. Camera dei Deputati, Roma
Patchett K (1982) Tecniques d'élaboration des lois. In: Principes et méthodes d'élaboration des normes juridiques. Actes du douzième Colloque de Droit Européen (Friburg, 13–15 octobre 1982). Conseil de l'Europe, Strasbourg, pp 131–139
Peces-Barba G (1996) La democracia en España: experiencias y reflexiones. Temas de Hoy, Madrid
Prieto de Pedro J (1989) Los vicios del lenguaje legal. Propuestas de estilo. In: Sainz F, Ochoa J (eds) La calidad de las leyes. Parlamento Vasco, Vitoria, pp 121–156
Prieto de Pedro J (1991) Lenguas, lenguaje y derecho. Civitas, Madrid
Renton L (1990) Current drafting: practices and problems in the UK. Statute Law Rev 11:12–17
Renton Committee (1975) The preparation of legislation. Report of a Committee appointed by the Lord President of the Council. H.M. Stationery Office, London
Ross A (1963) Sobre el Derecho y la Justicia. Eudeba, Buenos Aires
Rubin EL (1991/1992) Legislative methodology: some lessons from the truth-in-lending act. Geo Law Rev 80:283–308
Rylance P (1994) Legal writing and drafting. Blackstone Press, London
Sainz F, Ochoa J (1989) La calidad de las leyes. Parlamento Vasco, Vitoria
Salvador Coderch S (1989a) Elementos para la definición de un programa de técnica legislativa. In: GRETEL (ed) Curso de Técnica Legislativa. Centro de Estudios Constitucionales, Madrid, pp 45–85
Salvador Coderch P (1989b) Definiciones y remisiones. In: Sainz F, Ochoa J (eds) La calidad de las leyes. Parlamento Vasco, Vitoria, pp 157–182
Santaolalla F (ed) (2008) Técnica Normativa en la Unión Europea, 2 vols. Senado de España, Madrid
Schauer F (1991) Playing by the rules. A philosophical examination of rule-based decision-making in law and in life. Clarendon, Oxford
Schepsle KA (1972) The strategy of ambiguity: uncertainty and electoral competition. Am Pol Sci Rev 66:555–568
Thornton GC (1987) Legislative drafting, 3rd edn. Butterworths, London
Uhlmann F, Höfler S (eds) (2016) Professional legislative drafters. Status, roles, education. Dike, Zürich
UK Government (2010 [2018]) Guidance for Members of the Office of Parliamentary Counsel who are drafting bills to be considered in Parliament (20 October 2010, updated 17 July 2018). OPC, London
Uniform Law Conference of Canada (1989) Uniform acts drafting conventions. Uniform Law Conference of Canada, Ottawa
U.S. House of Representatives (Office of Parliamentary Counsel) (1997) Guide to legislation drafting, Washington, DC
U.S. Senate (1997) Legislative drafting manual. Washington
Voermans W (2011) Styles of legislation and their effects. Statute Law Rev 32(1):38–53

Wassermann R (1982) Loi et Efficacité. In: Principes et méthodes d'élaboration des normes juridiques. Actes du douzième Colloque de Droit Européen (Fribourg, 13–15 octobre 1982). Conseil de l'Europe, Strasbourg, pp 91–106
Wintgens LJ (2013) The rational legislator revisited. In: Wintgens LJ, Oliver-Lalana AD (eds) The rationality and justification of legislation. Springer, Cham, pp 1–31
Xanthaki H (2014) Drafting legislation. Hart, Oxford
Xanthaki H (2019) Misconceptions in legislative quality: an enlightened approach to the drafting of legislation. In: Oliver-Lalana AD (ed) Conceptions and misconceptions of legislation. Springer, Cham
Zagrebelsky G (1992) El derecho dúctil. Trotta, Madrid

Chapter 10
The Drafter's Deontology

10.1 The Drafter and the Genesis of Norms

The genesis of norms can be studied either from the perspective of demand, or from the perspective of supply, or even as a result of the system's own self-reproduction. According to the first perspective—the theory of demand—norms are the consequence of felt social needs, which become demands that are sometimes satisfied through the enactment of a norm. It is understood (see La Spina 1989, pp. 15 ff) that the legislator is a "receptive" actor who either limits himself to ratifying juridical models that are already given in society or "creates" a norm to give a solution to a certain social problem. Some Marxist, iusnaturalist, or sociologic accounts of law contain an explanation of this kind for the genesis of norms. And it is true that the pressure of events—rather than electoral programs[1]—can sometimes determine the normative production of an entire legislative session (Griffith and Ryle 1989, p. 309; Edwards and Wood 1999).

Another perspective tries to explain the birth of norms from the point of view of supply: it is the decision-makers themselves who determine or condition social needs. A public policy-making system, as Lindblom (1991, pp. 145 ff) says, has by itself a great effect on the aspirations, opinions and attitudes to which policies respond. It is not like a machine into which people introduce their desires and needs and which produces satisfactory solutions to them. Rather, it is the machine itself that produces those desires and needs. Only with regard to some primordial or basic issues do public authorities consistently give citizens what they say they want; yet, those citizens may have previously been indoctrinated to ask almost always for what governments want to give them (see Lindblom 1991, p. 153). In short, supply can

[1]Electoral programs have the virtue, not so much of advancing the specific policies that the government will carry out as of "showing the set of problems, the type of diagnosis that is made about them, and a pool of solutions or lines of action to undertake" without going into detail (Subirats 1992, p. 90).

V. Zapatero Gómez, *The Art of Legislating*, Legisprudence Library 6,
https://doi.org/10.1007/978-3-030-23388-4_10

also generate the demand for rules. When this perspective is applied to the genesis of norms, these can be said to be created by an interventionist legislator who does not limit himself to reflecting reality but takes the initiative to mould or shape it according to his own program (La Spina 1989, pp. 25 ff).

But neither the perspective of demand nor the perspective of supply of norms explain the whole norm production in our systems (Meny and Thoenig 1992, p. 112): a norm can be born because another pre-existing norm, in the course of its execution phase, poses difficulties, encounters obstacles, or modifies a previous situation in such a way that public authorities have to intervene again in another direction, on a different aspect, or by other means. In other words, public policies feed largely on themselves, as a result of the constant and necessary adjustment and readjustment of current norms, which we could attempt to explain through the concept of autopoiesis—i.e., trough the idea of a self-reproducing legal order.[2] For this reason, it is convenient to distinguish between norms that are born out of a strictly political impulse and those that originate in administrative instances, that is, between political and administrative norm projects.[3] The former—which some also call party politics—affect directly the position of political parties, their signs of identity and electoral possibilities. The latter, which do not ordinarily occupy the centre of public debate (industrial policy, finance, communications...) are the field of technocracy.[4]

These are the three clichés that have traditionally been used to explain the origin of rules. None of the three explains by itself the origin of each and every one of the thousands of norms that appear daily in our legal systems. And all three contain a part of the truth, because norms are sometimes the fruit of social demands, on other occasions they are the result of offers from public authorities and, much more frequently, they derive from the very functioning of the legal system. But whatever the impulse is to which they owe their birth, they all end up in the hands of the least studied and at the same time most decisive figure in the process of norm production: the norm-writer or *drafter*.

---

[2]For Luhmann (1981, p. 66), as noted in Chap. 6, law is a self-referential system: it "produces and reproduces by itself the elements of which it is constituted (. . .). A self-referential system can thus conduct operations only by means of self-contact; that is, in tune with other operations of its own (. . .). Every decision refers to other decisions and each of the decisions can express its own sense only through such an internal reference, as a contribution to the attainment or impairment of other decisions, as the rings of a chain". Law is thus conceived as a system that is continually self-reproduced: norms are daughters of other norms.

[3]Burton and Drewry (1970, 1981) distinguish between policy bills (which make substantial changes in public policies) and administration bills (which facilitate their implementation).

[4]"All this leads us to nuance the role of parties in the production of public policies. Their role is crucial in the phase of determining the elites of government and a certain capacity of control over the activity of the different governments (...). However, in the most *substantive* field, in the field of determining the policies that will be pursued by public authorities in specific areas of intervention, their protagonism is greatly reduced, to the benefit of other actors" (Subirats 1992, pp. 96–97).

At least in our parliamentary systems (see above Chap. 8), the vast majority of the drafts that will end up becoming laws pass through the hands of the drafters. The quality of our laws and therefore also the trust in law as an instrument of social direction depend to a great extent on the quality of the drafter's work. Traditionally, the drafter has been presented—in those few occasions in which this figure has merited the attention of legal science—as a mere technician, a loyal Weberian-style official, an expert in how to do the things that others decide need to be done. The ideal type of drafter is a politically neutral professional, with an excellent technical preparation and with the requisite ability to set aside his personal preferences in order to help politicians realise their own. But beyond this idealisation, reality shows us to what extent drafters are at the very heart of the norm-making process: their relationship with norms is not a technical relationship but a clearly political one. They are not, despite what one might think, mere scribes who limit themselves to translating political decisions into legal language (Marcello 1996, pp. 1439 ff); rather, their work as norm-writers is inherently political, in the sense that they not only determine the form but also usually the very substance and content of the norms they draft. As discussed in previous chapters, drafters do so by participating in the clarification of the objectives of norms, by evaluating and selecting the adequate instruments of legislative intervention, by choosing the degree of vagueness in the language of laws, by specifying the level of administrative or judicial discretion, by recommending delegations and implementation mechanisms... By doing all this—and inevitably all this has to be done—drafters cannot possibly elude the ethical and political implications of their profession.

10.2 Drafters and Jurists

The drafting of legislative texts normally remains, as we saw, in the hands of jurists. In a way, the relationship between the drafter and the political decision-makers resembles the lawyer–client relationship—understood in a broad sense.

As members of a legal profession, lawyers are at the same time representatives of their clients, agents of the legal system and citizens who have a special responsibility for the quality of the judicial system (American Bar Association 2004). As legal representatives, lawyers perform different functions. Lawyers are counsellors who inform their clients of their rights and obligations and of the practical implications of their actions, and give them advice on the best legal strategy. When it comes to litigation, lawyers defend their clients before the administration or the courts; and they are also negotiators who try to reach agreements which suit their clients' interests, or evaluators who assess their clients' legal affairs and inform them of their position. As agents of the legal system, lawyers also have an interest in its proper functioning, in its prestige and in the promotion of the trust that citizens have in it. And finally, lawyers are citizens who, as such, long for a better quality of the legal system and for a better and more accessible judicial system. Thus, lawyers defend their clients (ex post) and help them choose the best course of action (ex ante); but they also have obligations towards the system of administration of justice, towards their own colleagues and towards the citizens themselves. Even though their performance does not necessarily imply endorsing the behaviour or the political, moral or social views of their clients, lawyers do much more than translating their clients' wishes into legal terms. Hence the need for lawyers to assume, in addition to their legal obligations, a whole series of deontological norms which are usually enshrined in professional codes of conduct.

Traditionally it was considered that lawyers or jurists working in the public sector were not bound by deontological codes, since in principle these codes were intended for the free exercise of the profession. At first, it was even considered that such codes did not fully apply to corporate lawyers or to lawyers whose clients are companies, not private citizens. This may explain why, in Spain, lawyers in the public sector and corporate lawyers have remained for a long time beyond the scope of the codes of professional ethics—as can be inferred from reading the Deontological Code of Spanish Lawyers.[5] But this trend is changing, at least in the Anglo-Saxon world. And so, for example, the Model Rules of Professional Conduct in the USA include rule 1.13, explicitly devoted to the lawyer working for a corporation—"organisations as clients"—, who must comply with the stipulations of this ethical code.[6] There is a clear tendency to consider that not only the regular practising lawyer but also a wider range of legal operators are bound by deontological rules or standards. And this should also include jurists who work in the service of public authorities, be it in the legislative or in the executive branch. In fact, the claim is gaining ground that the codes of conduct of bar associations should be applied—with due adjustments—to jurists working for the administration or the legislature, and that these should be subject to similar duties as lawyers representing private citizens.

Among the jurists who work for the executive branch are those who have the task of drafting norms. The importance of their activity and the need for its adequate regulation cannot be overemphasised. As mentioned, the drafter's work is not a merely "translation" of his or her principal's wishes into legal terms: it includes providing and filtering the relevant information for decision making; advising politicians on the different courses of action they can follow, and on the implications of each option; providing reasons to justify the chosen options; negotiating different draft texts with the departments affected; monitoring the whole itinerary of the draft, including its parliamentary processing, etc. All these functions have a formidable impact on the quality of our legal system, on the preservation and progress of the rule

[5]Approved by the Plenary of the General Council of Spanish Lawyers on 30 June 2000.

[6]Further development of these rules can be found in the California Rules of Professional Conduct of 1 June 2007, in the Colorado Rules of Professional Conduct adopted by the Colorado Supreme Court on 12 April 2007 (effective from 1 January 2008), or in the Tennessee Rules of Professional Conduct.

of law principle and on citizens' rights and duties. In short: the realisation of very important values depends on the drafters' professionalism and commitment.

So, if most laws and regulations—both in concentrated and diffuse systems—are drafted by jurists who work within the Administration or for the Administration, and if their work has such a big impact on citizens in general (and not only on specific individuals as is the case with lawyers), it is only logical to ask whether they should be subject to certain ethical guidelines and, if so, whether these would be the same or similar to the codes that regulate the activity of lawyers in general. Until now, the dominant ideology used to present lawyers—and also jurists at the service of the administration—as legal representatives who do not endorse the political, economic or social activities of their clients, nor their ideological and moral commitments. The jurist thus appears as "morally encapsulated" (Clark 1999, p. 37), which makes sense when it comes to guaranteeing the defendant's right to defence but has little meaning when the jurist acts as an advisor, counsellor or mediator. The same can be said of drafters: their mission lies not in justifying or defending past behaviour but in establishing rules of conduct for the future. These rules, when poorly designed and drafted, can certainly cause irreparable damage to people and property. Do drafters hold any kind of responsibility—we are referring to moral and social responsibility—if they have indeed collaborated in the enactment of legislation that has harmful effects for individuals or for society as a whole? What is the responsibility of those experts in financial engineering who in 2008 caused the biggest economic crisis since the 1929 crash? It is not easy for jurists who participate in the making of socially harmful legislative or economic decisions to avoid—by hiding behind the hierarchical structure of the administration or of a large company—the weighty moral responsibility involved in their work. For even much better reasons than in the case of regular lawyers, legislative drafters cannot limit themselves to be simple "translators" of the wishes of their superiors or principals.

Yet, if drafters are to assume their responsibility, their specific duties as drafters—i.e., not their strictly legal obligations—should be first defined. It would at least be advisable to delimit the scope and boundaries of the special obligations that should bind drafters in the practice of their profession; the relation towards their immediate superiors, and towards the government or the parliament; and the criteria to follow when conflicts of responsibility arise. Rules of conduct of this kind—it must be remembered—do not constitute the basis for civil or criminal liability but aim, rather, to establish new parameters in order to improve the system, to share values amongst professional colleagues and counterparts, to drive constructive debate and to identify problems (Macnair 2004).

10.3 Materials for a Code of Conduct

The special nature of the work of jurists at the service of the administration prevents us from directly applying to them the deontological rules that guide the work of private lawyers. But comparative law, the Code of Ethics for Lawyers in Spain—

clearly insufficient and little adapted to the needs of the profession today—and some important doctrinal contributions from the Anglo-Saxon world,[7] among which Roger Purdy's work stands out,[8] can help us gather some materials with which to construct a code of conduct that could apply—with due specifications—to those who deal, in the heart of government or parliament, with the production of norms. Here and now, however, we will consider only the governmental phase of legislative drafting.

1. Perhaps the first duty of a norm drafter is, as is the case with any lawyer, the duty of professional competence. A lawyer should not accept a task he does not consider himself competent for, unless he works in collaboration with a lawyer who is.[9] More precisely, the ABA Model Rules of Professional Conduct remind us that the lawyer's duty of competence implies having the legal knowledge, the skills and the preparation which are reasonably necessary for legal representation. Furthermore, this competence comprises the diligence and the mental, emotional and physical ability which are required to adequately perform the legal service in question.[10] On this basis, Roger Purdy suggests the following first rule of conduct: a drafter must provide the legislator with competent advice and drafting technique. This presupposes that drafters must possess and utilise technical writing skills, and that they can prove to be knowledgeable about the legal area and the legal issues affected by draft norms, and eventually also about their possible political, economic or social repercussions. Drafters should not accept a commission if they are not capable of executing it in a competent manner—but they can accept it if they are capable of acquiring such a competence before having to put it into practice.

   The accreditation of adequate professional competence is what justifies Anglo-Saxon institutions such as the Office of Parliamentary Counsel, and should be taken into account when establishing entry filters to the official bodies—such as the technical general secretariats in Spain—that are entrusted with the drafting of norms. Those who work with draft norms should be able to demonstrate the possession of greater technical-legal knowledge and experience than the average civil servant, specifically in those abilities required for drafting. Offices or organs with lawmaking powers should elaborate handbooks and guidelines to orientate and homogenise writing techniques, as is already the case in many countries,[11] and

[7]See Cramton (1991), Donahoe (1989), Marcello (1996), Pennell (1994), Josephson and Pearce (1986), or Weinstein (1966).

[8]Roger Purdy (1987) made one of the most important contributions to this field, providing us with useful insights.

[9]See Art. 13 of the Dentological Code of Spanish Lawyers.

[10]See Rule 3-110 of the California Rules of Professional Conduct.

[11]In this connection, we can mention e.g., the legislative drafting handbooks issued in Australia (Office of Parliamentary Counsel of New South Wales and Queensland), Hong Kong (Department of Justice, Law Drafting Division), the UK (Parliament of Scotland) or India (Imachal Pradesh, Law Department, Legislative Wing); or in the U.S.: in Alaska (Legislative Affairs Office), Arizona

should also provide the necessary training. But in addition to legal drafting skills, drafters must also possess—or acquire—an adequate knowledge of the law applicable in their field of operation (industry, telecommunications, urban planning, environment, administration of justice, etc.), and at the different levels (regional, national or international). And since some of the norms they draft will end up serving to settle disputes in courts, drafters must also have a good knowledge of the respective case-law as well as of the canons of interpretation usually followed by the courts.

Without such skills and knowledge, no jurist should take on the task of drafting a law.

2. The drafter's mission is not to assume responsibility for the policy decision but to provide the best assistance and advice to public decision-makers. Drafters should not be "shadow" legislators who usurpate lawmaking powers that do not belong to them, but loyal collaborators of those who legitimately hold these powers. Their task consists in offering their technical skills and their legal knowledge to the policy responsibles—and this includes offering specialised advice on the best possible solutions. Of course it would make little sense to claim that drafters must be as independent as regular lawyers are—the latter have a "right to independence", which counterweights eventual pressures coming from clients.[12] But

(Legislative Council), Connecticut (Legislative Commissioner's Office) Hawai (Legislative Reference Bureau), Illinois (Legislative Reference Bureau), Indiana (Legislative Council), Maine (State Legislature, Office of the Reviser of Statutes), Massachusetts (Counsel to the Senate), Minnesota (Office of the Reviser of Statutes), North Dakota (Legislative Council), South Dakota (Legislative Research Council), Texas (Legislative Council), Utah (Legislature), or Washington (Statute Law Committee, Office of the Code Reviser); or the International Labour Organization's Labour Legislation Guidelines (chapters X and XI). There are also norm drafting manuals for use by governments, e.g., in Germany (Bundesministerium der Justiz 2008), Australia (Victoria, Department of Premier and Cabinet, Office of the Chief Parliamentary Counsel), in the U.S. (National Archives and Records Administration, Office of the Federal Register) as well as in the states of Alaska (Department of Law), Connecticut (Legislative Commissioner's Office), Indiana (Legislative Council), Minnesota (Office of the Revisor of Statutes) and Ohio (Legislative Service Commission). For the UK, see the OPC's Drafting Guidance, available at: http://www.cabinetoffice.gov.uk/media/427772/drafting-guidance-101002.pdf.

[12]As stated in Art. 2 of the Deontological Code of Spanish Lawyers: "1) The independence of the lawyer is a requirement of the rule of law principle and of the citizens' right to legal defence, so for the lawyer it constitutes a right and a duty. 2) In order to be able to adequately advise and defend the legitimate interests of his clients, the lawyer has the right and the duty to preserve his independence against all kinds of interference and against his own or other people's interests. 3) The lawyer must preserve his independence from the pressures, demands or complacency that limit it, be it with respect to public, economic or factual powers, to the courts, to his client or even to his own colleagues or collaborators. 4) Independence allows him to reject instructions that, contrary to his professional criteria, are intended to be imposed on him by his client, his partners, the other professionals with whom he collaborates or any other person, entity or current of opinion; the lawyer must cease to advise or defend the matter in question when he considers that he cannot act with total independence. And 5) his independence disallows the lawyer from exercising other professions or activities that limit him or that are incompatible with the practice of law *(ejercicio de*

drafters do need to be able to make free use of their knowledge, specialisation and experience when it comes to questions of legal technique, form, style, language, organisation, etc. Drafters cannot forget that the form may affect the substance, and that their technical contributions have a bearing on the rights and freedoms of citizens. Drafters are tied to the instructions coming from their superiors but they also have duties before the very society they serve.

Somewhat more complex is the issue of the implication of the drafter as an advisor on substantive policy issues. Most drafters have internalised their role as technicians who avoid any involvement in the political decision: it is not their function to determine in any way the legislative policy (Drieger 1953). The reasons alleged for this vary, ranging from the lack of preparation or legitimacy to the overwork or the politicisation that this would entail. But in fact drafters, consciously or unconsciously, do participate in the decisions by selecting the information they provide, by pointing out and filtering the panoply of legislative options and solutions, by evaluating the legal repercussions of each one of them, by helping their political counterpart to outline his objectives (initially, there is normally only a vague idea) and by participating in negotiations with other departments or even with parliamentarians (Marcello 1996, p. 2463). The question, therefore, is not whether drafters should deal with the substance of norms or only with their form, but, rather—since they inevitably contribute to the substance—, how to establish the limits and responsibilities of their activity as advisors. It seems logical that while technicians must be more demanding in matters concerning the form of legislation, they must ultimately defer to the wishes and instructions of their superiors in matters of substance. Their mission is to cooperate loyally and not to substitute or manipulate the will of their political counterpart, the person on whom the political responsibility for the decision lies.

3. The experience of normative drafting shows how sometimes the loyalty drafters owe to their superior can cause conflict with other no less powerful commitments. By giving assistance and advice to their political counterpart, drafters contribute to the proper functioning of the democratic system. But in exceptional circumstances the loyalty due to the political superior—a typical feature of the public administration in countries like Spain—and the loyalty due to the democratic system as a whole may collide. What should norm writers do they receive instructions that are clearly unconstitutional, illegal or harmful to public interests or to certain population groups? The answer must be found in the loyalty to the constitutional system as the first and principal obligation of every drafter.

In some systems, e.g., in the United States, a solution for this dilemma has been found in the analogical application of the deontological rules of the lawyer's profession to the drafters that work for the administration. Indeed, one of the peculiarities of the ethical model established for the legal profession in the U.S. is that it is also valid for corporate lawyers. It is understood that, if the interests of an

la abogacía), as well as from professionally associating or collaborating with persons or other professionals who exercise such activities (…)".

organisation come into conflict with the instructions or interests of its directors, the lawyer must first defend the organisation as such. Furthermore, lawyers must take a number of measures that include asking their superiors to reconsider the decision, explaining the negative consequences of the intended action, or even bringing the matter to the attention of the highest authority within the organisation.[13] It is therefore understood that the first and most important duty of the lawyer is the loyalty to the company itself.

If we were to apply these rules, by analogy, to drafters working in the public administration, we could argue that drafters, in the event of conflict, owe their loyalty not to their immediate superiors but to the Government and, above it, to the constitutional system itself. The same could be said when it comes to parliamentary work: drafters must be loyal to parliament as an institution, rather than to individual legislators or to the parliamentary staff or employees (Brown and Cartin 1996). This should be reflected in guidelines that foresee the procedure to follow by a drafter upon receiving instructions that are disloyal to the democratic system.[14]

4. The duty of confidentiality has special relevance in the work of the drafter. Just as the professional secrecy of lawyers is a necessary condition for a correct defence,[15] the confidentiality on the part of the drafter is needed for a successful

---

[13]See Rule 1.13 (Organization as Client) of the ABA Model Rules of Professional Conduct, https://www.americanbar.org/groups/professional_responsibility/publications/model_rules_of_professional_conduct/. See also Rule 3-600 of the Colorado Rules of Professional Conduct, as well as Rule 1.13 of the California Rules of Professional Conduct.

[14]In this sense, Roger Purdy (1987, pp. 77 and 78) proposes a second rule of conduct: "*Rule*: The drafter's primary duty is to the legislative process, and the legislature as a whole. In carrying out this duty, the drafter will work temporarily for one or more legislators on individual projects, but ultimately must act in the interest of the legislature, overall, rather than individuals. Usually these duties will not conflict, and the drafter will normally assist the legislator in achieving his or her goals. Where a reasonable argument supports the action requested by a legislator, the drafter should seek to inform the legislator fully of relevant considerations, but ultimately accept the legislator's wishes. Where a legislator, however, intends to act, acts, or seeks to have the drafter act in a way that is clearly violative of the rules of the legislature, in violation of law, substantially deceptive to the legislature, or substantially subverts or is prejudicial to the legislative process, the drafter should take reasonable steps to protect the interests of the legislature and legislative process pursuant to Proposed Drafting Rule 3.2".

[15]The Spanish Lawyers' Deontological Code establishes in its Art. 4: "The relationship between the client and his lawyer is based on trust". Art. 5 regulates professional secrecy: "Trust and confidentiality in the relations between client and lawyer, is based on the right of the former to his integrity and to not to declare against himself, as well as on fundamental rights of third parties, and imposes on the lawyer the duty and confers on him the right to keep secret all the facts or news he knows by reason of any of the modalities of his professional service (...). 2. The lawyer's duty and right to professional secrecy includes the client's confidences and proposals, those of the adversary, those of his colleagues and all the facts and documents of which he has become aware or has received by reason of any of the modalities of his professional service".

outcome. This outcome depends largely on the trust that is created between the political leaders and the technicians, a trust that would be impossible if they couldn't be sure that their comments, observations, proposals, suggestions or doubts will not be disclosed. The design of a legislative draft, the adequate materialisation of a project that is sometimes initially no more than a simple idea, requires an atmosphere of dialogue and understanding between technical specialists and policy makers that could not be generated if the confidentiality of reciprocal communications were not assured. Therefore—and notwithstanding the legal obligations derived from citizens' rights or from legitimate claims of public authorities to access official information—, norm drafters should not communicate to third parties the details of their work, unless this communication is expressly authorised by their superiors or strictly necessary to prevent an infringement of the constitution or the law, or a criminal act—in these cases, a drafter may try to persuade his superior or take any measure he deems necessary.[16] Obviously, the duty of confidentiality cannot be invoked to refuse parliamentary or judicial requests of information, nor used to hamper citizens' information access rights as regulated in the constitution. In short, drafters are public servants and they first and main loyalty is owed to the democratic system.

5. A code of ethics for norm drafting should also regulate such issues as incompatible posts and activities, conflicts of interest and, above all, conversations or negotiations with third parties or groups that have a special interest in the development of the norm.

The increasingly fluid transit between the public and the private sectors facilitates the "revolving door" effect—people who work in the administration and after their service are hired by the private sector. The due regulation of "incompatibilities" should also apply to norm drafters: it is better to eliminate the temptation of working in a sector one has contributed so decisively to regulate. On the other hand, drafters have the right to abstain from taking on a task that seriously undermines their deepest moral and political convictions. What is more: they have the duty to abstain from such a task as soon as they realise that the impartiality—or even the appearance of impartiality—which is needed to carry out their work is at risk.[17] It is difficult to imagine how a jurist who is openly opposed, for moral reasons, to the decriminalisation of abortion can correctly draft a law on this issue. Situations like

[16]In the deontological rules of the legal profession there is only the provision (art. 5.8) that in exceptional cases the lawyer may consult the Dean of the Bar. Much more explicit is the American regulation in this regard: see Rule 1.6 (Confidentiality of Information) of the ABA Model Rules of Professional Conduct, https://www.americanbar.org/groups/professional_responsibility/publications/model_rules_of_professional_conduct/.

[17]In Roger Purdy's (1987) proposal, drafters may also request permission from their supervisors to decline or withdraw from an assignment when "a) the drafter feels he or she cannot adequately perform his or her duties because of intense personal feeling regarding the bill, o b) a conflict of interest or potential conflict of interest makes the drafter's completion of the assignment difficult or would create the appearance of impropriety, or c) other good cause exists" (Rule 5.b).

this don't arise frequently, but they can occur exceptionally, in which case the drafter not only has the right to refuse but the obligation to do so.

The establishment of guidelines that regulate the drafter's communications with third parties, companies or groups that may have an interest in the drafting of a norm may be of greater interest. Unlike other countries,[18] pressure groups and lobbies are not regulated in Spain, even though their activities are increasingly visible—and not only in Brussels. This lack of recognition and regulation could and should be mitigated: rules or guidelines should be adopted that, as a minimum, require any contact of the drafter with third parties to be previously notified to and authorised by a supervisor, as well as the keeping of some publicly accessible register of such contacts.

The drafting of legislative texts is a task with powerful political components, and it therefore entails significant responsibilities. Of course, what we have presented here is no more than an outline of the norm drafters' deontological duties. The only intention of the above reflections is to highlight that, given the importance of their function in society, drafters must be granted a proper environment to carry out this function. This would surely contribute to having a better, more effective and efficient norm-making process without disrupting the course of democracy.

References

American Bar Association (2004) ABA model rules of professional conduct (updated in 2018). ABA, Chicago

Brown DG, Cartin DL (1996) The attorney–client relationship and legislative lawyers: the state legislature as organizational client. J Am Soc Legis Clerks Secretaries 2(1):57–64

Bundesministerium der Justiz (2008) Handbuch der Rechtsförmlichkeit, 3rd edn. Bundesministerium der Justiz und für Verbraucherschutz, Berlin. Published in the Bundesanzeiger 60, no. 160a, 22 September 2008. http://hdr.bmj.de/

Burton IF, Drewry G (1970) Public legislation: a survey of the session 1966/1969. Parliament Aff 23:154–183

Burton IF, Drewry G (1981) Legislation and public policy: public bills in the 1970–74 parliament. Macmillan, London

Clark K (1999) The ethics of representing elected representatives. Law Contemp Probl 61(2):31–45

Cramton RC (1991) The lawyer as whistleblower: confidentiality and the government lawyer. Geo J Legal Ethics 5:291–315

Donahoe KW (1989) The model rules and the government lawyer. A sword or shiel? A response to the DC Bar Special Committee on Government Lawyer and the Model Rules of Professional Conduct. Geo J Legal Ethics 2:897–1002

Drewry G (1981) Legislation. In: Walkand SA, Ryle M (eds) The commons today. Fontana, London

Drieger EA (1953) The preparation of legislation. Can Bar Rev 31:33–51

Edwards C III, Wood BD (1999) Who influences whom? The president, congress and the media. Am Pol Sci Rev 93:327–344

[18]See e.g., State of Colorado's Office of Legislative Legal Services (2004).

Griffith JA, Ryle M (1989) Parliament. Functions, practice and procedure. Sweet and Maxwell, London
Josephson W, Pearce R (1986) To whom does the government owe the duty of loyalty when clients are in conflict? How Law J 29:539–569
La Spina A (1989) La decisione legislativa. Lineamenti di una teoria. Giuffrè, Milano
Lindblom CE (1991) El proceso de elaboración de políticas públicas. MAP, Madrid
Luhmann N (1981) Teoria politica nello Stato del Benessere. Franco Agnelli, Milano
Macnair D (2004) Ethics and drafting. Ottawa, Department of Justice
Marcello DA (1996) The ethics and politics of legislative drafting. Tul Law Rev 70:2437–2462
Meny I, Thoenig J-C (1992) Las políticas públicas. Ariel, Barcelona
Office of Legislative Legal Services (State of Colorado) (2004) Guidelines for working with lobbysts. Revised version (updated in October 2008). Colorado General Assembly, Denver
Pennell JN (1994) Representations involving fiduciary entities: who is the client? Fordham Law Rev 62:1320–1356
Purdy R (1987) Professional responsibility for legislative drafters: suggested guidelines and discussion of ethics and role problems. Seton Hall Legis J 11(1):67–120
Subirats J (1992) Un problema de estilo. La formación de las políticas públicas en España. Centro de Estudios Constitucionales, Madrid
Weinstein JB (1966) Some ethical and political problems of a government attorney. Melbourne Law Rev 18:155–172

Chapter 11
Implementation

11.1 Implementation

Beyond a certain critical point, legal interventions on politics and society are either indifferent or have disintegrating effects or expose law to its own decay. In the light of Günther Teubner's (1987) well-known regulatory trilemma, the solution can only be one of these three: deregulation, self-regulation of each system, or improvement of the quality of norms. Having discarded the first two, which we have already discussed, those of us who believe that law continues to be the most legitimate instrument of social direction are left with the third option. And if the quality of norms is to be improved, due care for their efficacy and effectiveness is an absolute requirement—in other words, norm efficacy and effectiveness are essential components of any sound legislative policy (Bettini 1983). Starting in the 1970s, when the failure of the first major social programs began to be perceived, some started wondering what is it that guarantees that a given law achieves its objectives. American literature on this subject is perhaps the most interesting.[1] In Germany, the works of Renate Mayntz should be highlighted.[2] We find the same preoccupation in France (Morand 1993). Particularly important in this regard was also the Italian debate: in 1977 the *Archivio Italiano di Sociologia del Diritto* dedicated a special issue to studying the so-called "manifesto laws" (*leggi manifesto*), i.e., those laws that have no possibility of administrative execution, and this study opened a research path which has led to some interesting initiatives.[3] This topic has also been addressed in Spain (see Montoro 1989; cf. Galiana 2008, pp. 143 ff).

---

[1]Among other works, we can cite Wilson (1967), dedicated to studying the performance of public officials and servants in the implementation of public policies; Bunker (1972), Dertick (1972), or Pressman and Wildadsky (1973).

[2]See especially Mayntz (1977, 1980, 1983).

[3]For example, the High Council of Public Administration addressed the Presidency of the Council of Ministers exposing, among other issues, the "demand to dictate legislative norms accompanied

V. Zapatero Gómez, *The Art of Legislating*, Legisprudence Library 6,
https://doi.org/10.1007/978-3-030-23388-4_11

It goes without saying that clear and precisely drafted texts are a prerequisite for the success of laws, but this is not enough, as we have seen over the past century, in which the hopes placed in the whole legal *corpus* with which the social state was built have been followed by growing scepticism. Sometimes doubts have revolved around the capacity of science to design solid political decisions; other times around the capacity of governments to satisfy social promises and, finally—assuming that governments can and want to elaborate the appropriate norms—what was doubted was their capability to execute them correctly. This is how the symptoms of dissatisfaction with both the expectations created by rules and their costs began to be studied. That is to say, in the agenda of social and political science research, the problem of the implementation of norms appeared as a new object of study. Not only because of the theoretical interest of such matters, but also because a norm cannot be well constructed if the factors that determine its successful execution are not taken into account during the process of its elaboration. Identifying the factors that contribute to the success of a political decision is the subject of implementation analysis.

Preparing a norm is like drawing a sketch to build a machine that generates certain products. This machine is built by pieces, either from scratch or by assembling or using mechanisms belonging to other artefacts such as fiscal, budgetary and organizational resources administered by other bodies or owned by the citizens. The construction of a norm can therefore be seen as the process of assembling different elements whose ownership and control are generally in other hands (Bardach 1977, pp. 36 ff). The number and complexity of the parts is determined by the policy in question: the implementation of a scholarship policy for students does not have the same degree of difficulty as a program for the integration of immigrants or the eradication of gender based violence. But, in any case, the success of any public policy will depend on the correct assembly of all its parts.

The first requirement for the success of a norm, as we have seen, is clearly establishing its objectives. It is not usual for a norm to pursue a single objective, it

---

by the so-called administrative coverage, to avoid the unfortunate and widespread phenomenology of the inapplicability of those norms which, assuming the form of manifest laws, frustrate the legitimate expectations of citizens or consumers". This first position was followed by the Giannini Commission (1979), which presented a *Rapporto sui principali problemi della Admministrazione dello Stato* demanding either the enactment of a rule requiring a priori verification of the practicability of all draft laws or the creation of a unit within the Cabinet with the task of examining the practicability *(fattibilità)* of norms prior to their approval by the Government. Two years later, the Barettoni Arleri report on *Fattibilità e applicabilità delle leggi* (1983) was approved, focusing in particular on aspects relating to the proper preparation of the norm as well as the preliminary calculation of costs with analysis of the general burden of laws. A final Commission was appointed in 1983 by the Craxi Government (known as the Cassese Commission) to search for and eliminate all those norms that no longer had any justification. Among other proposals, the Cassese Commission suggested—successfully—the creation of a Central Office for Legislative Coordination (see above Chap. 8, Sect. 8.2). Thus, the three main subjects studied in Italy have been the applicability of rules, legislative technique stricto sensu, and the study of the preliminary calculation of costs. See Barettoni Arleri (1983).

is common practice to attribute several objectives to a norm in order to achieve maximum consensus. In these cases, the ambiguity or incompatibility of the various objectives can end up diluting or distorting the spirit and purpose of the norm, which is likely to make it fail. Implementation is the continuation of policy by other means: silent interests might be waiting to have their turn, and to gain in the implementation phase of the new law what they lost in the design phase (Bardach 1977, pp. 85 ff). Clearly established objectives must be followed by a no less precise prioritisation of these objectives. Unless the norm explicitly establishes a new office dedicated exclusively to its implementation, the new tasks are normally assigned to units of the administration already in charge of a multitude of functions. For this reason, a clear and precise hierarchy of the objectives of a norm is essential in order to establish what priority is given to each new directive in the department's program (Sabatier 1980, p. 545).

The success of the norm will depend, secondly, on the availability of sufficient material resources for its implementation. It is not uncommon to start an underfunded program in the hope of later collecting the needed financial resources: the 2006 Dependency Act[4] in Spain is a good example of this. But if resources are not allocated when the problem is the centre of attention and debate, they are much less likely to be obtained later on, when the problem has disappeared from the public agenda. The result are those *leggi manifesto* that Italian literature speaks of, laws that are nothing but mere declarations of intent, grandiloquent and impracticable. At best, they have a symbolic function; at worst, they are no more than pure rhetoric, if not simple manipulation of public opinion. It is therefore essential to allocate sufficient and adequate resources to the objectives declared in the norm and, obviously, once allocated, it is necessary to prevent their diversion or deviation.[5]

A third crucial point are the personal resources that are mobilised for the execution of any regulatory program—they are as important as material resources. For some, the implication of civil and public servants is even the most central element for the success of any norm (Wilson 1967). Although this implication may not always be the decisive factor, it is nevertheless important. The degree of commitment of civil servants will depend to a large extent on whether the public policy is implemented in accordance with the spirit and purpose of the norm. The prompt implementation of the policy also determines the attitude of civil servants: delay in the implementation process of any norm is a typical cause of its failure. Sometimes, delays are the result of the opposition to the project within the administration itself, but there are delays that nobody wants. Their causes can be found,

[4]Act on the promotion of personal autonomy and assistance to persons in situations of dependency (*Ley 39/2006 de Promoción de la Autonomía Personal y Atención a las personas en situación de dependencia*), usually known as "Dependency Act" (*ley de dependencia*).

[5]According to Bardach (1977), in the implementation process there are some adverse games: one of them is the "diversion of resources" that can be caused by the incompetence of public servants, ignorance, lack of serious incentives (positive and negative) for a professional performance of the function, obsession with forms (budgetary execution) independently of the control of substantial aspects or the recourse to the "pork barrel" of parliamentarians.

among others, in the time, the effort and the significant number of transactions that go into obtaining the necessary political support for the new norm (Bardach 1977, pp. 180 ff). Among the tools available to policy makers to incentivise a positive involvement of bureaucracy are: (a) assigning the development and implementation of the norm to those departments whose political orientation is consistent with the objectives pursued in it; (b) entrusting the implementation of the norm to a department with power and prestige; (c) selecting, as much as possible, the personnel responsible for the implementation among the officials most committed to the specific program; and (d) designing the appropriate incentive strategies, positive and negative, to face the eventual resistance or disinterest of bureaucracy (Sabatier 1980, p. 457).

The success of a norm also depends on the procedures followed in its implementation. The norm must be practicable with the lowest possible costs and frictions (Montoro 1989, pp. 75 ff), a goal that is not easy to achieve in our political systems, especially in federal or decentralised models, in which the majority of the competences of the different levels of government are shared. There are numerous, sometimes hundreds of small decisions that different actors have to make to ensure the success of a specific policy (Pressman and Wildadsky 1973): each of these actors, to a greater or lesser extent, has the capacity to veto or, at least, to delay the process of norm implementation—and this cannot always be prevented through incentivation policies. Coordination thus becomes the leitmotiv of politics in our time, in which the ability to negotiate and to reach intergovernmental agreements increasingly determines the success of policies (Dertick 1972). Without the active participation in the design phase of the norm of those who are to apply it,[6] and without an adequate coordination of all the actors involved, any norm—however perfect its drafting—is doomed to fail.

And lastly, the implication of the citizens to whom the new norm is addressed is likewise necessary for its successful implementation. Without the constant support of a sufficient number of citizens committed to a regulatory program and without a minimal media attention, the new norm will—sooner rather than later—also fail. The efficacy of a norm,[7] the level of observance by its addressees, has as much to do with the severity and probability of sanctions, as with the degree of awareness and

[6]In Spain, there are many bodies that must be consulted for an opinion or report before passing laws and regulations: the Council of State, the General Council of the Judiciary, the Economic and Social Council, the Fiscal and Financial Policy Council of the Autonomous Regions, the Telecommunications Council, the Water Council, the Nuclear Energy Council, professional associations, etc. Depending on the scope of the provision, trade unions and other organisations representing interested parties must (or may) also be consulted. The nature, objectives and justification of all these consultations vary.

[7]For William Evan (1980, pp. 554 ff), the factors on which compliance with the norm depends are, among others, the following: (a) the authority and prestige of the person who issues the norm; (b) the clarity of the norm and its correct legal drafting; (c) the establishment of a correct transition and adaptation regime for the new norm; (d) the degree of commitment of the agents in charge of enforcing it; (e) the establishment of a regime of positive or negative incentives; and (f) the support and protection of those individuals whose interests are harmed by the violation of the norm.

consensus around the objectives that the norm is able to arouse in society. Respect for the new law requires confidence in its values and the support from citizens, who must adhere both to the content of the new legislation and to its underlying goals (Braithwaite 1993). From this perspective, the participation of citizens in the development of norms should not be considered as a cost (in time or resources) to democracy but rather as a condition for the efficacy of laws. It was precisely with this concern in mind—the efficacy of norms—that from the 1970s onwards many governments initiated significant reforms[8] towards more open consultation processes. As a consequence, in recent years we have witnessed an increasing formalisation and regulation of consultation processes (where corporatist structures seem to have lost prominence while lobbies are gaining ground), as well as the creation of central regulatory structures to control or to stimulate consultations—which are often associated, in turn, with regulatory impact analyses.

A comparative examination of these practices in different countries shows that, although public consultations may entail certain drawbacks,[9] they do in fact have at least some of the following advantages and objectives (OECD 1994): (a) they serve to strengthen democratic values: consultations can be a good complement to the normative procedures formalised in democracies, while at the same time they enable the right to know of citizens, encourage their participation in decision-making and reinforce the legitimacy of institutions and their policies; (b) they serve to generate consensus around problems and their solutions by involving the organisations that represent certain interests in sensitive issues, reinforcing their legitimacy and facilitating the subsequent approval of the regulatory program both at governmental and, above all, parliamentary level; (c) they improve the quality of the norm by collecting relevant information: the addressees of the norm often have better information than

[8]For instance, in Canada, since 1986, citizens have to be consulted, and it is mandatory to notify draft norms and receive comments. In Germany, consultation about environmental norms has been compulsory since 1974 and a resolution was issued in 1989 to improve the consultation procedure for users. In Japan, directives on the management and operation of advisory councils were issued in 1994. In the Netherlands, in addition to consulting the Economic and Social Council, business circles have been consulted since 1985. In Portugal, public notification of projects was regulated by law in 1991 and a government plan to improve the transparency of the decision-making process was established in 1993. In Sweden, it is constitutionally mandated that citizens be consulted. In the United Kingdom, since 1985 business sectors have been consulted on the assessment of the costs of regulation; in 1990 consumer consultation was established on regulations concerning the management of private monopolies; and in 1993 working groups of business people have been established to reform 3700 existing regulations. In the United States, since 1946, when the first law on notification and public comment on draft regulations was passed, numerous regulations established impact analysis and the prior publication of the regulatory program. A law on the negotiation of regulations (1990) and a presidential order (1993) to improve consultations were also adopted. See OECD (1994).

[9]Among the drawbacks, we can highlight the unequal access of citizens to procedures that are often "captured" by powerful interest groups, the low quality of the information received, the absence of a real dialogue between the administration that dictates the norm and the citizens or sectors that make comments or observations, the time required (which is sometimes not compatible with the urgency of the decision), or the late stage in which the consultation occurs.

political decision-makers on the nature of problems, on the impact of the different solutions considered or even on linguistic, legal or constitutional issues; (d) with better information, the cost of implementing the new regulation for individuals, businesses and the administration is presumably reduced; and (e) they facilitate the reform of the administration itself.

These are some of the circumstances and conditions that must be taken into account in the process of drafting norms if Teubner's aforementioned regulatory trilemma is to be avoided.

11.2 Taking Memoranda Seriously

Few tasks in the legislative process are more important than writing memoranda; still, it is difficult to find a task to which less attention is devoted. When it does exists, the memorandum accompanying a norm is ordinarily nothing more than a document attached a posteriori, with the text of the norm is already closed, as a last formality in the process—a formality that must be completed but has lost its original value. It is more a justification of the work carried out than a foundation of the proposed program. It is worth while reflecting, albeit briefly, on the value of memoranda.

The most primitive and narrow conception of positivism reduced laws to commands, and commands to mere declarations or expressions of will. Anything other than commands, or fragments of commands, was considered to be an addition that obscured the purity of legislative language. It was just another way of confusing legislating and commanding, a misconception to which enlightened thinkers were unanimously opposed: "I do not understand at all—de Mably (1797, p. 192) noted—the notion of those politicians who recommend the legislative power to express itself with a majestic brevity: they want to reduce laws to ordering and prohibiting". Certainly, laws have to establish rules of behaviour, but they have to do so by reasoning. The idea of the need for the motivation of norms was stressed by Montesquieu, who probably took it from Plato (1988, pp. 87 ff). A few years later it was picked up again by Schmid d'Avenstein (1821, pp. 363 and 364) who presented the legislator as a family father whom he recommended to "present the motivation of laws at the time of creating them": "It certainly seems to me as despotic pride and untimely haughtiness to make subjects feel the strength of the bridle that governs them, and to claim as the sole motive of laws the pleasure of commanding". Already at the dawn of the French Revolution, the need to motivate laws was a central idea, based on the principles of rationality and human dignity. Rousseau (1971, p. 278) had already said that "the power of law derives much more from its own wisdom (*sagesse*) than from the severity of its ministers", and that "the public will derives its full force from the reason that dictates it". In short, laws are the fruit of will, yes, but good laws are the product of a will enlightened by reason. Therefore, in the face of narrow-minded legal positivism, it is always important to remember that giving orders alone is not enough. If law wants to be an effective and legitimate instrument of social direction, the legislator must explain his reasons: in a democracy, legislating is not synonymous with commanding.

This old and persistent enlightened ideal of giving reasons for decisions represents a way of understanding the exercise of power—of all powers—which has gradually consolidated. The fight against arbitrariness and in favour of human dignity has ended up forcing administrations, under penalty of nullity, to motivate their decisions. For the same reasons, the decisions of the judiciary have to be properly motivated and the absence of a correct, consistent motivation is a sufficient ground for appeal. But what is nowadays obvious for the executive and judicial powers seems to be forgotten when it comes to the legislative power: we, legal scholars, are most concerned with articulating detailed theories about judicial decision-making, with the aim of eliminating arbitrariness in adjudication and rendering courts' rulings more controllable and responsible; but we allow legislators to take decisions without seriously demanding reasons from them. This indulgence explains why legislative statements of reasons and justificatory memoranda have passed to a second or third level priority in the making of laws—in spite of the fact that legislative reason-giving may be a constitutional requirement.[10] Recovering the enlightened ideal of legislation implies taking memoranda seriously (Seidman 1992).

Jurists and other technicians are in charge of writing memoranda. Drafters have to explain and justify the legislative proposal, and become key actors in any legislative project aiming to filter the maximum rationality into the final legislative decision. An action or a decision becomes rational if it can be explained and defended with arguments acceptable to a public audience, and the only acceptable arguments in public debate are those that refer to the public interest. Even political decisions that can be perfectly explained by the pressure of powerful interest groups need to be disguised or adorned with considerations about their general interest. The peculiar position of drafters in the legislative process forces them to justify the legislation they drafts from the public interest point of view, using facts and reason as tools. If a theory of legislation is to be useful for drafters, it must therefore conceive law as reason informed by experience (Seidman 1992). In our time, it is this form of reason—and not pure reason, far less tradition—that has proved to be the most powerful tool when it comes to taking public policy decisions.

A drafter, as we saw, is not a partial lawyer whose mission is to defend a client. A drafter who participates in the legislative process owes loyalty first and foremost to the legislative process itself. And it is this loyalty to the process that obliges drafters to explain the legislative proposal and to give reasons for it. Unlike what happens in judicial argumentation, and in the absence of a consolidated theory of legislation, determining the canonical content of a memorandum is not easy. This is what

[10] Thus, Art. 88 of the Spanish Constitution establishes that "Government bills shall be passed by the Council of Ministers, which shall refer them to Congress, accompanied by a statement setting forth the necessary grounds and facts in order for them to reach a decision thereon"—the same provision is included in Art. 109 of the Congress Standing Orders.

explains the heterogeneous contents of explanatory reports, or the fact that in many cases they only refer to costs and benefits of the proposed norm. But if we really take memoranda seriously and make them the documents that feed public debate by giving reasons for envisaged norms, then their content must be congruent with the meaning and purpose of the legislative process—as we have tried to explain throughout previous chapters. And this means that the memorandum must contain, at least, the following elements.

In the first place, a memorandum has to explain what exactly the problem is that the norm is trying to solve. As we have seen, defining a problem consists—with all the difficulties that this implies—in looking for the causal relationship that generates an undesired situation. Second, a memorandum has to explicitly state the objectives the norm aims at, so that, once stated, these objectives can be discussed; the congruence between them and the proposed solutions can be debated; and a mechanism to evaluate ex post whether, and to what extent, they have been achieved can also be established. Third, if a memorandum is to be loyal to the legislative process, it must, furthermore, analyse and evaluate all the alternative solutions that have been considered but not applied. And, fourth, it must justify why the option presented is the best among all the considered solutions. This is how memoranda fulfil, or should fulfil, the double task of explaining and justifying a norm. By explaining, they substantiate and justify. And by doing so, they discipline the legislative process because the requirement to justify all measures—not to simply approve them—has the effect of conditioning the type of measures that end up being proposed and approved (Sunstein 1985). This is one of the central advantages that memoranda have.

Some progress has been made, albeit very slowly, in the field of specifying what the canonical content of the memorandum should be. The Government of Spain approved in 1992 a Questionnaire for the Evaluation of Projects submitted for consideration to the Council of Ministers. On its part, the OECD Council—after a long series of studies and debates—approved on 9 March 1995 a recommendation for the improvement of the quality of norms. For the representatives of the OECD member governments, the quality of norms has a clear impact on the efficacy of government action and on economic growth. The recommendation contains an evaluation questionnaire, which must be completed for the draft laws of the respective member countries, which contains the following ten principles in the form of questions that should guide the drafting of any memorandum:

1. Is the problem correctly defined?
2. Is government intervention justified?
3. Is regulation the best form of government action?
4. Does the regulation have a legal basis?
5. What are the appropriate administrative levels for this action?
6. Are the benefits sufficient to offset the costs?
7. Is the distribution of effects within society transparent?
8. Is the norm clear, consistent, understandable and accessible to users?
9. Have all the affected groups had the opportunity to express their views?

10. How will compliance with the norm be ensured?

The list of criteria that was approved in the form of recommendations has been drawn up on the basis of the experiences of 15 important countries.[11] An examination of the different lists of criteria used by the different governments makes it possible to group the issues that arise around one of the following items (OECD 1993): (a) the role of the State in the norm-making process: evaluation questionnaires normally require, in the first place, to establish the need for intervention, to reflect on the different alternatives available to legislators and to determine the level or instance of government at which the decision should be made; (b) the costs and benefits of the norm: at this point, the various questionnaires differ in terms of the level of detail in the evaluation of costs and benefits, and as to whether or not they consider the costs that the norm implies for citizens and companies; (c) the impacts of the new regulation: these impacts refer to a great variety of concerns governments have, which usually reveal their political priorities: employment, environment, competitiveness, health risks, gender policies, etc.; (d) the commitment to the principles of constitutionality and legality that are implicit in the draft norm, as well as the formal quality of the text; (e) the alignment of the draft norm with the political priorities of public authorities; and (f) the alignment and compatibility of the norm with international laws and agreements.

The use of seriously elaborated memoranda makes it possible to publicly explain government policy, to guarantee that the management of legislative policy responds to political priorities, to ensure that decision-making procedures and competences are respected, to increase the technical quality of norms, to improve the design and implementation of regulatory programs, to facilitate the supervision of the legislative process, and to promote cultural change within the administration. The key to the neo-republican project, Seidman (1992, p. 77) argues, is ensuring that legislation rests not on private interests but on practical reason. Or as Bentham (1981, p. 574) had put it much earlier: in order to write laws it is enough to know how to write them, and in order to enforce them it is enough to have enough power: "the difficulty—he was right to nuance—lies in making good laws, and good laws are those in favour of which good reasons can be claimed". It is these good reasons that the drafter has to find and expose in the legislative memorandum.

[11] In various reports the OCDE has analysed progress made since the first OECD Reviews of Regulatory Reform—carried out between 1998 and 2006. Drawing on these comparative experiences, in 2008 the EU15 project "Better Regulation in Europe" was launched in order to assess, through individual reviews of 15 member states, the capacities for effective regulatory management across the EU. This project, carried out by the OCDE in co-operation with the European Commission focuses on strategy and policies, institutional capacities, transparency, development of new regulation, simplification and burden reduction, compliance, enforcement, appeal, and relationships between sub-national and national governments, and between the latter and the EU. See OECD (2011). On the recent developments of the EU better regulation agenda, see European Commission (2016, 2017a, b).

11.3 Analysing the Impact of Norms

A key element of the documentation attached to a draft norm is the analysis of its impact. The concern for the impact of new norms is relatively recent: it could be traced back to the 1970s, when the great social programs of the welfare state matured and the need to control public spending gained momentum. Until very recently, governments, urged by this demand to contain public deficit, were only worried about calculating the costs that any law implies for the public treasury in the form of personnel expenses, first establishment expenses, operating expenses, subsidies and other current expenses, investment expenses, fiscal expenses or expenses derived from capital transfers and financial operations. When it comes to enacting a norm, it is necessary not only to foresee the cost of its implementation but also the resources that will finance it (revenues generated by the norm, decrease in surplus budget appropriations, new budget allocations or sources of extra-budgetary financing). Actually, assessing the budgetary costs of each norm is an obligation that already binds most governments. For instance, in 1958 the German Government approved the Joint Rules of Procedure of the Federal Ministries (updated in 2000), which already introduced an obligation to prepare regulatory impact analyses, including items related to consultations (within and outside government), structure of bills, justifications or statements of reasons, legal scrutiny, procedures for bill submission to the Cabinet and to parliament, promulgation, etc. (OECD 2004). In 1984, the German Cabinet endorsed the "Blue List" which evaluated both the legal drafting and the economic effects of the norms.[12] Since 2000 the focus has been mainly on the impact of regulation and the efficiency of the public sector. The establishment of the powerful and independent National Regulatory Control Council (*Normenkontrollrat*)[13] in 2006 has been the most important change as concerns the improvement of the quality of legislation.[14] A similar interest in prospectively

[12]The *Prüfliste für bessere Rechsetzung* requires the proponent of a new regulation to answer whether the new regulation changes or derogates other laws, as well as further questions on the correctness and comprehensibility of the draft, on the need of official regulation, on the intended and foreseeable effects, on the consultation to others departments, on the report of *Normenkontrollrat* and on the review of the systematicity and formal correctness of the text by the Ministry of Justice (Bundesministerium der Justiz 2008, pp. 263–265).

[13]*Gesetz zur Einrichtung eines Nationalen Normenkontrollrates* (14 August 2006), BGBl I.S 1866.

[14]The ex ante procedure is designed to prevent unnecessary bureaucracy and compliance costs. Before the Federal Cabinet adopts any piece of legislation, the *Normenkontrollrat* (NKR) reviews the ministries' estimates of compliance costs for citizens, businesses and public authorities. The annual and one-off compliance costs that are to be expected are critically assessed. The NKR also examines: information regarding the aim and necessity of any regulation for its comprehensibility, considerations relating to other possible solutions ("alternatives"), considerations regarding the effective date of a regulation, time limits and evaluation, information concerning simplifications of legal and administrative procedures, information concerning the one-to-one transposition of EU law. Under the Joint Rules of Procedure of the Federal Ministries, the NKR is incorporated into the legislative process in the same way as a ministry. Draft regulations are required to be submitted to the NKR no later than the start of the coordination process within the Federal Government. In

assessing the cost of norms can be witnessed in many other countries (such as the U. S., Canada, The Netherlands, Sweden, Finland, the UK, Austria, Japan, etc.).

But what was initially a tool fundamentally aimed at controlling the fiscal repercussions of new norms has been gradually extended to other areas of activity—following the political priorities of governments. And so, other assessments have begun to be required, such as those referring to the impact of laws and other regulations on competitiveness, on companies,[15] on employment,[16] on risks to

practice, the ministries often involve the NKR at an earlier date. The NKR prepares a draft opinion for each regulatory initiative. These are presented to the NKR plenum for adoption. The NKR sends its comments to the lead ministry. The draft law or regulation is then submitted, together with the NKR comments—and as applicable, with a response of the Federal Government—to the Federal Cabinet for deliberation. The Bundestag and Bundesrat always receive the government drafts together with NKR opinions. The comments form part of the papers printed for parliamentary deliberations and are accessible to everyone at that point in time. The NKR reviews draft regulations from the Bundesrat when the Bundesrat refers these to the NKR. It comments on draft legislation from the floor of the Bundestag only at the request of the parliamentary group or members introducing the bill. See the Federal Government's document *National Regulatory Control Council. Bureaucracy Reduction and Better Regulation* at: http://www.normenkontrollrat.bund.de.

[15]The test on the effects of rules on companies approved by the Dutch government must be applied to all those norms that are likely to have an impact on companies, market operations and economic and social development. The test—compliance with which is monitored by the Ministers of Economy and Justice—requires answers to the following questions: (a) What type of companies can the draft norm affect?; (b) What is the most likely nature and level of costs and benefits of the draft for the affected companies? The report should cover: whether the effects will be structural or cyclical, the distinction between financial and compliance effects, the certainty of costs and benefits and the level of uncertainty, the comparison in the distribution of effects between (categories of) companies or the consequences for administrative costs; (c) What is the comparison of the costs and benefits of the draft with the resources of the companies in question?; (d) What is the position regarding this type of regulation in the countries that can be considered as the most important competitors of the Dutch economy in this area? What are the consequences of the draft for market operations?; and (e) What are the social and economic effects of the draft (on employment, production, etc.)? See the Dutch Business Test Checklist and Notes-Effects of Draft Legislation (Ministry of Economic Affairs, The Netherlands, September 1995).

[16]The French Government—having noted that the explanatory memories and reports accompanying the projects are often no more than a summary of the general objectives of the project—decided that, as from 1 January 1996, draft laws and decrees must be complemented by an impact study illustrating to government and, where appropriate, to parliament the scope of the policy decisions. The impact study must involve a precise analysis of the expected benefits of the norm, for which a quantitative assessment of the benefits (or, if this not feasible, a qualitative assessment) must be carried out that should include ate least the following items: (a) expected benefits: the study in question must highlight, in the clearest and most precise way, the benefits expected from the adoption of the norm. To this end, the study must analyse the existing legal regulations and their shortcomings, and demonstrate that the objectives pursued cannot be achieved by means other than the enactment of the norm. Finally, the expected benefits must be calculated in figures in order facilitate comparisons with other effects of the norm. (b) Impact on employment: the direct or indirect impacts on employment of each norm must be evaluated. However "general" a norm may be, the study must consider the nature of the jobs and the categories of persons affected, the short- and medium-term effects on the labour market, as well as the effects the funding of the proposed measures on employment. And (c) impact on other general interests: the possible impact of the norm on other general interests such as environmental protection must also be assessed. See the

health, on the environment, on the reduction of administrative burdens and procedures, on gender issues and policies, on the powers or competences of other levels of government, etc. Of course, a comparative examination of the use that different governments make of these assessment techniques shows remarkable differences. First, there are differences in the methodology: some countries are only concerned with the analysis of the budgetary cost of norms, others also deal with compliance costs for companies (cost-benefit analysis is usually preferred, but they can also apply cost-efficacy or risk analyses). Second, there are differences regarding the bodies responsible for the impact assessment (a centralised governmental body, the affected ministries, the ministry of finance, bodies under parliamentary supervision). Third, countries also differ in the type of norms (laws, decrees, orders) for which an impact evaluation is mandatory as well as in the greater or lesser publicity of the results. But in any case, there does seem to be a tendency to rely more and more on this type of decision-making tool (Morand 1993; Mader 1985; Galiana 2008, pp. 279 ff).[17]

The need to anticipate the effects of legislation has paved the way for a related idea which has an evident ideological load: the idea of evaluating the total cost of the entire norm-giving activity of the state—i.e., the cost of regulation. The claim is that governments ordinarily care first and foremost about the budgetary costs of each norm, but the principle of efficiency also requires looking at other costs, which governments sometimes don't consider at all or only insufficiently, such as the costs of complying with laws for citizens, businesses and society as a whole.[18] It is certainly difficult to make a comprehensive economic assessment of the entire regulatory activity (OECD 1993). Firstly, because the data available about the total effect of regulation are insufficient: apart from the expected, intentional, direct and specific costs and benefits, any regulation may have unforeseen undesired,

---

Circulaire du 21 novembre 1995 relative à L'experimentation d'une étude d'impact accompagnant les projets de loi et de décret en Conseil d'Etat (Journal Officiel de la République Française 1 décembre 1995).

[17]On regulatory impact assessment, see further Dunlop and Radaelli (2017).

[18]An interesting experience in this regard is the recourse to what has been called the "regulation budget", which would contain the expenses induced by the norms to individuals and companies. This would make it possible to set a maximum ceiling of costs induced, globally and by programmes, and allow for a more precise knowledge of all the economic costs generated by a norm. This knowledge is all the more necessary given that the global macroeconomic effects of norms (for example, regulations on hygiene, environment, etc.) can be as important as the effects of a country's ordinary budget. To develop its social and economic policy, the state could thus use both instruments (state budget and regulation budget). The ultimate objective of these experiences would be to follow the model of the ordinary budget and include in any new law that imposes certain costs on the private sector a regulatory cost ceiling (Morral 1992). In this scheme, any new law should set a ceiling on all the costs that agencies could impose on the private sector in the application of the law. Agencies would monitor the estimated costs entailed by regulation. Once the ceiling set by the law has been reached, any new regulation would need either the adoption of a new text raising the permitted ceiling, or a compensatory modification in other regulations in order to keep the overall costs borne by the private sector and arising from compliance with the rules within the limits (Morral 1992).

Table 11.1 Annual social cost of regulation (Hopkins 1992)

Type of regulation	1977	1988	1991
Environment	42	87	115
Other regulations	29	30	36
Economy regulation	120	73	73
Procedure regulation	122	343	343
Total	313	343	413

perverse, indirect or symbolic effects (Mader 1985) that are very difficult, if not impossible, to quantify. Secondly, because we do not have the means to assess the impact of every norm correctly, nor do we have well-established, accepted indicators to make the relevant comparisons. It is a well known fact that budgetary cost is only a part—and sometimes not the largest—of the cost of rules (National Performance Review (U.S.) 1994, p. 32). A 1992 study in the U.S. (Hopkins 1992, quoted in Wiscusi 1995) provided the following data on the annual social costs of regulation estimated in billions of dollars (Table 11.1).

As these figures show, the costs for citizens and businesses of complying with environmental regulation, health and safety regulation and economic regulation together with administrative expenditure appear to be significant: in 1991, it is said, they accounted for 7.3% of the U.S. gross domestic product. But there is really no comprehensive reliable data (Morral 1992): nobody knows the net result of a law, among other reasons because social benefits are rarely calculated, and social costs are not budgeted even if they are ultimately paid for by citizens, especially in their role as consumers. Surely, however, if the efficiency of norms were to be precisely evaluated, it should be possible to calculate, not only their direct, budgetary cost, but also their indirect cost. Of course, it should also be possible to calculate their benefit. The insufficient evaluation of benefits is one of the most notable shortcomings of this important tool. For some governments, it is the cost of each legislative proposal that needs to be highlighted (and highlighted in thick characters), as an effective way of eluding regulation: in fact, what this has sometimes led to is not better government but simply less government (Tolchin and Tolchin 1983, pp. 111 ff). In other words, many have seen the economic evaluation of norms—insisting only on costs—as the best way to justify deregulation.

But even if such a policy is not shared, the cost-benefit analysis has an obvious limitation: there are benefits that are almost impossible to evaluate monetarily and therefore to compare with costs. How to evaluate the economic benefit of safe streets, breathable air, clean water, reducing the mortality rate, or increasing the interest for art or literature of the population? Or, to put it more emphatically: how much is the benefit of saving a life? It is true that since Dublin and Lotka (1946) offered a formula for calculating the cost of damage to life—the profits that a victim would have obtained during his life, minus the predicted personal consumption, adding some intangibles such as the pretium doloris or the loss of quality of life—, setting the price of a life or a part of the human body has worried governments and, above all, insurance companies. Still, our sensitivity and dignity make the idea of attributing a monetary value to life repugnant to us, and it would be degrading if by setting this monetary value, we were to establish a market price that would allow the buying and selling of people or parts of their bodies. We are left with the uneasiness of not knowing if this will be a possibility in our future societies. According to the ILO, human trafficking directly affects more than 2,500,000 people worldwide and fuels a transnational business that generates more than 7000 million dollars annually, ranking third among lucrative illicit businesses, after drug trafficking and arms sales. The need to persecute both human and organ trafficking[19] is proof of the dangers we face in this regard. If there is one idea in Marx that is still relevant today, it is probably his warning about the fact that in a market economy everything can end up being treated like a commodity (Kleinig 1961, p. 147). Today, fortunately, our societies do not seem willing to go as far as putting a monetary value to human life.[20] In the meantime, it is clear that while an approximation to the cost of regulation is possible, it is not so easy to determine its benefits, especially social ones.

Comparative experiences in the application of these instruments by different countries show some notable shortcomings.[21] Nevertheless, impact analysis of norms is a very useful decision-making tool that does not supplant the responsibility of politicians (although unfortunately they often do hide behind it) but provides them, systematically and consistently, with the empirical data they need for an informed decision. Of course, it is not only these economic analyses that determine the regulatory decision, but to do without them would seem clearly irresponsible. Impact analysis of regulation can make at least four important contributions: (a) it serves to improve our understanding of the real impact of government action, including both the costs and benefits of norms; (b) it facilitates the integration of multiple and mutually interdependent objectives that are often present in policy decisions: economic efficiency, effects on employment, trade, competitiveness, the

[19]Cf. the United Nations Convention against Transnational Organised Crime and the Protocol to Prevent the Smuggling of Migrants by Land, Sea and Air (15 December 2000), as well as the Council of Europe Convention on Action against Trafficking in Human Beings (Warsaw, 16 May 2005).

[20]In those cases in which monetary evaluation is not possible, the application of the cost-benefit method can be facilitated by determining what is gained (number of lives saved, reduction of certain risks) in exchange for what it costs: as Wiscusi (1993) suggests, one can thus calculate the cost per life saved or the cost per genetic injury; and it will be possible to make a comparison—between different regulations and policies—regarding the price to be paid in exchange for what is obtained. These comparisons make it possible to establish the opportunity costs of each health programme, for example, by objectifying and giving maximum transparency to decisions about life and death.

[21]Among these shortcomings, some authors highlight that the different methods (cost-benefit analysis, cost-effectiveness analysis, compliance cost analysis, business impact analysis, budget analysis, risk assessment or risk/risk analysis) are not fully developed; that data collection is costly or does not exist; that the methods are too costly to be practical; that resistance to their application is high when the results contradict the aspirations or interests of certain groups; that there are no incentives for regulators to resort to such methods; that in some cases the decision may be economically inefficient but legally binding; that sometimes there is no time to do this type of analysis; or that their quality is not always adequate and there is a lack of well-prepared experts (see Jacobs 1997).

environment, and so on; (c) compared to other decision methods—that tend to be more opaque, such as negotiations and transactions—impact analysis improves transparency and facilitates consultation and debate, and (d) it raises the standards of accountability for governments, which have to demonstrate that the regulation is created in the public interest, that is, that there are good reasons for it.

References

Bardach E (1977) Implementation game: what happens after a bill becomes a law. The MIT Press, Cambridge

Barettoni Arleri A (1983) Fattibilità ed applicabilità delle leggi. Relazione conclusiva della Commissione di studio per la semplificazione della procedure e la fattibilità ed applicabilità delle leggi. Maggioli Editore, Roma

Bentham J (1981) De la promulgación de las leyes. In: Tratados de legislación penal y civil. Editora Nacional, Madrid

Bettini R (1983) Il circolo vizioso legislative. Efficacia del diritto ed efficienza degli apparati pubblici in Italia. Franco Angeli Editore, Milano

Braithwaite J (1993) L'amelioration du respect de la réglementation: stratégies et applications pratiques dans les pays membres de l'OCDE. OECD, Paris

Bundesministerium der Justiz (2008) Handbuch der Rechtsförmlichkeit. Bundesministerium der Justiz für Verbraucherschutz, Berlin, 3.Auflage. Published in the Bundesanzeiger 60, no. 160a, 22 September 2008. http://hdr.bmj.de

Bunker DR (1972) Policy sciences perspectives on implementation processes. Policy Sci 3:71–80

de Mably L'A (1797) De la législation ou Principes des Lois (Œuvres Complètes), vol 9. Chez Bossange, Masson et Besson, Paris

Dertick M (1972) New towns in-towns. The Urban Institute, Washington, DC

Dublin LI, Lotka A (1946) The money of a man. Ronald Press, New York

Dunlop CA, Radaelli CM (eds) (2017) Handbook on regulatory impact assessment. E. Elgar, Cheltenham

European Commission (2016) Better regulation: delivering better Results for a Stronger Union [COM (2016) 615 final]

European Commission (2017a) Completing the Better Regulation Agenda: Better Solutions for Better Results [COM (2017) 651 final]

European Commission (2017b) Better Regulations Guidelines (Working Document) [SWD (2017) 350]

Evan W (1980) Law as an instrument of social change. In: Evan W (ed) The sociology of law. The Free Press, New York

Galiana A (2008) La ley, entre la razón y la experimentación. Tirant lo Blanch, Valencia

Giannini Commission (1979) Rapporto sui principali problemi della Admministrazione dello Stato (In Il Foro Italiano V: 250–272)

Hopkins TD (1992) Cost of regulation: filling the gaps. Report prepared for Regulatory Information Service Center (August 1992). Regulatory Information Service Center, Washington, DC

Jacobs SH (1997) An overview of regulatory impact analysis in OECD countries. In: Regulatory impact analysis. Best practices in OECD countries. OECD, Paris

Kleinig J (1961) Valuing life. Princeton University Press, Princeton

Mader L (1985) L'Évaluation législative. Pour une analyse empirique des effets de la législation. Payot, Lausanne

Mayntz R (ed) (1983) Implementation politischer Programme II: Ansätze zur Theoriebildung. Westdeutscher Verlag, Opladen

Mayntz R (1977) Die Implementation politischer Programme: Theoretische Überlegungen zu einem neuen Forschungsgebiet. Die Verwaltung 10:51–66
Mayntz R (ed) (1980) Implementation politischer Programme I: Empirische Forschungsberichte. Athenäum, Königstein
Ministry of Economic Affairs, The Netherlands (1995) Business test checklist and notes-effects of draft legislation. The Hague
Montoro MJ (1989) Adecuación al ordenamiento y factibilidad. Presupuestos de calidad de las normas. Centro de Estudios Constitucionales, Madrid
Morand CA (ed) (1993) Évaluation législative et lois experimentales. Presses Universitaires d'Aix-Marseille, Aix-en-Provence
Morral JF (1992) La maîtrise des coûts de la réglementation: le recours à la budgétisation des réglementations. OECD, Paris
National Performance Review (U.S.) (1994) Creating a government that works better and cost less. Report of the national performance review. U.S Government Printing Office, Washington
OECD (1993) Mise au point et utilisation des listes des critères à prendre en compte pour l'élaboration des réglementations. OECD/GD (93)181. OECD, Paris
OECD (1994) Procédures de consultation pour l'élaboration de consultation: pratiques et expériences de dix pays de l'OCDE. OECD, Paris
OECD (2004) Regulatory Reform in Germany. Government capacity to assure high quality regulation. OECD Reviews of Regulatory Reform. OECD, Paris
OECD (2011) Regulatory policy and governance. Supporting economic growth and serving the public interest. OECD Publishing, Paris
Plato (1988) Las leyes. Porrúa, México
Pressman J, Wildadsky AB (1973) Implementation. How great expectations in Washington are dashed in Oakland. University of California, Berkeley
Rousseau JJ (1971) Discours sur l'oeconomie politique. In: Oevres Complètes, vol 2. Seuil, Paris
Sabatier P (1980) The implementation of public policy: a framework of analysis. Policy Stud J 8 (4):545–560
Schmid D'Avenstein GL (1821 [1776]) Principios de Legislación Universal. Imprenta Roldán, Valladolid
Seidman R (1992) Justifying legislation: a pragmatic, institutionalist approach to the memorandum of law, legislative theory and practical reason. Harv J Legis 29:1–79
Sunstein CR (1985) Interest groups in American public law. Stan Law Rev 38:29–87
Teubner G (1987) Juridification: concepts, aspects, limits, solutions. In: Teubner G (ed) Juridification of social spheres. A comparative analysis in the areas of labor, corporate, antitrust and social welfare law. Walter de Gruyter, Berlin, pp 3–48
Tolchin SJ, Tolchin M (1983) Dismantling America. The rush to deregulate. Boston, Houston Miflin Company
Wilson JO (1967) The bureaucracy problem. Pub Int 6:3–9
Wiscusi WK (1993) L'amélioration du respect de la réglementation: stratégies et applications pratiques dans les pays membres de l'OCDE. OECD, Paris
Wiscusi WK (1995) Regulation and its impact on competitiveness. A paper commisioned by the U.S. Competitiveness Council. Washington

Chapter 12
Government and Parliament

12.1 The Legislative Agenda

So far, we have dealt with the work of legislative drafters as experts in the writing of laws, a role not sufficiently highlighted—if not openly undervalued—due to the persistent cliché according to which politicians decide *what* to do and technicians merely propose *how* to do it. Let us now talk about the role of governments and parliaments in the production of norms, and especially of laws.

A schematic and simplistic vision of the legislative process would consider the government as the only institution that drives it. The basic idea is that political leaders who know the problems to be solved and the relevant solutions, offer them to citizens through their programs. But a closer examination of reality reveals the existence of other impulses that set the norm-making process in motion (Denninger 1986).

If we stop to look at the electoral programs of political parties we will find that they include only some of the laws intended for enactment, and that, among these, only a few end up being approved.[1] Electoral programs explain little when it comes to the origin of laws: they can be a source of inspiration at the beginning of the legislative term but their importance declines as the term advances (Miers and Page 1982, p. 61). That is why the broad outlines of any government's policy can only be perceived retrospectively; it is the pressures of daily events and not programs that determine government action (Griffith and Ryle 1989, p. 309). The meaning of electoral programs, increasingly vague and ethereal, is to offer a broad explanation

[1]The first thing that stands out when examining the electoral programs in Spain between 1982 and 1992 is that they contained fewer and fewer legislative commitments. If in the electoral program of the Socialist Party (PSOE) in 1982 (II Term after the 1978 Constitution) there was a promise to send 99 bills to the Chambers, in its program for the III Term 52 bills were proposed, and only 29 bills for the IV Term. Of these bills, only 65, 34 and 10 respectively ended up being approved as laws. This figure contrasts with the 426 government bills that the socialist cabinet actually presented and the 379 the parliament approved between 1982 and 1992 (II, III and IV Terms).

V. Zapatero Gómez, *The Art of Legislating*, Legisprudence Library 6,
https://doi.org/10.1007/978-3-030-23388-4_12

of a legislative policy rather than a proper legislative program: they serve to showcase the problems that seem relevant to a party as well as the manner in which they will be approached (Subirats 1992, p. 90).

Something very similar can be said about the government program that the presidential candidate exposes to Congress in Spain.[2] Although the activity of the ministers offers more information on the legislative plans of a government,[3] the analysis of legislative activity as it happens in real life tells us that, as the term advances, "party projects" (those that affect the identity and the electoral prospects of a party) decrease, and what Drewry (1981) calls "administrative projects" grow in proportion.[4] Trying then to explain legislative activity solely through the initiative of parties or even governments leads to a somewhat short-sighted vision of reality. This is so even in the most rational model of normative production, the Anglo-Saxon one, with its Office of Parliamentary Counsel, in which the government seems to lead and fully dominate the legislative process.[5]

The genesis of public policies is much richer: they can have their origin in supply or demand, or they can be the product of self-generation (Meny and Thoenig 1992, pp. 110 ff). The same can be said of laws. Viewed from the supply point of view, it is politicians who take the initiative by offering certain laws (the ones they want to offer depending on their ideological principles), and hoping that citizens will consent to them (Lindblom 1991, pp. 145 ff). Seen from the perspective of demand, laws are the result of felt needs that become demands, and are eventually satisfied through legislative action: the legislator, from this perspective, is a receptive agent (a listener) who either limits himself to conferring formal sanction to models of behaviour that are already given in reality or creates a new law to solve a specific social problem (La Spina 1989, p. 66). But also, norms feed on other norms: a norm is often promulgated because another already existing norm, in its phase of execution or implementation, poses difficulties, encounters obstacles or modifies situations that force authorities to intervene with new regulation (Luhmann 1983, p. 66). Government regulatory programs, therefore, explain only the genesis of a small number of norms.[6] Political science prefers to use the idea of public agenda to explain the origin

---

[2]With regard to the legislative promises of the candidate for President, there were 48 laws for the II Term (only 28 were passed), 6 for the III Term (all were passed) and 12 for the IV Term (7 were passed).

[3]In their first address to the competent Congressional Committee, ministers usually set out a more ambitious legislative program. Thus in the II Term they announced 146 bills (of which 81 were approved), in the III Term they promised 76 (33 were approved) and in the IV Term they promised to send 69 (of which only 21 were approved).

[4]See also Burton and Drewry (1970), who, as noted earlier (Chap. 10, note 3), distinguish between policy bills (which make substantial changes in public policies) and administration bills (which facilitate their implementation).

[5]See Zander (1994, Chap. 1); cf. also Miers and Page (1982, pp. 25 ff). On his part, Sir Gramsville Ram (1951), once First Parliamentary Counselor, carefully describes the steps to be taken when it comes to preparing and implementing legislative programs.

[6]If one focuses the examination on the 1982–1992 legislative period and compares the electoral programs, the government programs and the laws finally passed in each term, one can see that most

of norms[7] since it covers not only the norms that are the result of government initiative, but also those other norms—certainly more numerous—that have their origin in the demands of certain population groups and in the need to permanently update the normative system.

What is known in political science as a formal agenda brings together, for our purposes, all those social issues that, whatever their origin, political leaders have seriously taken into consideration. In Spain, for instance, the best proof of the government taking these issues seriously is their inclusion in the agenda of the Committee of Secretaries and Undersecretaries of State. What existed up to that moment was a multitude of studies, reports and proposals contained in the thousands of drafts dealing with the most varied problems that fill the archives of ministries. What now begins is a purely political phase in which specific legitimised bodies—government and parliament—will decide whether to create a binding law out of what was previously nothing more than a proposal put forward by technicians. Let us see what is in that black box of government.[8]

---

of the laws passed did not appear in these programs. As regards the II Term, only 38% of the laws finally passed were included in the government's program (understood in a very broad sense), while 72% of the laws finally passed were the result of a logical reaction to unforeseen events. The conclusion is similar with respect to the III Term: only 26% of the laws passed were provided for in the programs, compared to 74% of those that did not appear in any program. A similar conclusion is drawn by Sabino Cassese (1992, p. 315) regarding legislative activity in Italy: only about a third of the laws adopted during the life of a government are in fact provided for in its program. Another third is made up of laws announced in programs of previous governments and the last third are laws adopted by Parliament on its own initiative.

[7]For Cobb et al. (1976, 1982) the public agenda is made up of all those issues that are the subject of broad public attention, require some form of action in the opinion of a considerable proportion of people and fall within the competence or jurisdiction of some public body. The formal agenda, on the other hand, includes all those issues that politicians have seriously accepted to take into consideration. It is when a problem enters the formal agenda of a society that the gestation of a public policy—including legislation—actually begins. There are three models of agenda-building: the external initiative model, the mobilisation model and the internal initiative model. The external initiative model accounts for those processes through which certain groups external to the Government raise a problem, extend it to place it on the public agenda and sometimes manage to place it on the formal agenda of public officials. The mobilisation model, on the other hand, tries to explain the evolution of issues or problems that are raised within the Government, which are normative objectives pursued by the Government but which, in order to guarantee their success, are presented to public opinion. Finally, the internal initiative model describes the process followed by certain issues that arise within the government sphere and whose promoters do not extend to the general public but rather try—as quietly as possible—to place in the formal agenda.

[8]In what follows (Sect. 12.2), I will largely confine myself to the Spanish experience.

12.2 Government and the Production of Laws

Once a preliminary draft has been produced and all the requisite conditions have been met—consultations, opinions, evaluation questionnaires and the preparation of memoranda—, it is the government's turn to act.

The studies referring to this phase of the elaboration of laws do not abound (García Escudero 2000a), either because it is considered a specifically political moment that has its own internal logic, or because the actions of the executive bodies in charge are not made public. The truth is that this last phase of the legislative decision constitutes a kind of black box whose content is largely unknown. Despite the importance of this phase, it lacks adequate formalisation: its regulation is usually contained in the Prime Minister's circular notes[9] or in agreements of the Council of Ministers that regulate the functioning of the collegiate bodies of the government.

Particularly important in this process in Spain is the work of the Committee of Secretaries and Undersecretaries of State, which has become one of the most active and relevant instruments of coordination in legislative production. If coordination is the act of unifying and harmonising the sectorial policies of the different ministries so that they are inserted coherently and without contradictions in the *continuum* of government action (García Fernández 1992, p. 47), the Committee of Secretaries and Undersecretaries of State is the key piece in this task.[10] This Committee makes a useful contribution to the technical purge of draft laws. The Council of Ministers has

---

[9]In the case of France, see *Circulaire relative aux règles d'élaboration, de signature et de publication des textes au Journal Officiel et à la mise en oeuvre de procédures particulières incombant au Premier Ministre* (21 May 1985) and the *Circulaire* of President Rocard of 2 January 1993. As for the UK, some processing requirements can be found in the Questions of Procedure for Ministers (Cabinet Office 1992).

[10]Roughly, the procedure and the formalities are as follows. The proposing Department requests the inclusion of the debate on the preliminary draft (*anteproyecto*) in the agenda of the Committee of Secretaries and Undersecretaries of State entrusted with the study and preparation of matters submitted for deliberation by the Council of Ministers. This Committee does not adopt any agreement but only informs the Council of Ministers on each and every one of the matters it deals with. In order to obtain the inclusion of the preliminary draft in the agenda, it is assumed that the competent Minister has given a first approval to the text. But normally, unless the envisaged piece of legislation is particularly important, the request for its inclusion in the agenda of the Committee of Secretaries and Undersecretaries of State is made by the Secretary or Undersecretary of the affected ministry without the need of prior authorisation of the Minister. To be included in the agenda, the draft must be distributed to all members of the Committee with sufficient anticipation—requisite studies, reports or opinions are also distributed along with to the draft text. In the case of preliminary drafts of bills (*anteproyectos de ley*), background information and explanatory statements must also be submitted. Once these procedural steps have been completed, the preliminary draft is included in the so-called black index or agenda of the Committee of Secretaries and Undersecretaries of State. From this moment, and until the is debated in the Committee (i.e. approximately one month for draft laws and two weeks for other provisions), there is a phase of purification of the text in which all the Departments can participate through the so-called "observations". These observations are made in writing, and must be answered by the proposing Department, also in writing, until the day before the session is held.

Table 12.1 Types of "observations" debated in the Committee of Secretaries and Undersecretaries of State, ordered by affected ministries (1988–1991)

Ministry	Substantive	Competence	Procedure	Form	Other	Total
Foreign affairs	245	23	14	107	1	330
Justice	497	60	32	718	14	1321
Defence	52	47	4	36	2	141
Economy	499	65	57	440	6	1067
Interior	510	90	57	751	3	1411
Public works & Urban devl.	305	48	15	309	1	1067
Public works & transport	14	0	4	30	0	48
Education	120	36	7	137	1	301
Labor	209	30	29	311	0	579
Industry	265	43	22	202	8	540
Agriculture	203	53	21	337	1	615
Public administration	794	362	69	772	4	2001
Transport	193	58	5	48	2	306
Culture	60	5	1	46	0	112
Health	333	51	23	105	0	514
Parliamentary relations	1682	234	269	3230	1	5419
Social affairs	152	3	12	208	1	379
Total	6073	1211	641	7789	45	15,759

relatively little time to examine the drafts in depth, so the filter of the Committee is in fact a pre-evaluation of the policy contained in the draft, of the competence issues and conflicts both between the different departments and between the central administration and the rest of the administrations, of the observance of procedural requirements on which the validity of the draft may even depend, and of the formal questions of legislative technique. All of this is evidenced by examining the cross-observations between the different ministries in the cases the Committee dealt with from January 1988 to June 1991 (Table 12.1).

As we can see, the largest volume of observations (almost half of them) refer to questions of legislative form and technique (i.e. to "norm depuration") which are of interest to all departments but especially to horizontal ministries such as Parliamentary Relations (now Ministry of the Presidency), Public Administrations, Justice and Economy. A second level of concern is that of substantive issues or observations that refer to the policy underlying the drafts—such observations accounted for 41% of the total of observations made in the studied period. In this phase, other departments are enabled to examine the procedural problems and conflicts of competence that the proposed norm may cause. The proposing ministry usually has a special interest in obtaining a favourable report from the Committee of Secretaries and Undersecretaries of State. To this end, it has to argue for each proposal, correct the detected errors and, in the case of substantive differences, negotiate the final text or submit the differences to the Council of Ministers itself.[11]

Among the collegiate bodies of the Spanish government, the most relevant is the Council of Ministers. Under the direction of the president, it assumes the most important constitutional functions, such as the executive function (for which it is responsible to Congress), or the direction of domestic and foreign policy, as well as of civil and military administration. But more interestingly for us, it holds the regulatory authority (i.e. the authority to issue regulations and lower-ranked legal provisions), and it approves bills for their referral to the houses and enacts the decree-laws it deems necessary.[12] The Council of Ministers is, together with the chambers, the capital organ in the legislative production process. A brief reflection on its activity is therefore in order.

A classic model of governmental management of the legislative process is the Anglo-Saxon system, in which the drafting of bills by the Office of Parliamentary Counsel is preceded by ad hoc political instructions formally approved by the cabinet. The observance of these instructions is monitored by the government through the Legislation Committee. In Spain, there is a deficit in the political management of the legislative process, which is restricted to the proceedings of the Committee of Secretaries and Undersecretaries of State: Approval is the usual result of any project that passes through the filter of this Committee, and it is not unusual for the Council of Ministers to become aware of the content of the project in the same session in which it is approved. Possibly one of the cause of this lack of political direction lies in a model of legislative production in which it is not compulsory to previously inform the Council of the outline of the projects of greater relevance that are in planning phase.

Another cause of this deficit of leadership of the Council of Ministers in the Spanish legislative process is the lack of time. Between December 1982 and June 1992, the Council of Ministers approved 38,536 matters, including 340 bills, 91 royal decree-laws, 14,477 royal decrees, 11,706 case files and 11,922 agreements. All this in 432 sessions. And although the structure of the Council's agenda in two indexes—green and red—allows the debate to concentrate on the capital issues, each

[11]Of the total of 15,763 comments circulated in the period that goes from January 1988 to June 1991, 7809 were replied to in writing: 3729 accepted and 4080 rejected. It is evident that in this procedure the most important work is carried out outside the Committee of Secretaries and Undersecretaries of State and prior to it by means of bilateral or multilateral meetings of the different Departments. The Committee in question, throughout the approximately 3 h of each weekly session, establishes and, if necessary, formalises the agreements and disagreements between the different Departments; this establishment will determine the type of treatment to which the draft law will be subject from that moment on. If there is an agreement, it will be reported favourably and included in the so-called green index. If there is no agreement, it will be included in the red index. The first implies that there is a very high probability that the Council of Ministers will not debate it and will limit itself to approving it as it is. The red index means that the Council will discuss it and, if necessary, modify it.

[12]As noted in Chap. 2, "decree-laws" are pieces of legislation issued by the Cabinet in cases of extraordinary and urgent need (Art. 86 of the Spanish Constitution).

session lasts 4 h at most, which gives an idea of how little time can be devoted to the debate of norm projects.

But perhaps the main factors that limit the control of the Council of Ministers over legislative production are neither the lack of time nor the inadequate articulation of the procedure. Other phenomena must be taken into consideration that have developed throughout these years of democratic life, such as the presidentialist drift of our government model,[13] the suspension of the principle of collegiality and the strengthening of the autonomy of ministerial departments.[14] For the legislative process, this has meant it is ministers who ordinarily decide on the package of norms that they will present to the council and that the council rarely rejects or modifies them if they are supported by the president.

The conclusion to these considerations is not very encouraging: it is true that the government approves the bills it sends to the houses, but it is also true that, except in matters affecting party identity, the government rarely knows in depth the bills it approves. There is no need to mythicise the Anglo-Saxon model or to alter the diffuse system of legislative production followed in Spain, but it is obvious that some procedures of the British tradition deserve to be considered. For example, the need for a regulatory program approved by the government for each parliamentary period, the obligation for the government to approve the outline of the proposed norms prior to their drafting and the convenience of having an administrative body verify that the draft that is resubmitted to the Council respects the policy that was defined. And as long as no measures are taken in this direction, a better balance of the technical and political components of legislative production will not be possible.

---

[13]In the Spanish constitutional system, the President of the Government is not a *primus inter pares* but a body endowed with very important powers and faculties that do not require a collegiate exercise. It is only the President who draws up the political program of the cabinet he intends to form; he and his program receive the confidence of the Congress of Deputies; it is he who proposes the appointment of Ministers to the King, directs the action of the government and coordinates its functions, and who may raise a so-called question of confidence (*cuestión de confianza*) to the Congress, propose the calling of a referendum to the King, lodge an appeal of unconstitutionality, dismiss the ministers or propose the dissolution of the Houses. All these powers are constitutionally attributed to him. To this constitutional design we must add a series of circumstances that have strengthened his leadership: the social demand for a solid executive in the face of the country's difficult situation, the configuration of political parties around certain leaders or the electoral system that chains Deputies and Senators to party discipline, among other circumstances. On this subject, see, among others, García Canales (1995).

[14]The Spanish Constitution recognises the "direct competence and responsibility of Ministers in their management" as heads of Department. There is, therefore, a number of competences and responsibilities for each Minister that are not shared with the Council of Ministers, and that the President must be aware of. The President is responsible for "coordinating" the functions of each Minister with those of other Ministers and with those of the Government as a whole ["The President directs Government action and coordinates the functions" of the ministers, "notwithstanding the power (*competencia*) of the latter to carry out their duties and their direct responsibility for it" (Art. 97.2 of the Spanish Constitution]. The "departmental principle" was respected to the extent that in the 1980s ministers ended up, in practice, defining unilaterally, and to a very large degree, the normative program that they would present to the Chambers.

12.3 The Role of Parliament

It is often said that, in practice, the first mission of parliaments is to control governments (García Fernández 1994). And surely the importance of this parliamentary function cannot be underestimated, but we cannot forget the legislative function of parliaments. When Bodin (1992), enumerated the true attributes of sovereignty, he concluded that the essential and exclusive elements of sovereignty were not jurisdiction—"because it is common to the prince and the subject"—, nor the appointment or dismissal of officers. For Bodin "the first attribute of sovereign power is the power to give laws to all in general and to each one in particular". In our constitutional democracies, this essential function of lawmaking, the essential attribute of sovereignty, is entrusted to the parliament made up of representatives who act on our behalf and are not subject to any imperative mandate.[15] This is how, in a democracy, the laws are expected to temper their heteronomous character.

But here we find an important paradox: while it is precisely the houses that draft bills in presidential systems, in a parliamentary democracy it is usually the government who presents the projects that will be discussed and approved or (rarely) rejected by parliament. Except for the so-called "legislative proposals" viz. parliamentary motions or private member bills—which are as scarce as they are unlikely to succeed—, parliamentarians work on texts already laid down by government, so the correct drafting of these texts will determine, to a large extent, the quality of the final laws. In theory, they can amend a bill in whole or in part, they can even reject it outright, but in practice, parliaments tend to ratify the draft presented to them. Moreover, lost in an ocean of technicalities that only interests those most directly affected by a bill—and its amendments—, they allow the bill to pass without a clarifying public debate on its substance, on the public policy embodied in the text. Of course, on occasions, there is a confrontation between alternative options and parliament connects with the needs and interests of those represented, but these occasions are rather exceptional. Normally form prevails, and the substance is clouded by it. Now, the exercise of legislative power that our societies deserve requires much more. What society is interested in and what its representatives can and must offer is not the technicalities—for which the parliamentary groups and parliament itself have well prepared specialists—but the thorough debate on each public policy. And for this type of debate, an eminently political body such as parliament doesn't lack the time nor the preparation.

It is true, then, that parliamentarians in parliamentary democracies do not usually take the legislative initiative. There is no point in regretting it. But democracy

---

[15]Spanish constitutional law scholars have already produced invaluable literature on the exercise of the legislative function by the parliament. See the monographic issue on laws and legislative procedures ("La ley y el procedimiento legislativo") of the *Revista Española de Derecho Constitucional* 16 (1986); Biglino Campos (1995, 1997); Santaolalla (1998, pp. 20 ff); or García-Escudero (2000b).

implies that representation be open to any citizen, as long as he earns sufficient support from the members of his community. What citizens need is that their representatives perform, at least, some of their tasks, to ensure that laws are the result of reason informed by experience and not populist laws that create great expectations but have no foundation. Among these tasks, the following deserve special attention. Firstly, parliament should debate and clarify the public policy that the bill is intended to develop. This involves establishing the problem to be solved, debating the various solutions proposed and explaining the reason for choosing the specific solution embodied in the submitted text. Secondly, parliament should asses the practicability of the projected law, that is, whether it runs the risk of becoming a "banner law", or it has the personal and material resources necessary for its implementation. Thirdly, parliament should verify that the necessary procedures and rules are in place for the proper implementation of the law, as well as make sure that the citizens or officials on whose commitment to the project the success of the future law depends, have been consulted. And, finally, it should confirm that the predicted costs and benefits of the new law are known and can be quantified. The answers to these questions can only be made accessible to all citizens through the public debate in parliament.

Parliament can also exercise its legislative power by following up on the fate of newly adopted laws. "Decretinism" was that Bolshevik disease—Karl Renner said—by which a good decree was enough to solve any issue. To think that the mission of parliament, when confronted with a social issue, ends with the drafting of a new law is proof of a certain decretinism. Respect for its very own actions obliges parliament to verify that newly implemented laws are accepted by their addresses, that the proper resources are in place, that the objectives proclaimed in the law are being fulfilled. *Ex post* evaluation of public policies is already increasingly institutionalised within governments (see OECD 2003) and there is no reason why parliaments should not do just the same with the laws they enact. If parliaments are to take the exercise of legislative power seriously they must carry out an evaluation of the rules they issue. In order to do so, they need to be provided with some sort of public policy office.

Taking the exercise of legislative power seriously also means reviewing existing laws and repealing or modifying the ones that are outdated or clearly detrimental to society. Our societies, especially since the 1980s brought the progressive globalisation of the economy, have come under pressure in favor of strong deregulation. It was not only or mainly a question of eliminating all those obsolete or irrelevant laws that settle over the years in accumulative strata and produce minimal social benefits. Rather, the focus of attention and pressure was directed towards laws that burden the competitiveness of the economy and the globalisation of markets: laws that establish prohibitions on activities, that create monopolies, that stipulate requirements for the exercise of a profession or an activity, production quotas, quality standards that become entry barriers, price controls, opening hours, geographical limitations on certain activities, exclusive concessions to certain industries or people, and so on. Some states have undertaken ambitious programs to revise existing legislation,[16] programs that continue to be fundamentally in the hands of governments. But... do parliaments have really nothing to say about this? Is this legislative operation not important and delicate enough for the legitimate representatives of the citizens to consider?

Together with the control and guidance of the government, taking the exercise of legislative power seriously is a responsibility of parliament. And this also means supervising and guiding the whole process of legislative production. This process must begin with the elimination of all those obsolete rules that pollute our legal systems and produce no social benefit. The impact of these laws must also be evaluated ex post.[17] But parliament also has to evaluate the net benefit to society—and the public interest—of the many laws that have accumulated over time. In this case, it is a question of evaluating the legislation in force ex post. From a technical point of view, this operation is easier than the ex ante evaluation, since data—and not just estimates of costs and benefits—are often available. However, from a political perspective, this kind of evaluation is more likely to fail because of the strength of the interests already created around existing laws and the little attention they receive from the public. Parliament—given its limitations of time and resources—should establish certain priorities in terms of the sectors of society subject to scrutiny (Jacobs 1997), and at the same time supervise the deregulatory activity carried out by the executive. This requires parliaments that are more aware of their mission and backed by stronger resources.

We are living in times of deregulatory fury, times in which governments, captured or manipulated by pressure groups and carrying the banner of national economy competitiveness, often have no objection to the elimination of controls or mechanisms that protect citizens on health, consume and environment matters. Day after day, without public participation or even knowledge, decisions are taken in these fields that affect our interests. Who is to decide on the quality of the air we breathe? Who should set standards for the medicines we take, the food we eat or the cars we drive? Although their opinion is of course relevant, this cannot be done by the industry or the government alone. If we are to build a deliberative democracy, it would be desirable for parliament to have its own agenda in this debate, because deregulation is in many cases—as we have seen lately—simply the deliberate dismantling of a social welfare system that has taken a lot of effort to build (Tolchin and Tolchin 1983, p. 37).

[16]Perhaps one of the most ambitious countries in this field has been Australia with the signing (by all States and the Commonwealth) of the Competition Principles Agreement (1995), which sets in motion a whole process that culminated in the revision of more than 1500 norms. See Holmes and Argy (1997).

[17]The analysis of the impact of existing rules is virtually identical to that of draft laws. It must be applied to determine whether the rule in question is achieving its intended objectives, and what is the result of comparing the benefits and costs it is generating. The advantage in this case is that to calculate costs and benefits we already have real data and not estimates: the effects are already known facts, not assumptions. See Rex Deighton-Smith (1977).

The major decisions affecting our society cannot be left to governments only. Issues such as global warming, genetic engineering, nuclear energy, biodiversity, use of pesticides or food hygiene cannot be decided at governmental level alone. A public debate on these issues is needed. When governments are compelled to give reasons both paternalism and populism are avoided. We demand that public authorities take the necessary measures to prevent all kinds of risks in our lives and, in Europe at least, we have opted for the precautionary principle as a guide.[18] But everything involves risks, living is already a risky activity. What we need to know is what risks we in fact consider intolerable and what are the costs for reducing them. We are opposed to genetic modification because we do not know the hazards it involves, we want drastic measures to prevent global warming, many people oppose nuclear energy, or the use of certain pesticides, or the smoke from factories because of the risks they involve. But to ban genetic modifications, reduce pollution, do without nuclear energy and limit the use of certain pesticides by applying the precautionary principle, as is the custom in the countries of the European Union, also means depriving our societies of certain benefits such as improvements in food production that could substantially reduce world hunger, cheaper energy or a sustained level of economic development. What are the levels of risk that our society wants to assume? And how much are we willing to pay for the benefits? What do we give up in each case? These are questions that cannot be decided by a government. We need our representatives to deal with the issues that are most relevant to our lives by debating them in public and by giving reasons and exchanging arguments. This is the mission of parliament.

References

Biglino Campos P (1995) Procedimiento legislativo. In: Enciclopedia Jurídica Básica, vol 3. Civitas, Madrid

Biglino Campos P (1997) El procedimiento legislativo. In: V Jornadas de Derecho Parlamentario. Congreso de los Diputados, Madrid

Bodin J (1992) Los seis libros de la república. Centro de Estudios Constitucionales, Madrid [The Six Books of a Commonwealth, Harvard University Press, Cambridge (MA), 1962]

Burton IF, Drewry G (1970) Public legislation: a survey of the session 1966/1969. Parliament Aff 23:154–183

Cabinet Office (1992) Questions of procedure for ministers. Cabinet Office, London

Cassese S (1992) Introduzione allo studio della normazione. Rivista trimestrale di diritto pubblico 2:307–330

Cobb R, Ross J-K, Ross MH (1976) Agenda building as a comparative political process. Am Polit Sci Rev 70(1):126–138

Cobb R, Ross J-K, Ross MH (1982) Participation in American politics. The dynamics of agenda building. Allyn and Bacon, Boston

Deighton-Smith R (1977) Regulatory impact analysis: best practices in OECD countries. OECD, Paris

[18] On the precautionary principle, see the illuminating work of Sunstein (2005).

Denninger E (1986) El procedimiento legislativo en la República Federal Alemana. Revista Española de Derecho Constitucional 16:11–59
Drewry G (1981) Legislation. In: Walkand SA, Ryle M (eds) The commons today. Fontana, London
García Canales M (1995) La huella presidencialista en el constitucionalismo español. Revista Española de Derecho Constitucional 44:99–127
García Fernández J (1992) La coordinación intragubernamental como principio del derecho constitucional del Gobierno. Revista Vasca de Administración Pública/Herri-Ardura Laritzazko Euskal Aldizkaria 34:43–64
García Fernández J (1994) La función de control del Parlamento sobre el Gobierno. Revista de las Cortes Generales 31:31–69
García-Escudero P (2000a) La iniciativa legislativa del Gobierno. Centro de Estudios Políticos y Constitucionales, Madrid
García-Escudero P (2000b) La iniciativa legislativa en la Constitución Española de 1978. Revista Española de Derecho Constitucional 59:57–91
Griffith JA, Ryle M (1989) Parliament. Functions, practice and procedure. Sweet and Maxwell, London
Holmes S, Argy S (1997) Reviewing existing regulations: Australia's national legislative review. OECD, Paris
Jacobs SH (1997) An overview of regulatory impact analysis in OECD countries. OECD, Paris
La Spina A (1989) La decisione legislativa. Lineamenti di una teoria. Giuffrè, Milano
Lindblom CE (1991) El proceso de elaboración de políticas públicas. MAP, Madrid
Luhmann N (1983) Teoria politica nello Stato del Benessere. Franco Agnelli, Milano
Meny I, Thoenig J-C (1992) Las políticas públicas. Ariel, Barcelona
Miers DR, Page AC (1982) Legislation. Sweet and Maxwell, London
OECD (2003) Regulatory performance: ex post evaluation of regulatory policies. OECD, Paris
Ram SG (1951) The improvements of the statute book. J Soc Public Teachers Law:447–449
Santaolalla F (1998) Elaboración de las leyes. Comentarios al capítulo II del título III de la Constitución. In: Alzaga O (ed) Comentarios a la Constitución española de 1978, vol 7. Edersa, Madrid, pp 17–26
Subirats J (1992) Un problema de estilo. La formación de las políticas públicas en España. Centro de Estudios Constitucionales, Madrid
Sunstein CR (2005) Laws of fear. Beyond the precautionary principle. Cambridge University Press, Cambridge
Tolchin SJ, Tolchin M (1983) Dismantling America. The rush to deregulate. Houston Miflin Company, Boston
Zander M (1994) The law-making process, 4th edn. Butterworths, London

Chapter 13
Legislators and Judges

13.1 The Judge as an Agent

It is surprising how little attention the doctrine has paid to the problems involved in the legislative process until relatively recent times (see Posner 1983). Our silence on the subject contrasts strongly with our philosophical loquacity when it comes to judicial activity. On few occasions do philosophers of law deal with legislative activity and when they do, it is usually to present a demonised image of politics as the realm of ignorance, of incompetence or obscure manipulation, of stark struggle for power. To this picture they oppose the idealised image of judges who, equipped with their vast preparation, their prudence and their selfless search for justice, only aspire to find the law, not to create it (Waldron 1999). The latter only seek justice, the former reign in the impure realm of politics, an activity that cannot be subjected to rules and reason. On this account we have good and solid theories of legal argumentation, but we still lack a mature, well-developed theory of legislation: occupied with finding out what judges do, legal philosophy has disregarded what legislators do. And this disinterest has logically aroused criticism—which, fortunately, is already beginning to be heard (Eskridge and Frickey 1987, p. 691).

One of the consequences of this disinterest has been the disconnection between the theory of legislation and the theory of interpretation. Once the theory of legal interpretation has been disassociated from the theory of legislation, it loses its foundation, and its proposals run the risk of falling into arbitrariness. Because any theory of interpretation has to be explicitly based on a theory of democracy. It has to be firmly anchored in a clear conception of the functions that pertain to legislators and judges—or what is the same, of the relations between parliament and the courts.

The foundation of the classical conception of democracy is the idea of the supremacy of legislative power, defined as the first power of the state. The state in turn is based on national sovereignty, expressed periodically through free elections. The rule of majorities (with equal rights for minorities, as Elías Díaz always reminds us) and the idea of the responsibility that all powers ultimately hold towards citizens

V. Zapatero Gómez, *The Art of Legislating*, Legisprudence Library 6,
https://doi.org/10.1007/978-3-030-23388-4_13

are consubstantial principles of this classical conception of democracy. In this scheme judges and courts are placed in a subordinate position regarding the law. The function of the judge (an unelected and politically unaccountable body) is limited to faithfully applying the will of the legislator (elected and accountable) expressed in the legislative text. That is why all the literature of that time—from the first Enlightment thinkers, through Montesquieu, to Bentham—focused on how to prevent the judge from usurping legislative functions. Before the approval of Napoleon's civil code, the Organic Decree of 16/24 August 1790 created a legislative *référé* requiring that the judge, in case of obscurity or contradiction in the norm, remit the solution of the problem to the legislator. The same year witnessed the creation of the Court of Cassation—separated from the judiciary—as an extension of the legislative power, in charge of "supervising or inspecting the application of the law" by judges and magistrates. But the promoters of the civil code themselves, like Cambacérès or Portalis, maintained more open criteria regarding the role of judges. They were aware of the fact that even the most refined code could not provide an answer to all the problems that the application of the law might present. The judge could not be constrained to being the silent mouth of an always imperfect law: what was desired was to affirm the primacy of the law and to force the judge to decide "penetrated by the spirit of the law", but assisted in this task—as Portalis wanted—not only by customary usage, but also by maxims and doctrine, converted into the necessary complements of laws. It was the jurists of the School of Exegesis who later deified the law and tried to reduce the work of the judge to resolving a syllogism in which the law was the major premise, the facts of the matter the minor premise and the sentence their mechanical conclusion. But, these exceptions made, the conception of the judge as a loyal agent of the legislative was not intended to eliminate all margin of discretion for judges but simply to prevent them from usurping legislative functions. Such is the idea of the judge as an agent of parliament; in this model, the theory of interpretation was embedded in a clear theory about the division of powers.

In general terms, the model has worked successfully until now, although not without notable criticism in Europe. Among the opposing voices we can highlight Geny (2000 [1899]), the Free Law School represented among others by Kantorowicz (1949 [1906]), or more recently the alternative use of law (López Calera et al. 1978) made fashionable by Pietro Barcellona (1976) or Luigi Ferrajoli (1973). In England the resistance of common law judges to accept the authority of the British Parliament to make laws was clamorous: parliament was doing the work of a newcomer, neither expected nor desired, who had arrived to alter what judges understood by rule of law. That is why it has been said that Bentham was the least British of all British thinkers. The same thing happened in the U.S. when the tension erupted between the growing legislative interventionism of the social state (Sunstein 1989) and the judicial resistance to President Roosevelt's new deal, which was also presented in the form of a controversy between common law and legislated law. U.S. courts—as Jerome Frank (1949, p. 292) summed up—, until very recently, considered the laws coming from the chambers as intrusions that had to be interpreted in such a way as to alter precedent laws as little as possible, for the courts' feeling was: "here we have a stable body of rules which provide legal certainty. We ourselves barely change them, and when we do, we do so with the utmost care. But the chambers pass new laws, often without proper examination, that break legal certainty. Chambers do their work capriciously, superficially, on the basis of the few subjective impressions of a few members of the legislative commission. Why, in view of all this, should we have such great regard for such products?" Curiously, in the current Public Choice theory, there are clear echoes of these old arguments (Rubin 1991). Anyway, generally speaking, the model that conceives judges as agents of the legislative is the one that has worked in practice over the last century.

13.2 New Proposals

What is being questioned today is precisely this classical conception of the relationship between judges and parliament. At the same time proposals have been advanced to replace this model with a new understanding of the principles of the division of powers, rule of law and of national sovereignty itself. Some have called these new ideas "meta-democracy" (Schachter 1995), and it is in these new interpretations of democracy that the most fashionable proposals regarding the role of judges vis-à-vis legislators are nurtured. These proposals were born in the U.S. and, to a large extent, imported into European thought, although in a certain sense they repeat arguments from the oldest European theories on interpretation.

To add to the criticism that we mentioned at the beginning of this work—effects of a globalisation without control over the legitimacy of norms, normative inflation, inefficacy, inefficiency and ineffectiveness of norms—, there is now a rebirth of the scepticism around the capacity of legislative language to establish clear directives of behaviour. Much of the theory of law in the past and the present century has devoted its best efforts to "remind" us—since it has always been known—of the impossibility of law responding to every specific situation faced by its interpreter when it comes to applying it. The legislator cannot possibly foresee the details of all the real situations that the interpreter of a norm will encounter. As noted earlier, this is due to our relative ignorance of the facts, to the relative indetermination of the legislator's purposes and to the very limitations of language (Hart 1968, p. 160). Legal formalism, navigating through the paradise of concepts, did not perceive the inevitable open texture of norms that, in practice, makes interpretation of the norm in many cases an open choice between different alternatives. To reaffirm the open texture of norms might be a harmless trend, but the scepticism towards rules that bloomed at the beginning of the twentieth century (think e.g. of the Free Law School) seems to have dominated the method and, therefore, even the theory of legal sources. As Hart says, formalism and scepticism are the Scylla and the Caribdis of legal theory, they are great exaggerations that are healthy only when they correct each other. I have the impression that scepticism towards rules is now the most dangerous path which should be avoided. Too often now, the interpreter of the law does not operate inside the marginal areas in which the legislator has delegated the normative powers (empowering him to make an informed and reasoned choice between alternatives). Rather, the applier simply tries to create the norm, distilling it from the most heterogeneous components that his or her imagination provides and among which, of course, sometimes the law also appears.

But above all, what has called into question the traditional conception of the relations between legislators and judges has been the criticism of the model of parliamentary representation. Attacks from opposing fronts try to highlight the shortcomings of parliaments, which are either not able, not knowing or not willing to hear the voice of the marginalised—feminism (Sherry 1986), republicanism,[1] *critical legal studies*—, or are "captured" by pressure groups (Public Choice theory). These limitations of parliament, some argue, would justify assigning a new and more active role to judges: society—now believed to be better represented by judges—could then hear also those voices that are not usually represented in the chambers; and limit the power of parliament through a restrictive judicial interpretation of legislative texts, because, as the classics used to say, "the best government is the one that governs least".

Perhaps the two orientations that have distanced themselves today more clearly from the traditional model of democracy are, according to Schachter (1995), those who seek to reconstruct politics through judges and those who want to reduce democracy through judges. Among the former are those who demand that judges use their discretion—which very few have in fact denied—to advance a whole agenda of progressive social transformation. Within this group we can place new republicanism (Sunstein 1990, pp. 14–16; Yale Law Journal 1988; Eskridge 1987, 1989), the critical feminist discourse, the fight against racial exclusion, etc. Despite the differences between all of them, these critics have some points in common: (a) their anti-positivism and their conception of laws as dynamic processes that begin with the legislator but end in the judge; (b) a certain "epistemological pluralism" that has to be transferred to judicial activity; and (c) a conception of democracy as non-domination, as inclusion and not only as procedure. In this way, democracy demands the conscious task of "listening" to the voice of those historically excluded from the realm of politics, and this task is attributed to judges and courts. From a neo-republican perspective, laws must be interpreted in favour of the disadvantaged because a fully deliberative and inclusive legislative process would have arrived at that result (Schachter 1995, p. 626). To this end, Cass Sunstein offers a whole series of principles to be applied by judges in the interpretation of laws, among which he cites: constitutional principles in favour of federalism, political responsibility, protection of disadvantaged groups, attention to certain immaterial values, the sympathy for deliberative democracy and the antipathy for transfers to pressure groups, and so on (Sunstein 1990, pp. 160 ff, 235 ff). Similar principles are offered by Eskridge (1989).

This reconstructionist concept of politics also includes critical discourses that reject that extreme positivism for which there is only one truth (that of the legislator)

[1] For a history of the republican tradition, see Pocock (1975).

and therefore only one correct interpretation. Numerous current ideas are connected to a certain "epistemological pluralism" (Minow 1990), according to which the meaning of words is closely linked to the identity, experiences or relationships of the interpreter: "family", for instance, does not have the same meaning for a homosexual as it has for a heterosexual. The judge must know how to "listen" to these new meanings and thus include the perspective of the oppressed.

The other interpretational model of democracy comes from those who try to discipline legislators through the restrictive interpretation that judges will make of their texts. The "disciplinary" conception starts from a vision of politics as the realm of abuse and arbitrariness perpetrated by legislators, governments and officials. On this account, it is claimed that we should contain democracy, and nothing will do so better than a strict, literal interpretation of the texts that limits the scope of laws.[2] The representatives of this vision are judges like Antonin Scalia and Frank Easterbrook as well as Jonathan Macey, and their ideas are usually based on—or at least compatible with—the Public Choice theory. For Easterbrook (1984, pp. 92–94) the judge must declare any ambiguous text inapplicable. Obscurity and ambiguity are not a fault or defect, but a byproduct of the legislative process itself. Somewhat more radical is Calabresi's (1982) proposal: the judge should simply not apply the law when it is incoherent with the system as a whole. For Macey (1986), the judge must apply the "plain meaning" of the legal text, and must use a whole series of resources or techniques aimed at revealing the "hidden interests" behind each law, thus disciplining legislators and avoiding the "capture" of legislation by interest groups.

But the most significant figure in this field has been conservative judge Scalia (Brisbin 1997), who advocates the strictest textualism as the best way to educate and to "reform" the legislator. For Scalia (1997), legislators often avoid making sensitive decisions and like to pass the responsibility on to judges. The solution is not to look to legislative records for guidance because they are not laws that passed through both houses and because they are often nothing more than the expression of interest groups or the incompetence of legislators. What the judge has to do is to strictly apply the enacted text following only the ordinary, most common meaning of the legislator's words. This methodology, in his opinion, is not a definitive solution, but it does contain important preventive and healing elements. By making it clear to congress that the courts will not go beyond the text of the law, the courts end up forcing legislators to take better care of what they explicitly state and what they omit in laws.

All these proposals are, to a certain extent, old acquaintances. The former remind us of the so-called alternative use of law, so fashionable in the 1970s, which was intended to undermine dictatorships such as Franco's or to judicially implement certain programs with a strong social content. The latter bring us the echoes of both

[2]This does not mean that all literalism has the purpose of limiting democracy. Proof of this is found in the work of Francisco Laporta (2008) which contains a rigorous defence of literalism and formalism precisely in order to make the regulative ideal viz. *regulative Idee* of the rule of law a reality.

the School of Exegesis and economic liberalism of the nineteenth century. Both proposals, even though with opposing aims, have a point in common: they struggle to make judicial activism compatible with a democracy in which citizens have reserved for themselves the right to establish and change policies through their elected representatives (Franck 1996), and not through judicial decision-making.

These trends, which encourage judicial activism, are not only found in the United States, they have spread to European countries too, due in large part to a confusion between constitutional interpretation and interpretation of laws. It is true that courts have to be the counter-majority watchdog, that they have to protect minorities from possible abuses by majorities (Mikva 1987). But does it make sense to transfer this function to the interpretation of laws in general without jeopardising the democratic principle that majorities have the right to change laws and establish new policies? What legitimises judges to assume that they represent the excluded better than an elected legislator who is accountable to citizens? And finally, how can we ensure that the parameters of one judge can be made generalisable to the rest of the judges?

13.3 Interpretation and Theory of Legislation

If one is not prepared to abandon in haste—and without any clear alternative—the principles that are inherent to our model of rule of law, a theory of interpretation anchored in a political theory that is compatible with our parliamentary democracy will be necessary. The development of such a theory can only be approached by using and improving the knowledge and the study of the legislative process,[3] since most of the problems faced by the interpreter have generated at some stage of this process (Twining and Miers 1991).

In the first place, a norm may fail *already before it is even drafted*, due to an erroneous, incomplete or inadequate apprehension of the context and facts, to an inappropriate categorisation of the problem to be solved, to contradictory or inconsistent political objectives, because the norm was intended to solve a situation that would have required another type of regulatory instrument, or because the existing institutional framework makes the correct solution difficult or impossible. Secondly, the new norm may also fail *in the drafting phase*, because it causes doubts about the legislator's intention (meaning of the words, intended scope, desired effects, supposed consequences, reasons for dictating the rule) or about the integration of the new norm within the preexisting system, because of the inadequate formulation of its objectives, because of defective wording (inappropriate choice of terms, gaps, structural inconsistency, intentional darkness), of a deliberate delegation of normative powers (use of vague terms and indeterminate concepts), or of undue urgency in its processing. Thirdly, the new rule can fail *at the stage of governmental decision*: the government can cause doubts if it neglects certain procedural requirements on

[3]Cf. recently Nourse (2016) or Rosen (2017).

which the validity of the norm may depend, or uses ambiguous terminology to sweeten the content of the norm in order to avoid its rejection by parliament or society, or if it unnecessarily uses (too) indeterminate concepts. Fourthly, *parliament and legislators* must be mentioned as responsible for some of the loopholes, ambiguities and contradictions in norms: the need to achieve certain majorities or to reach consensus may lead to modifications of the draft that create ambiguity, reduce the clarity of the original text or alter its logic through last-minute amendments. And finally, a new norm might fail if it finds further obstacles in the *publication phase*: doubts can be caused by errata that may occur throughout the entire drafting process (many hands rewrite the successive versions of a draft) or during the publishing phase itself (printing errors).

It is therefore here, in the legislative phase, that some of the problems originate that the interpreter of a norm will subsequently face. That is why the interpretation of legislation would be greatly improved if the interpreters were to take parliament more seriously and reach a better understanding of how the legislative process actually works.

To take Parliament seriously means, as Hart and Sacks (1958, p. 147) claimed in their influential *The Legal Process*, to start from the premise that "unless proven otherwise, parliament is composed of reasonable persons who reasonably pursue reasonable objectives". And the actions of reasonable people usually follow an objective: law is about doing something, it is a finalist activity, a continuous attempt to solve the basic problems of society (Hart and Sacks 1958, p. 148). Laws are directives for the future and people in their right mind do not approve future directives that do not have an objective. We can accept as an established premise that every law or every other legal instrument, has some kind of purpose or objective, however vaguely expressed, however difficult it may sometimes be to agree on its exact wording. The legislator, when dictating rules—and very especially in a democracy—does not think of citizens as puppets he can foolishly manipulate: if he orders, prohibits or allows certain behaviours it is because he wants to reach certain goals: a better air to breathe, cleaner water to drink, safer roads, education for all, and so on. The legislator believes he will be able to achieve such results if the rules are complied with, if they are efficacious. It is these desired results—not only the means or methods for their achievement—that matters, i.e. that justifies regulatory activity itself. That is the first meaning of taking parliament seriously.

Moreover, taking parliament seriously implies taking its words seriously. This is the great truth of literalism and the reason why, from the point of view of the rule of law principle, the text is the fundamental key to the interpretation of norms—a text for which it is not necessary to create an interpretation but already has a clear meaning derived from its words and shared by the linguistic community and the specialists (Laporta 2008). That is why it was traditionally suggested that the first and main source of meaning is found in the "proper", conventional sense of the words in the legal text. The advantages of clinging to words are more than evident (Sunstein 1989): they have a special legitimacy given that they are the words of parliament itself, they offer greater security than other canons because they usually only have one plausible meaning. Above all, by following only words, the abuse in which the judge often incurs when he tries to interpret the intention of the legislator by other means, would be avoided. It is true, then, that literalism, as proposed by Laporta (2008), offers the strongest anchor for making the rule of law principle a reality. It is more necessary than ever to state clearly that the interpretational moment of laws cannot be arbitrary, that it must be subject to a pattern and that this pattern is fundamentally the legislative text itself.

But the study of the legislative process has evidenced how this capital interpretative anchor, the words of the legislator, does not always give the clear answer sought by the applicator of the law. Of course, a reform of the norm-drafting process, as we advocate here, should improve the quality of norms by making them more precise and clear. But it could never achieve such precision as to make it unnecessary in all cases to search for a sense or meaning of the text. Unfortunately, as we have seen, not even the most expert drafters can completely control the vagueness of legal language, nor can the requirement of brevity to which they are bound prevent the ambiguity of certain expressions, causing the text to cover a semantic field greater than desired (over-inclusiveness) or smaller than necessary (under-inclusiveness). Norm drafting technique also shows that the drafter cannot possibly say everything and must take for granted that all what can be considered implied in the text itself or even in other texts (co-text) is clearly understood. The study of the legislative process shows, moreover, that the legislator often avoids clear settling of certain delicate questions but rather, through the use of vague terms, refers the determination of their precise meaning to the administration or the courts. Finally, a good number of the doubts caused by a normative text are simply the result of drafting errors. So, as we see, words are the essential reference, the anchor of interpretation, but sometimes, as even the most textualist judges have to acknowledge, the interpreter of law needs other tools.

Traditionally, the other instrument often needed to discover the meaning of the words in legislative texts has been the analysis of the intention of the legislator. This is what Justice Holmes proposed, with obvious exaggeration—"if my fellow citizens want to go to hell, I will help them". Much has been discussed (Waldron 1999, pp. 25 ff) around the legislator's intent since the first Enlightenment scholars began to rely on it to avoid judicial despotism. In our times too, attempts have been made to find this intent through parliamentary debate (Breyer 1991/1992).[4] And it is true that sometimes the study of what parliamentarians say in public debate can shed some light on the interpretation of norms. In this regard, both parliamentary proceedings and legislation that has not yet come into force are sometimes used as interpretative aids[5]; the Spanish Constitutional Court itself has

[4]For recent approaches to legislative intent, see e.g. Ekins (2012) or Frieling (2017).

[5]See Aulis Aarnio (1991, pp. 123 ff) about the value of parliamentary works as a source. In this connection, the Spanish Supreme Court's Judgment of 1 December 1992 (third Chamber), when dealing with a judge's request of compensation for the advancing of the retirement age introduced by an ordinary law, stated (Ground 8): "the Act on Public Administrations and Common Administrative Procedure (...), while not yet in force, is orientative of the legislator's will to regulate this matter for the first time; and this Act does limit compensation to individuals for the application of

based some of its decisions on parliamentary works.[6] But critical voices abound.[7] The virtuosity of this instrument depends to a large extent on the liveliness of parliamentary life, on the interest of parliamentarians in the legislative debate, on the very parliamentary structure and dynamics. Moreover, as we saw in the previous chapter, parliamentary procedure in Spain clearly offers room for improvement. That is why some of these voices have concluded that we should not waste time looking for the legislator's intent because it simply does not exist, and trying to rebuild it is nothing more than an exercise in logomachy (Easterbrook 1983a, b).

But what is not logomachy is to try to search for a precise meaning for the more obscure passages of a legal text in the expression of the public policy that the law pursues. In order to do so we do not need to waste excessive time trying to detect the will of each and every one of the legislators. The recourse to parliamentary proceedings, to the documentation that must accompany each legal project, to precedents, etc., does not aim at understanding the motivation that was behind the approval of the norm (to these effects it doesn't matter if it was more or less generous, more or less explicit) nor the mental state of each and every one of the legislators. What we can and must find out is if there was a problem that our representatives wanted to solve, what it consisted of and what were the instruments they articulated to solve it. Because that is what citizens demand of their governments and parliaments: that they confront the social, economic and political problems of our societies and do so with rules, with laws, because these are the most worthy instrument of government and the most respectable source of justice. This is what citizens need governments and parliaments for.

It is not a question, then, of searching for the will of the legislator and trying to cope with all the problems that such an operation entails. It is not even a question of looking for the reasons that lead the legislator to dictate a norm, as the Public Choice

non-expropriatory legislative interventions in three aspects: 1) that they should not have the legal duty to bear [the consequences of the legal intervention]; 2) that this compensation be established in the statute itself; and 3) that the compensation will be granted in the terms specified by the statute". Accordingly, the Supreme Court concludes that there is no place for the compensation requested. For its part, the Madrid Appelate Court's (*Audiencia Provincial*) Judgment of 10 May 1992 reads as follows: "Article 2.3 of the Organic Law 8/1984 of 26 December 1984 [regulating the system of appeals available to conscientious objectors to military service] clearly condemns 'anyone who refuses to comply with the substitutive social service' and both in letter and in spirit is subordinating the moral duty or duty of conscience to compliance with that legal obligation. From the preparatory works of this Act, parliamentary debates and other precedents, it can only be concluded that the legislator took into account and discussed all the questions raised about the possibility pointed out by some parliamentary sectors of establishing a professional and voluntary army".

[6]See e.g. the Constitutional Court's Judgment of 30 January 1981 (STC 2/1981): the principle *non bis in idem*, while not expressly included in Art. 9.3 of the Constitution, has actually constitutional rank, because "it was understood by the parliamentarians in the Committee on Constitutional Affairs and Public Freedoms of the Congress od Deputies (...) to be intimately linked to the principles of legality and typicity of infractions which are enshrined mainly in Art. 25 of the Constitution".

[7]See e.g. Easterbrook (1988). In a similar sense, Laporta (2008, pp. 175 and 216).

theory pretends. Nor is it a question of transferring to the judicial decision our own understanding of what the law should have said, which is what the Dworkinian "Hercules method" can lead to. Within an instrumental conception of law, which makes law the most dignified instrument for the solution of social problems, what interests us most is the underlying public policy. Every norm—beyond the reasons why it was approved by the government and/or the parliamentarians—is created to deal with a problem, and to reach a new state of affairs by influencing the behaviour of citizens. Of course, a reform of the norm-making process—e.g. by resorting to directives as is already common in the EU, by taking seriously the memoranda that have to accompany each bill and by improving parliamentary debate—would make it easier to understand the public policy that underpins a specific bill. But, even with the current limitations, it is possible to distinguish in every bill the policy that is being implemented by it. Therefore, leaving aside the situations in which the literal wording of the legislative text is clear and pristine—which are the majority of cases—, what matters is not to uselessly follow the subjective will of the legislator but to answer to the question of what problem did parliament try to solve with the law upon focus and to interpret the text, if it is in fact unclear, in the sense that allows a better answer to the problem that gave rise to this law. Taking parliament seriously—something that is particularly necessary in a parliamentary democracy—involves discovering what the spirit and purpose of norms is, the public policy they serve. This should be the main canon for courts and judges willing to respect the legislative supremacy of parliament, without which we cannot properly speak of rule of law.[8]

Obviously, an orientation such as the one suggested here—the connection between norm and public policy—does not solve all the problems posed by the interpretation of norms, although it does solve many more than is normally believed. Because it is true that a rule can have several objectives and that these can be sometimes contradictory. There are other pending problems such as regulation that, far from being the expression of a public interest, is nothing more than a contract between private groups and parliamentary groups intended to protect faction interests (Macey 1986). Also the problems derived from updating obsolete laws have yet to be resolved (Aleinikoff 1988). It will always be difficult to find solutions for difficult cases: that is, cases for which there is no authoritative regulatory text (loopholes), cases for which the judge has nothing but contradictory norms (antinomies) or extreme situations that challenge the common sense of justice (not the sense of the judge, which is of little interest). The solution to these cases must be found within the framework of that theory of interpretation that best corresponds with the political theory of rule of law. Therefore, instead of giving free rein to the

[8]In the "Note on the Rudiments of Statutory Interpretation" at the end of *The Legal Process*, Hart and Sacks (1958, p. 1374) insist on the attitude with which a judge must fulfil his task: respect for the position of Parliament as the main agency of political direction of society subject only to constitutional limitations, respect for the procedures followed in the approval of the law, deference to the interpretation that the agencies have made in good faith and with common sense, awareness of the nature of language as well as the fact that every law is part of the legal system.

creative imagination of judges, it would be better for them to stick as closely as possible to the legal system as a whole and, leaving aside Dworkin's Hercules method, to find the solution to those difficult cases "under the shadow of the law", as Portalis intended centuries ago, that is, in implicit law, in analogy, in jurisprudence and, of course, once again, in the purpose of laws (Laporta 2008, pp. 193 ff). Either the solution is found in this way or we will see the triumph of its alternatives (Macey 1986), that is, the abandonment of representative democracy in favor of either the anarchy of direct participation or the tyranny of judicial despotism which is where judicial activism can lead.

This position implies going beyond the theory of the judge as an agent of parliament, but not so far as to exempt judges from their duty of loyalty to the legislative process. The point is to consider them—in a certain sense as Ronald Dworkin does, but without endorsing his "noble dream"—not as subordinates of the legislator but as those agents who are called upon to finish painting, loyally and without manipulation, the same picture—not another—that, in its general lines, was designed by parliament (Dworkin 1986, pp. 313 ff). The judges' role is not, therefore, to be the silent mouth of the law nor to opt for the interpretation that seems to them personally to be the fairest, but to give laws—the inexcusable starting point—the meaning that results from the best interpretation of the legislative process as a whole.

13.4 Interaction Between Legislators and Judges

In any case, it is evident that legislators and judges—being, as they both are, necessary agents for the correct functioning of the system—do not know each other: legislators do not usually worry excessively about how their laws are applied in courts and are judges are not very preoccupied with the process of producing them. The subject has begun to be addressed in the legal scholarship, and studies begin to appear in this regard (Katzmann 1988, pp. 21 and 25) that focus primarily on three aspects: whether judges, through their decisions, have an influence on the legislative activity, whether there are institutions in place that work for parliament studying judicial decisions and whether there are channels, in addition to the official ones, through which a judge can influence parliament (Abrahamson and Hughes 1991). This is to say, if up until now the separation of judges and legislators has rightly been insisted on, now the relevant question is whether or not there is room for a more fluid relationship between them that, without risking judicial independence, would result in the improvement to the entire legal process.

With regard to the first type of studies—whether judicial decisions influence the legislative activity—, and leaving aside the ones devoted to examining the reaction of Congress to the rulings of the Supreme Court (see Eskridge 1991, p. 331), consider for instance Katzmann's (1992) analysis of the attitude of legislators towards the decisions of the rest of the courts.[9] This study, carried out within the framework of the Governance Institute—and aimed at improving the drafting of laws, the expression of legislative will and the assessment of laws following their enactment—has revealed the following relevant facts which, mutatis mutandis, would be applicable to our case: (a) except for the cases that reach the public opinion or are brought to the chambers by social collectives or pressure groups, parliamentary attorneys and advisors are generally unaware of the judicial rulings that apply the laws they contributed to draft; (b) when they do know of any judicial decision, they are aware of the ruling but rarely of its rationale and justification; (c) in spite of the above, the majority of the consulted consider that it would be interesting to know about such decisions and reasonings with a view to reforming specific laws; (d) a majority considers equally convenient that courts should have knowledge of decisions taken by parliament as a reaction to their rulings and justifications; (e) a majority of attorneys and advisors does not agree on any proposal that could harm their autonomy, but would accept some kind of relationship model between parliament and courts provided it were relatively inconspicuous and respectful of their competences; and (f) the only judicial opinions that would be acceptable to the majority of parliament attorneys and advisers would be "technical" opinions, which stay out of political considerations or substantive proposals (Katzmann 1992). The parliamentary committees that receive such opinions should therefore be free to take them into account or not. In our parliamentary democracy, there is much that could be done in this field.

Also, in an effort to modernise, clarify and correct laws in the U.S., many states have taken steps to allow the review of laws in the light of judicial decisions. In some cases, these mechanisms are created by the executive to support parliaments: this is the case of the mandate received by some general attorneys to examine judicial opinions in order to propose reforms. Sometimes it is parliament itself that sets up committees to review court judgements and to reform laws. Occasionally, external commissions—similar to the Codification Commission in Spain—are created with the task of making ad hoc proposals. And there are even states, such as Mississippi, Idaho or Illinois, where the law or the constitution itself imposes on judges and courts the obligation to review existing legislation and suggest appropriate reforms to the houses. But all these mechanisms, as Abrahamson and Hughes (1991) concludes, are not without their problems: (a) the examination of judicial rulings by an office created by the executive may be partial; (b) it is difficult to know to what extent such a body can cause an effective reaction in parliament; (c) the success of the review proposals stems fundamentally from the authority and personality of the parliamentarians who receive them; (d) the proposals made by bodies which have the capacity to present legislative initiatives are more effective; and (e) the established parliamentary procedure sometimes conditions the success of these review proposals.

Despite all the shortcomings noted, these measures aim at improving legislation and its interpretation without altering the model, and increasing the mutual visibility

[9]Cf. also Gluck and Schultz Bressman (2013, 2014).

and cooperation of both agents, legislators and judges. As Abrahamson and Hughes (1991, p. 1093) conclude, judges need to know more about how parliament works and what parliamentarians think about the role that legislative records and committee and plenary minutes should play. Judges need to draw the attention of legislators to problems that are either unresolved or poorly settled in legal texts. In turn, legislators need to know the conventions and canons that judges apply when interpreting and applying laws. Finally, both have a common interest: the improvement of the quality of laws and of the administration of justice, which is what citizens ultimately need. In order to do this, judges and legislators must be united by a relationship of loyalty, loyalty not to one another but to the parliamentary democratic system, which is how our state is defined by the constitution.

References

Aarnio A (1991) Lo racional como razonable. Centro de Estudios Constitucionales, Madrid

Abrahamson S, Hughes RL (1991) Shall we dance? Steps for legislators and judges in statutory interpretation. Minn Law Rev 75:1045–1093

Aleinikoff T (1988) Updating statutory interpretation. Mich Law Rev 87(1):20–66

Barcellona P (1976) El Estado y los juristas. Fontanella, Barcelona

Breyer S (1991/1992) On the uses of legislative history in interpreting statutes. S Cal Law Rev 65:845–874

Brisbin R (1997) Justice Antonin Scalia and the conservative revival. John Hopkins University Press, Baltimore

Calabresi G (1982) A common law for the age of statutes. Harvard University Press, Cambridge

Dworkin R (1986) Law's empire. Fontana Press, London

Easterbrook FH (1983a) Statutes' domains. Univ Chic Law Rev 50(2):533–552

Easterbrook FH (1983b) The court and the economic system. Harv Law Rev 98(1):4–60

Easterbrook FH (1984) Legal interpretation and the power of the judiciary. Harv J Law Policy 7:87–99

Easterbrook FH (1988) The role of original intent in statutory construction. Harv J Law Policy 11:59–66

Ekins R (2012) The nature of legislative intent. Oxford University Press, Oxford

Eskridge WN Jr (1987) Dynamic statutory interpretation. Univ Pa Law Rev 135:1479–1555

Eskridge WN Jr (1989) Public values in statutory interpretation. Univ Pa Law Rev 137:1007–1104

Eskridge WN Jr (1991) Overriding the Supreme Court's statutory interpretation decisions. Yale Law J 101:335–423

Eskridge WN Jr, Frickey P (1987) Legislation scholarship and pedagogy in the post-legal process. Univ Pitt Law Rev 48:691–731

Ferrajoli L (1973) Magistratura democratica e l'esercizio alternativo de la funziolne giudiziaria. In: L'Uso alternativo del diritto. Laterza, Roma-Bari

Franck MJ (1996) Against the imperial judiciary: the Supreme Court vs. the Sovereignity of the People. University Press of Kansas, Lawrence

Frank J (1949) Courts on trial. Myth and reality in American justice. Princeton University Press, Princeton

Frieling T (2017) Gesetzesmaterialien und Wille des Gesetzgebers. Mohr Siebeck, Tübingen

Geny F (2000) Método de interpretación y Fuentes del derecho Privado Positivo [1899]. Granada, Comares

Gluck AR, Schultz Bressman L (2013) Statutory interpretation from the inside—an empirical study of congressional drafting, delegation, and the canons: part I. Stan Law Rev 65(5):901–1026
Gluck AR, Schultz Bressman L (2014) Statutory interpretation from the inside—an empirical study of congressional drafting, delegation, and the canons: part II. Stan Law Rev 66(4):725–802
Hart HLA (1968) El concepto de derecho. Abeledo Perrot, Buenos Aires. [The concept of law. Clarendon Press, Oxford, 1961]
Hart HM, Sacks AM (1958) The legal process: basic problems in the making and application of law. Tentative ed, Cambridge (MA) [Foundation Press, Westbury, 1994]
Kantorowicz H (1949) La lucha por la Ciencia del Derecho [1906]. Losada, Buenos Aires
Katzmann RS (ed) (1988) Judges and legislators: towards institucional comity. The Brookings Institution, Washington, DC
Katzmann RS (1992) Bridging the Statutory Gulf between Courts and Congress: a challenge for positive political theory. Geo Law Rev 80:656–670
Laporta F (2008) El imperio de la ley. Una visión actual. Trotta, Madrid
López Calera N et al (1978) Sobre el uso alternativo del Derecho. F. Torres, Valencia
Macey JR (1986) Promoting public-regarding legislation through statutory interpretation: an interest group theory. Colum Law Rev 86(2):223–268
Mikva A (1987) Reading and writing statutes. Univ Pitt Law Rev 48:627–637
Minow M (1990) Making all the difference: inclusion, exclusion and American law. Cornell University Press, Ithaca
Nourse V (2016) Misreading law, misreading democracy. Harvard University Press, Cambridge
Pocock JGA (1975) The Machiavellian moment: florentine political thought and the Atlantic Republican Tradition. Princeton University Press, Princeton. [El momento maquiavélico. Tecnos, Madrid, 2002]
Posner R (1983) Statutory interpretation in the classroom and in the courtroom. Univ Chic Law Rev 50:800–822
Rosen A (2017) Statutory interpretation and the many virtues of legislation. Oxf J Leg Stud 37 (1):134–162
Rubin EL (1991) Beyond public choice: comprehensive rationality in the writing and reading of statutes. N Y Univ Law Rev 66:1–65
Scalia A (1997) A matter of interpretation: federal courts and the law. Princenton University Press, Princeton
Schachter JS (1995) Metademocracy: the changing structure of legitimacy in statutory interpretation. Harv Law Rev 108:595–663
Sherry S (1986) Civic virtue and the femenine voice in constitutional adjudication. Vand Law Rev 72:543–616
Sunstein CR (1989) Interpreting statutes in the regulatory state. Harv Law Rev 103:408–505
Sunstein CR (1990) After the rights revolution. Reconceiving the regulatory state. Harvard University Press, Cambridge
Twining W, Miers D (1991) How to do things with rules, 3rd edn. Weidenfeld & Nicholson, London
Waldron J (1999) The dignity of legislation. Cambridge University Press, Cambridge
Yale Law Journal (1988) The Republican Civic Tradition (symposium). Yale Law J 97:1493–1851

Chapter 14
Epilogue: The Art of Legislating and Globalisation

The leitmotiv of this work can easily be summed up: states are still necessary today to manage a large part of the problems that arise in our societies. One of the most valuable tools we can apply to this aim are laws, the quality of which can and must be improved. All of this is best synthesised in the idea of the dignity of legislation.

The fact that these ideas are not very new does not mean that we should not assert them permanently, especially when they are abused, as in recent times, by the demonisation of states and the deification of markets. As we have said throughout these pages, the market is a good instrument for allocating resources, so good that we have to take special care of it because it has a permanent tendency to suicide. The fact that this is not a purely ideological appreciation is confirmed by the disturbing economic crisis with which the first decade of the twenty-first century ended. A few years will pass before we can properly assess what has happened and what the causes were. But if one thing is clear at this point it is that the reason for the current problems cannot be found in the excess of regulation but rather in its insufficiency, in its defective design, in the systematic undermining of the public sphere and the state—to which a certain spirit of modernity, or even snobbery, of academia has contributed—, in the scant appreciation—if not disdain—for norms or in the eventual "capture" of regulation by the regulated groups. At the beginning of the twenty-first century there is little doubt as to what happens to societies when laws are systematically put under suspicion. Only those who want to be blinded by ideological prejudices will refuse to admit that, if any institution needs constant and intensive care, that is the market.

The necessary intervention of states does not have the purpose of drowning society in an ocean of rules that often have a more than dubious justification from the perspective of the general interest. This is another of the lessons of the twentieth century. The regulation that is needed does not aim at replacing the market with massive interventions that do not correct the problems at their root. It is paradoxical, by the way, that those responsible for this situation, investment bankers and financiers, claiming for the salvation of the system, now implore for massive interventions from public authorities or demand that the laws of the market are temporarily put in

V. Zapatero Gómez, *The Art of Legislating*, Legisprudence Library 6,
https://doi.org/10.1007/978-3-030-23388-4_14

brackets. And just as we should not take those voices seriously that once asked to thin out the state at any price and now say they need public money shovelled into the financial system, we should also beware of the two dangers that lurk permanently in all regulatory politics: obesity and anemia. The past century has incurred in both.

Reclaiming the dignity of regulation at the beginning of the twenty-first century requires reiterating once again what its objectives are. As we have explained throughout this work, it is a question of creating through regulation the necessary conditions so that markets are born where they do not yet exist, and their failures can be corrected where they are already in place. This way, citizens will have the necessary information to make relatively safe decisions with regard to the food they eat, the medicines they take, the quality of the air they breathe or the water they drink, as well as the credibility of the banks that take care of their deposits, the reliability of the risk rating agencies or the honourability of those who manage all types of funds. Alongside these economic and social objectives justifying the need for regulation, there is the question of distribution of income (salaries, basic incomes, compensation for the dependent) and the need to satisfy certain collective desires (quality television, for example, or certain cultural goods that lack a strong demand) or to attend to the rights of future generations (protection of the planet and its diversity). These economic and social objectives constitute the main reason why we should provide ourselves with norms that protect us and improve our lives. In the realisation of these objectives lies the justification of the intervention of public authorities.

In addition to having clear objectives, the concern for the dignity of regulation also requires seeking the best procedures and techniques to guarantee it, associating experts and specialists in the production of norms. This is what this work has advocated for, with the conviction that the system of norm production, or in other words, the governance of our societies through norms, must and can be improved. For this to happen, regulation cannot be reduced to an act of pure authority, but must be the result—as the thinkers of the Enlightenment desired—of a will illuminated by reason. This means that science has much to contribute to this goal: linguistic research applied to legal language can improve the quality of norms; examination of public policy can improve data collection, analysis, policy design and implementation; sociology of law can help make rules more effective; economic analysis can make rules more efficient; constitutional and comparative law suggest new approaches to reforming regulatory procedures. All this valuable knowledge can be applied to making rules more efficacious, effective, efficient and fair. This is the art of legislating that Filangieri understood as the voice that reason directs to the throne.

But if the enlightened art of legislation still has a meaning today, it is only on the basis of a search for solutions to the challenges of our time. We are facing a relatively unknown world, with new problems that require new solutions and old problems that resist old recipes. One of these new problems—at least in its magnitude—is the progressive fragmentation of the powers of the state as we knew it. Power, on the one hand, is being devolved into territorial sub-units which, as in the case of Spain, already manage most of the public resources autonomously. On the other hand, a large part of the power of states, including regulatory authority, is delegated to bodies managed on the basis of their independence and expertise: central banks, national commissions for securities, energy, telecommunications, etc. This fragmentation is intensified by the proliferation of all kinds of non-governmental organisations possessing strong resources and knowledge, which provide services but, above all, exert decisive pressure on legislators. These phenomena undoubtedly affect the exercise of power, including norm-making power.

The progressive blurring of the borders between public and private law is another of the characteristics of our current legal systems (Picciotto 2006, 2007). We have seen how public administrations are increasingly turning to private law to sell their assets, providing services indirectly via concessions to private companies, using private contracts to fulfil their missions, creating foundations for the management of certain services, and so on. At the same time, the state is increasingly replacing hard law based on regulation with soft law based on more or less binding codes of conduct, guidelines and recommendations.

This fragmentation of state powers, as well as the changes in the relationship between public and private law, raise the urgent question of how to legislate in decentralised states that want to guarantee not only the technical quality of their norms but also their legitimacy. New ideas are needed. Innovation is not the exclusive domain of individuals, not even of companies. More than ever governments need to innovate in their legislative production systems. Innovating in regulation means perfecting the performance of regulatory functions, which implies changes in the ways of identifying and specifying the problems to be solved; in the collecting and processing of data as well as in the design and implementation of appropriate regulatory techniques (Black 2005, pp. 12 ff). Innovation also means reviewing decision-making structures and creating new bodies—e.g. legislative policy evaluation agencies, as we have proposed—as well as updating procedures for the production of norms. The experience of the last decades and their dramatic conclusion with the financial crisis does not justify a simple return to the old modes of norm production (designed for the initial stages of the welfare state), but requires, rather, a rigorous investigation into how the state can better regulate our societies in the twenty-first century. A good strategy, at this stage, is to draw knowledge out of comparative experience (Berry and Berry 1999, pp. 169 ff). Much progress has been made in this respect thanks to the transnational dissemination of public policies (Dolowitz and Marsch 2000) and the speed with which ideas and programs now circulate between regions and states (Walker 1969).

But the reform of our national regulatory processes—as we have proposed here—is not enough: we need regulatory production systems that are fully open to their environment, that look beyond national borders. It is this international perspective that has remained in the background until now, despite the fact that the regulatory activity of national states has shown limitations when it comes to managing some of the major problems of our societies. The institutional horizon in which studies on legislation have so far been framed was always the nation state, but whether this is the right political unit to solve part of the problems that modern societies suffer has long since been questioned. Securing peace, eliminating poverty, dealing with major natural and humanitarian disasters, ensuring financial stability, protecting our habitat, fighting organised crime, achieving sustained development or guaranteeing universal respect for the hard core of human rights are objectives that no state, however powerful, can achieve on its own. The instrumental capacity of the nation state is decisively insufficient in the face of the globalisation of problems and their solutions (see especially Castells 2001a, pp. 271 ff). The traditional way to tackle these new challenges has been to appeal to cooperation and coordination of national policies, that is, relying on the classic mechanisms of international law understood fundamentally as inter-state law.

But is this strategy the one that best fits the nature of the global problems faced by humanity? Shouldn't the art of legislating also reflect on the new modes of regulation that are appearing not within states or between states but also on the margins of states and, in many senses, above them?

If the changes in the national procedures for legislative production have been important, much more intense and profound are the changes in international regulation caused by globalisation and the appeal to replace the government of states with the so-called *world governance* (see Commission on Global Governance 1995; World Bank 1997). These changes involve the agents, the procedures and the characteristics of the new international regulation. Alongside the increasingly strong presence of the traditional supranational organisations (UN, WTO, World Bank, OECD, etc.) with their own normative regimes and their demand for greater protagonism, two new phenomena have appeared that condition this new global regulation (Picciotto 1996): the emergence of a new type of statehood and the impressive development of international regulatory networks.

Indeed, regulatory regimes produced by a type of *offshore* statehood that does not fully fit into the traditional structure of nation-states have long been emerging. One of the oldest examples of this is the service and administration of ships, with convenience flags formally under convenience states (Liberia or Panama, for example), whose regulation and management may not imply a physical presence in these states because in reality these regimes are a set of standards, public and private, national and international. Something similar can be said of the tolerated existence of tax havens that have also become offshore financial centres. Along similar lines, we can mention the existence of legal enclaves and special jurisdictions (economic zones) created to attract industries by relaxing or exempting them from state rules on taxation, employment or social protection. All these new realities defined as *offshore* are not a marginal phenomenon: the OECD identifies more than 40 countries with financial centres of this type that constitute systems of regulation driven solely by competition, without an adequate control by regular international law, which implies a sort of privatisation of sovereignty.

A second characteristic feature of globalisation has been the emergence of international regulatory networks driven primarily by the revolution of information technology that expands the capacity to communicate and thereby strengthens the power of individuals and groups while diminishing traditional authority (see Castells 2001a; cf. also Majone 1996; Slaughther 1997; Braithwaite and Drahos 2000). The result is not a global government but what has been called *governance*, a system based on the interaction of an infinite number of networks made up of states, companies, citizen organisations, ethnic groups and a long etcetera. In many cases these are more or less formalised intergovernmental organisations that negotiate and take decisions on common problems (G-7 Groups, G-21, Conference of Bank Governors, etc.): even the European Union has been described as a network state (Castells 2001b). These networks tend to the use of a soft law consisting of guidelines or memoranda of understanding which, although lacking binding force, can be more effective and efficient than the hard law of states. In any case, this kind of soft guidelines tend gradually to be transferred into state law.

The liberalisation of financial markets has also resulted in a system of regulation consisting of a labyrinth network of banks and financial corporations, public and private—with their corresponding associations—that perform regulatory functions (codes of conduct, good practices, standards, guidelines, resolutions, technical norms or recommendations) as well as coordination functions (Zapatero 2006). But perhaps the most prominent phenomenon of late is the proliferation of networks generated by public interest activism and formed by transnational non-governmental organisations that not only promote new ideas and pressure states through mobilization and protest, but sometimes actively participate (as they did, for instance, in the Rio de Janeiro Earth Summit of 1992) in treaty negotiations as members of numerous delegations (Mathews 1997; cf. also Keck and Sikkink 1998).

This regulatory activity (usually called soft-law) is justified in many ways, depending on the type of network and activity involved. In general terms, this kind of regulation is accepted because of the greater competence, professionalism and political independence of the entities that form these networks. And it is true that a large part of the activity of international regulatory networks is nourished by those epistemic communities formed by a multitude of specialists and activists with their own world-shared discourses, values and knowledge (see Haas 1992, 1993; cf. also Zapatero 2003, pp. 477 ff). But all of this poses some problems that still remain unresolved, the most important of which is probably legitimacy. How can we legitimise, from a democratic perspective, the so-called governance? What kind of legitimacy can we articulate for policies and rules emanating from this poliarchic system of management? Do we have to worry about examining this type of regulation with the same parameters of efficacy, effectiveness, efficiency, technical perfection and adaptation to the principles of democracy that we apply to state rules? In short, does the art of legislating have anything to say in this new regulatory field that is growing in importance, quantitatively and qualitatively? This is a capital question for which, to this day, there is no single answer.

On the extreme end of the spectrum we find a kind of *neo-medievalism* that proclaims and celebrates the end of nation-states which are dissolving above, below and on the sides in supra-states, sub-states and para-states. In fact, according to this position, states will be replaced by the most diverse organisations that intersect, directing the destinies of the world in an immense network that includes such actors as Microsoft, Doctors without Borders, Caritas, Greenpeace, the Catholic Church, or Amnesty International, as well as the UN, the WTO, and the "remaining fragments" of states. This is how—it is said—the powers of the old nation state should be distributed, giving greater legitimacy to a new way of exercising power and resolving, in passing, the democratic deficit from which state powers suffer. The already diminishing power of states will continue to decline until perhaps—it is concluded (Mathews 1997, pp. 66 ff)—the nation states will cease to be the natural political unit in which the problems of society are collectively solved. Local governments will thus satisfy the growing desire of citizens to participate in decision-making, while transnational, regional and even local entities will be better adapted to the magnitude of global challenges.

The truth is that this network of institutions and regulations has even a greater deficit of legitimacy than nation states, but they are already unquestionable realities that mark an inevitable trend in the development of humanity. The only thing we can do with them is to demand that their function be in accordance with capital principles of democracy such as transparency, accountability, responsibility and participation (Picciotto 2001).

An arrangement, equally new but much more real, with less fanfare and richer substance, is suggested by Anne-Marie Slaughther (1997), for whom the state is not disappearing but fragmenting into separate units—courts, regulatory agencies, specialised executive bodies or parliaments—that network with their counterparts abroad, creating a dense web of connections that most certainly represent a new way of dealing with the great challenges of humanity. The problems of our world—terrorism, organised crime, environmental degradation, money laundering, financial policies, tax fraud, etc.—are being increasingly tackled through international cooperation, with networks established by governments and ranging from the European Union, the Basel Committee of Central Banks, the OECD, the WTO, the G-7 to Interpol or the international courts of justice. This type of regulation, supervision and coordination activity carried out by government bodies working in an international network is the sign of our time. This is how offices and officials of all kinds manage antitrust policies, market regulation, environmental policy, criminal policy and banking or insurance policy. Unlike *medievalism*, this other way of managing the affaires of humanity, which Slaughther calls *trans-governmentalism*, leaves control of all institutions and networks in the hands of the national representatives who are accountable to their citizens both for their domestic activities and their external actions. It is a new kind of organisation because new is the emerging force coming from the network of government officials; and it is realistic because it grows out of the still strong and necessary reality of nation states (Mesa 2004): governance without governments is government without power, and government without power—as we have seen at the beginning of this century—rarely works. But even if it did work, citizens would hardly accept any form of international regulation that they cannot control through their voice and their vote. Trans-governmentalism, therefore, practised by states committed to the values and procedures of democracy, can contribute to a better management of the wrecks caused by globalisation, especially if it is accompanied in this task by a greater presence, participation and control of parliaments, and if parliamentarians from all countries are encouraged to network.

The proposals analysed here are possibly already insufficient today.[1] The most progressive internationalist approach will continue to seek for the solution to the new regulatory problems in the consolidation of transnational organisations, with universal and centralised capacity, legitimised by democratic principles and duly controlled by citizens, as for example the United Nations ideally should be. This aspiration has its roots in Kantian cosmopolitanism (Petersmann 1998; Held 1997; cf. also Zapatero 2003, pp. 570 ff) but has not yet borne all its fruits due to the resistance of states to surrender part of their powers and sovereignty. As this utopia—which fortunately resists the ravages of time—progresses, it will be necessary to demand, in the first place, that those multiple transnational networks with regulatory powers respect certain standards of transparency, responsibility, accountability and participation. And it will also be necessary, as we move towards cosmopolitanism, to foster the development of fully democratic inter-state regulatory networks.

In any case, the magnitude of the problems and the depth of the possible answers needed highlight the limitations of any minimalist approach to the art of legislation and call for a much more ambitious approach that does not reduce its scope to the technical perfection of norms—its instrumental rationality—but goes deeper into the study of the fundamental issues—political, social, institutional and ethical—posed by legislation in the so-called era of globalisation. These are the new areas to be explored by a theory of legislation that is a continuation of the enlightened ideal of governing through norms guided by reason.

References

Berry FS, Berry WD (1999) Innovation and diffusion models in policy research. In: Sabatier P (ed) Theories of the policy process. Westview Press, Boulder, pp 169–200

Black J (2005) What is regulatory innovation? In: Regulatory innovation. A comparative analysis. Edward Elgar Publishing, Cheltenham, pp 1–15

Braithwaite J, Drahos P (2000) Global business regulation. Cambridge UP, Cambridge

Carrillo JA (2005) Globalización y orden internacional. Universidad de Sevilla, Sevilla

Castells M (2001a) La era de la información. Economía, sociedad y cultura II. El poder de la identidad. Alianza, Madrid

Castells M (2001b) La era de la información. Economía, sociedad y cultura III. Fin de milenio. Alianza, Madrid

Commission on Global Governance (1995) Our global neighbourhood. Oxford University Press, Oxford

Dolowitz D, Marsch D (2000) Learning from abroad: the role of policy transfer in contemporary policy-making. Governance 13:5–24

Haas TP (1992) Introduction: epistemic communities and international policy coordination. Int Organ 46(1):1–36

[1]Carrillo (2005) makes an interesting suggestion on how to govern globalization on a threefold level: world authority, international organizations, and states.

Haas TP (1993) Epistemic communities and the dynamics of international cooperation. In: Rittberger V, Mayer P (eds) Regime theory and international relations. Clarendon Press, Oxford, pp 168–201
Held D (1997) Cosmopolitan democracy and global order: a new agenda. In: Bohman J, Lutz-Bachman M (eds) Perpetual peace. The MIT Press, Cambridge
Keck M, Sikkink K (1998) Activists beyond borders: advocacy networks in international politics. Cornell University Press, Ithaca
Majone G (ed) (1996) Regulating Europe. European Public Policy. Routledge, London
Mathews JT (1997) Power shift. Foreign Aff 76(1):49–66
Mesa R (2004) Pórticos del nuevo milenio. In memoriam Roberto Mesa. Fundación El Monte, Sevilla
Petersmann E-U (1998) How to consitutionalize International Law and Foreign Policy for the benefit of civil society. Mich J Int Law 20:1–30
Picciotto S (1996) The regulatory criss-cross: interaction between jurisdiction and the construction of regulatory networks. In: Bratton W et al (eds) International Regulatory Competition and Coordination. Clarendon Press, Oxford, pp 89–123
Picciotto S (2001) Democratizing the new global public sphere (democratizing globalism). In: Drache D (ed) The market or the public domain: global governance and the asymmetry of power. Routledge, London, pp 335–359
Picciotto S (2006) Regulatory networks and global governance. In: The retreat of state: challenges to law and lawyers. W.G. Hart Legal Workshop 2006, Institute of Advanced Legal Studies, London
Picciotto S (2007) Law and legitimacy in multi-level governance. Centre for Globalisation and Regionalisation, Warwick
Rio de Janeiro Earth Summit (1992) United Nations Conference on Environment and Development (UNCED). Rio de Janeiro 3–14 June 1992
Slaughther AM (1997) The real new world order. Foreign Aff 76:183–197
Walker JL (1969) The diffusion of innovations among the American states. Am Polit Sci Rev 63:880–899
World Bank (1997) World development report: the state in a changing world. World Bank, Washington, DC
Zapatero P (2003) Derecho del comercio global. Thompson-Civitas, Madrid
Zapatero P (2006) Searching for coherence in global economic policy making. Penn State Int Law Rev 24(3):595–627

Index

V. Zapatero Gómez, *The Art of Legislating*, Legisprudence Library 6,
https://doi.org/10.1007/978-3-030-23388-4

The manufacturer's authorised representative in the EU is Springer Nature Customer Service Centre GmbH, Europaplatz 3, 69115 Heidelberg, Germany. If you have any concerns regarding our products, please contact ProductSafety@springernature.com

Printed and bound by CPI Group (UK) Ltd, Croydon, CR0 4YY
30/09/2026
02225450-0013